SAP HANA SYSTEM REPLICATION SCENARIOS

About the authors

Giridhar Kankanala is an experienced professional in SAP administration and related tools, with extensive expertise in managing complex SAP landscapes, implementing upgrades, and optimizing performance. He has worked across industries to ensure seamless SAP operations, focusing on building scalable, efficient, and secure solutions for enterprise clients. Giridhar's contributions to SAP technology have been recognized in various projects that span multinational organizations.

Acknowledgements:
I want to express my deepest gratitude to my wife, Likhitha and my kids for their patience and unwavering support. To my mother, and my in-laws, who taught me the values of resilience and hard work, and to my gurus, peers, colleagues, mentors over all these years who have made this journey so rewarding. A special thanks to the SAP community, whose shared knowledge and collaboration have been instrumental in my career.

Sudheer Amgothu (co-author) has built a remarkable career specializing in DevOps, cloud technologies, Kubernetes, and Site Reliability Engineering (SRE). He has contributed significantly to modernizing infrastructures in large-scale enterprises and startup environments, focusing on implementing CI/CD pipelines, automating cloud infrastructure, and ensuring operational excellence. Sudheer holds multiple certifications in Kubernetes and cloud platforms and has been a mentor in fostering best practices in containerization and scalability.

Acknowledgments:
I would like to thank Sudheer's wife, Ramya, for her endless support and understanding of my passion for technology. To my parents, who instilled in me a love of learning and perseverance, and to my mentors, who guided me through the complexities of my field. A special thanks to my colleagues, who continuously inspire me to innovate and improve.

First Reviewer:

Dr. Naveen Naik Sapavath is an Assistant Teaching Professor at Northeastern University, Boston, MA. He holds a Ph.D. in Electrical and Computer Engineering from Howard University and a Master of Engineering from IISc Bangalore. With over eight years of teaching experience, he has excelled in educating undergraduate and graduate students in Computer Science and Electrical Engineering.

Dr. Sapavath's research expertise spans next-generation communication systems, including 5G/Next-G Cellular Networks, O-RAN Architecture, AI/ML for Wireless Optimization, Cybersecurity, and IoT Security. He has contributed to advanced research projects at George Mason University, Iowa State University, and UC Davis, with a focus on wireless networks, resource allocation, and security.

An accomplished researcher, Dr. Sapavath has published over 10 articles in prestigious journals and conferences and serves as a reviewer for leading IEEE journals. His dedication to academic excellence and groundbreaking research enriches the scholarly contributions of this book.

Second reviewer:

Sudheer Devaraju is a Staff Solutions Architect, trusted advisor and recognized expert in Cloud Technologies, HR Information Systems (HRIS) and DevOps, with over 14 years of experience delivering transformative HRIS solutions for industry leaders, including retail giants like Walmart and top consulting firms such as PricewaterhouseCoopers (PwC). A well-known figure in Information Systems research and applications, Sudheer's work has been featured multiple times on Walmart corporate sites and in news media, showcasing his impact on enterprise-wide HR and payroll solutions. His technical expertise spans Workday HCM, Integrations, Recruiting, Talent, and Compensation, as well as cutting-edge cloud and DevOps methodologies. Leading a team of engineers in a Staff-level role, Sudheer is celebrated for his ability to align technology with strategic business goals, driving efficiency and innovation.

Beyond his professional accomplishments, Sudheer enjoys playing the piano and flute in his free time, channeling his creativity through music. Known for his depth of knowledge, strategic insight, and dedication to pushing HRIS innovation forward, Sudheer continues to shape the future of HR technology across industries.

Table of Contents

1.1. BASIC INTRODUCTION

What is SAP ?

As we all know SAP is an ERP – Enterprise Resource Planning set of principles, patterns, trends and best practices that used by an organization to implement SAP products in their landscape, it's can be implemented in multiple ways in customer OnPremises, Cloud environments/hyperscalers, Private Cloud environments or Hybrid deployments

SAP Architecture

Architecture includes **Presentation**: Client-Server Architecture – it has client, an **Application Layer:** application server and a **Database Layer**: database server, they are interpreted within its associated components and using SAP GUI (Graphical User Interface) application is reached which will get its required data for processing from underlying database server, it allows navigation between applications and menus, based on which SAP product to use.

It has landscape for Development, Quality & Production environments, before making anything to Production it has to be developed in Devlopment and for testing code is moved to Quality and finally to Production environment based on business cases.

Core of SAP Strategy

SAP All-in-one: this includes the same software as the SAP Business Suite, offers predefined standard processes, and is deployed in on-premise architecture

SAP Business suite: this includes comprehensive SAP ERP system and CRM – Customer Relationship Management, SCM – Supply Chain Management, SRM - Supplier Relationship Management, PLM, MDG so on several other applications offers a complete functional set of undefined processes and is their deployments

SAP Business by Design: this includes functional set of predefined processes which is hosted on defined processes, and is deployed in on-premise architecture

SAP Business One: offers only basic functions, targets small business and deployed in a hosted environment

SAP Application Server: this is central foundation of entire SAP software stack, it holds multiple technical components and integration with other vendor 3rd party application softwares associated with SAP NetWeaver architecture: it has both SAP ABAP (AS ABAP - Application Server ABAP) & SAP JAVA (AS JAVA - Application Server Java) stack

The AS Java architecture is comprised of:

- **AS Java Cluster Architecture:** Involves the building units of each application server, including all the components that allow user requests to be processed accurately and efficiently.

- **SAP JVM:** Involves the implementation of the Java Virtual Machine, the runtime platform of AS Java.

- **AS Java System Architecture:** Involves the logical layers of the AS Java system components and the relationships between them.

- **Zero Administration:** Involves a dynamic configuration environment that simplifies technical configuration tasks within AS Java.

AS ABAP is made up of a few core components, including:

- **Work processes:** Facilitates the execution of ABAP work processes and applications and links each application to a memory area that contains the context of each one.

- **Gateway:** Acts as the interface for communication protocols of the SAP NetWeaver AS ABAP system and initiates communication between other ABAP application servers, SAP systems, and non-SAP systems.

- **Dispatcher queue:** Provides a link between work processes and the users logged in to the ABAP application server, receives requests for dialog steps from SAP GUI, and directs screen output to the appropriate users.

- **Shared memory:** Offers a common main memory area to save concepts for work processes or buffer data in the local environment.

Database Server:

SAP Supports multiple databases to host SAP application on SAP owned databases and other 3rd party

SAP HANA DATABASE

SAP HANA (High-Performance Analytic Appliance) is an in-memory, column-oriented, relational database management system developed by SAP SE. It is designed to handle both transactional and analytical data processing in real-time, making it an ideal choice for businesses that require rapid access to large volumes of data. Below is an overview of the key features and components of the SAP HANA database server

1.2.   OVERVIEW OF SAP HANA DATABASE SERVER

1.2.1. ARCHITECTURE

- **In-Memory Database**: SAP HANA stores data in-memory, allowing for faster data retrieval and processing compared to traditional disk-based databases.

- **Columnar Storage**: Data is stored in columns rather than rows, which enhances performance for analytical queries and compresses data more effectively.

- **Multi-Model Processing**: SAP HANA supports multiple data models, including relational, graph, document, and spatial data, allowing for versatile applications.

1.2.2. KEY FEATURES

- **Real-Time Data Processing**: SAP HANA enables real-time analytics and transactional processing, which is crucial for businesses that need timely insights.

- **Advanced Analytics**: The platform supports advanced analytical functions, including predictive analytics, text analytics, and geospatial processing.

- **Data Integration**: SAP HANA integrates seamlessly with various data sources, enabling real-time data replication and ETL (Extract, Transform, Load) processes.

- **High Availability and Disaster Recovery**: Features like system replication, backup, and recovery ensure data availability and protection against data loss.

1.2.3. DEPLOYMENT OPTIONS

- **On-Premise**: Organizations can deploy SAP HANA on their own hardware, providing control over the environment.

- **Cloud**: SAP HANA is available as a service (SAP HANA Cloud) on public or private cloud platforms, offering scalability and flexibility.

- **Hybrid**: A combination of on-premise and cloud deployments allows businesses to balance performance and cost.

1.2.4. SYSTEM ADMINISTRATION

- **SAP HANA Studio**: This integrated development environment (IDE) provides tools for database administration, modeling, and monitoring.

- **Database Administration Console (DBACockpit)**: A web-based interface for monitoring and managing SAP HANA databases.

- **Performance Monitoring**: Tools for analyzing system performance, workload management, and troubleshooting.

1.2.5. USE CASES

- **Business Intelligence**: Organizations use SAP HANA for reporting and data visualization, enabling better decision-making through insights from data.

- **Enterprise Resource Planning (ERP)**: SAP HANA is the underlying database for SAP S/4HANA, the next-generation ERP suite.

- **Data Warehousing**: Companies leverage SAP HANA for real-time data warehousing, allowing for consolidated reporting and analytics.

1.2.6. ASSUMPTION

SAP HANA is a powerful database server that combines advanced data processing capabilities with high performance and scalability. Its architecture and features make it suitable for various applications, from analytics and reporting to enterprise resource planning and big data processing. Organizations leveraging SAP HANA can achieve greater agility and responsiveness in their operations, enabling them to thrive in today's data-driven business landscape.

2. PURPOSE AND SCOPE OF DOCUMENT

This document contains various test cases for SAP MDG system in the Preprod HA environment. This comprehensive guide explores the critical components of achieving high availability (HA) in SAP HANA environments through effective system replication strategies. It delves into the architecture of SAP HANA, detailing how system replication can be configured to ensure business continuity, minimize downtime, and protect against data loss.

The book covers various replication techniques, including synchronous and asynchronous modes, and explains their advantages and limitations. It includes best practices for implementing and managing high-availability configurations, monitoring performance, and conducting disaster recovery tests.

Real-world case studies illustrate successful deployments and the lessons learned from organizations that have navigated the complexities of SAP HANA high availability. Additionally, the book offers troubleshooting tips, maintenance strategies, and insights into emerging trends in database replication and HA solutions.

Whether you are an SAP administrator, architect, or IT manager, this book equips you with the knowledge and tools necessary to design, implement, and maintain a robust SAP HANA system replication setup, ensuring your organization's operations remain uninterrupted and resilient.

This description captures the essence of the book and highlights its key themes and intended audience.

3. HARDWARE / SOFTWARE ENVIRONMENT

The SAP HANA hardware and software environment is designed to support high-performance, real-time data processing and analytics. Organizations must carefully consider their hardware configurations, operating systems, and supporting software components to ensure optimal performance and scalability. Choosing certified hardware and following best practices in deployment will enable organizations to fully leverage the capabilities of SAP HANA.

If you have any specific questions or need further details about any aspect of the SAP HANA environment, feel free to ask!

The SAP HANA database is designed to operate in a robust hardware and software environment that maximizes its performance and capabilities. Below is a detailed overview of the hardware and software environment required for SAP HANA.

3.1.1. SAP HANA HARDWARE ENVIRONMENT

System Requirements

- **Processor**:

    - Minimum of 2 sockets with a multi-core processor (Intel or AMD) supporting Intel 64 or AMD64 architecture.

    - Recommended: there are several SAP certified hardware/appliances by several manufactures based on the need, scalability, landscape environment Intel Xeon processors (e.g., Skylake or later) or AMD EPYC processors for optimal performance.

- **Memory**:

    - Minimum: 64 GB RAM (for small deployments).

    - Recommended: Starting at 256 GB RAM for production systems; larger deployments may require several terabytes of RAM depending on the workload.

- **Storage**:

    - High-performance, low-latency storage systems (e.g., SSDs) are recommended for the best performance.

    - Disk space should accommodate the size of the database, backups, and logs; typically, a 2:1 ratio for memory-to-disk is suggested.

    - RAID configurations (RAID 10 is commonly recommended) for redundancy and performance.

- **Network**:

    - Gigabit Ethernet (1 Gbps) or higher network interfaces for internal and external communication.

    - Low-latency connections are critical for high availability setups and data replication.

3.1.2. REFERENCE ARCHITECTURES

- SAP provides reference architectures that outline hardware configurations for various use cases (e.g., small, medium, large). These include certified hardware from SAP HANA hardware partners (e.g., Dell, HP, IBM, Cisco, Lenovo) that have been tested for compatibility and performance.

3.1.3. SAP HANA SOFTWARE ENVIRONMENT

Operating System

- **Supported OS**:

    - SUSE Linux Enterprise Server (SLES) for SAP Applications

o   Red Hat Enterprise Linux (RHEL) for SAP

- **Kernel Version**: Ensure that the OS kernel is compatible with the SAP HANA version being used.

SAP HANA Software

- **SAP HANA Database**: The core component that provides in-memory database capabilities for real-time data processing.

- **SAP HANA Studio**: An integrated development environment for administration and modeling.

- **SAP HANA Cockpit**: A web-based interface for monitoring and managing SAP HANA instances.

- **Client Tools**: SAP HANA client libraries for connectivity (e.g., JDBC, ODBC).

Additional Software Components

- **SAP NetWeaver**: Middleware that can be used alongside SAP HANA for various integration scenarios.

- **SAP BusinessObjects**: For reporting and analytics on top of SAP HANA data.

- **SAP Data Services**: For data integration and transformation tasks.

- **SAP Landscape Management (LaMa)**: For managing SAP HANA system landscapes, including provisioning, monitoring, and optimizing resources.

4. INSTALLATION INFORMATION

SAP S/4HANA is SAP's next-generation enterprise resource planning (ERP) suite, built on the SAP HANA platform. It leverages the capabilities of the HANA in-memory database to provide real-time processing and analytics. Understanding the deployment options for both SAP S/4HANA and SAP HANA is crucial for organizations looking to optimize their IT landscape. Below, you'll find a detailed overview of these deployment options.

Deployment Options

- **On-Premise**: Organizations can deploy SAP HANA on their own hardware infrastructure.

- **Cloud**: SAP HANA is available as a managed service on cloud platforms (e.g., SAP HANA Cloud, AWS, Microsoft Azure, Google Cloud Platform), providing flexibility and scalability.

- **Hybrid**: Combining on-premise and cloud deployments for optimized performance and resource management.

Cluster setup activity performed by Infra team, Both SAP S/4HANA and SAP HANA provide a range of deployment options tailored to the needs of modern enterprises. Organizations can choose between on-premise, cloud, and hybrid models based on their specific requirements for control, flexibility, scalability, and cost-effectiveness. Each deployment option has its own advantages and is suited for different business strategies, regulatory requirements, and IT capabilities.

If you have more specific questions or need further information on any of these deployment options, feel free to ask!

5.1.1. SAP S/4HANA DEPLOYMENT OPTIONS

SAP S/4HANA offers several deployment models to suit different business needs and IT strategies:

5.1.1.1. ON-PREMISE DEPLOYMENT

- **Description**: SAP S/4HANA is installed and run on the organization's own hardware infrastructure. This model provides full control over the system.

- **Key Features**:

  - Customization: Organizations can extensively customize their system according to specific business processes.

  - Control: Full control over the environment, data, and security protocols.

  - Integration: Easier integration with existing on-premise systems.

- **Use Cases**: Suitable for businesses that require high levels of customization, have strict regulatory or security requirements, or prefer to manage their own IT infrastructure.

5.1.1.2. CLOUD DEPLOYMENT

- **Description**: SAP S/4HANA is offered as a service in the cloud, managed by SAP or third-party providers.

- **Key Features**:

  - Flexibility: Resources can be scaled up or down based on demand.

  - Lower Initial Investment: Reduced upfront costs as organizations do not need to invest in hardware.

  - Automatic Updates: Regular updates and maintenance are handled by SAP, ensuring that the latest features and security measures are implemented.

- **Sub-Options**:

- o **Public Cloud**: Multi-tenant environment where multiple customers share the same infrastructure, optimized for standard processes.

  - o **Private Cloud**: Dedicated resources for a single organization, offering more flexibility and customization than the public cloud while still benefiting from cloud advantages.

- **Use Cases**: Ideal for businesses seeking flexibility, lower total cost of ownership, and less burden on internal IT resources.

5.1.1.3. HYBRID DEPLOYMENT

- **Description**: A combination of on-premise and cloud deployment where certain components are managed on-site while others are run in the cloud.

- **Key Features**:

  - o Balance: Allows organizations to maintain control over critical processes while leveraging the scalability of the cloud for less sensitive applications.

  - o Flexibility: Organizations can transition to the cloud at their own pace and manage workloads across environments.

- **Use Cases**: Suitable for enterprises with complex IT landscapes that want to gradually migrate to the cloud while maintaining certain operations on-premise.

5.1.2. SAP HANA DATABASE DEPLOYMENT OPTIONS

SAP HANA also offers various deployment options tailored to different business needs:

5.1.2.1. ON-PREMISE DEPLOYMENT

- **Description**: SAP HANA is installed and operated on an organization's own hardware.

- **Key Features**:

  - o Full Control: Organizations have complete control over their data, infrastructure, and security.

  - o Performance: Optimized for local performance, with dedicated hardware tailored for specific workloads.

- **Use Cases**: Best for organizations with strict data governance, compliance, or performance requirements.

5.1.2.2. CLOUD DEPLOYMENT

- **Description**: SAP HANA can be deployed on cloud infrastructure, either through SAP's own cloud services or through third-party cloud providers.

- **Key Features**:

- o   Scalability: Easily scale resources up or down as needed.

  - o   Cost Efficiency: Reduces the need for significant capital investment in hardware.

  - o   Managed Services: SAP or cloud partners handle maintenance, updates, and security.

- **Sub-Options**:

  - o   **SAP HANA Cloud**: Fully managed cloud service that provides in-memory computing capabilities.

  - o   **Third-Party Cloud Providers**: SAP HANA can be deployed on services like AWS, Microsoft Azure, or Google Cloud Platform.

- **Use Cases**: Ideal for businesses that want to reduce IT overhead, increase flexibility, or scale quickly.

5.1.2.3. MULTI-CLOUD DEPLOYMENT

- **Description**: Utilizing multiple cloud providers to host different components of the SAP HANA system, providing redundancy and flexibility.

- **Key Features**:

  - o   Avoid Vendor Lock-In: Organizations can select the best services from various providers.

  - o   Optimized Performance: Different cloud environments can be optimized for specific workloads.

- **Use Cases**: Suitable for businesses wanting to leverage the best features of multiple cloud providers.

6. PACEMAKER SETUP

Pacemaker is a popular open-source high-availability (HA) cluster resource manager for Linux, used to manage and control the availability of critical services on a cluster of servers. It works with **Corosync** (for cluster communication) and **Heartbeat** (for failure detection) to provide high availability, fault tolerance, and disaster recovery.

Pacemaker is often used in environments where systems need to be highly available, such as for database clusters (like **SAP HANA**), file systems, and web services. It helps ensure that services are automatically restarted or moved to another node if the current node fails.

Basic Concepts

- **Cluster**: A set of machines (nodes) that work together to provide high availability for services.

- **Resource**: Any application or service that you want to manage with Pacemaker, such as a database, web server, or file system.

- **Resource Agent**: A script that defines how a resource is started, stopped, and monitored.

- **Nodes**: Individual machines in the cluster that run Pacemaker and provide the services.

- **Failover**: If a node fails, Pacemaker can move the services to another node in the cluster.

- **Quorum**: The minimum number of nodes required to be active and communicate within the cluster to ensure that it is functional.

Steps to Set Up Pacemaker on a Linux Cluster

Below is an overview of the basic steps required to set up a **Pacemaker cluster** to provide high availability for services:

6.1.   PREREQUISITES

- **Linux Nodes**: At least two Linux-based systems (preferably RHEL/CentOS, SUSE Linux, or Ubuntu) to form a cluster.

- **Root Access**: You need root privileges on all nodes in the cluster.

- **Network Connectivity**: The nodes must be able to communicate with each other over a reliable network (usually a private network for internal communication).

- **Install Pacemaker and Corosync**:

  - On all nodes, install the required packages. For example, on a CentOS/RHEL-based system, you would use:

```bash
Copy code
sudo yum install pacemaker corosync pcs
```

  - On a Debian/Ubuntu system:

```bash
Copy code
sudo apt-get install pacemaker corosync pcs
```

6.2.   CONFIGURE AND START COROSYNC

Corosync is responsible for the cluster communication and fault detection between nodes.

- **Edit the Corosync configuration** (/etc/corosync/corosync.conf) to reflect the nodes in your cluster:

```bash
Copy code
totem {
  version: 2
  secauth: on
  transport: udpu
  cluster_name: my_cluster
}
```

```
nodelist {
  node {
     ring0_addr: node1
     nodeid: 1
  }
  node {
     ring0_addr: node2
     nodeid: 2
  }
}
```

- **Start the Corosync service** on all nodes:

```bash
Copy code
sudo systemctl start corosync
sudo systemctl enable corosync
```

- Verify that Corosync is running on both nodes:

```bash
Copy code
sudo systemctl status corosync
```

6.3.   CONFIGURE PACEMAKER

Pacemaker manages the actual resources and decides which node should run a service.

- **Enable and start the Pacemaker service**:

```bash
Copy code
sudo systemctl start pacemaker
sudo systemctl enable pacemaker
```

- **Check Pacemaker status**:

```bash
Copy code
sudo crm status
```

If everything is configured properly, the nodes should form a cluster and you should see both nodes in the cluster status.

6.4.   AUTHENTICATE THE CLUSTER

You need to authenticate the nodes with **PCS** (Pacemaker Command Line Interface) for cluster management.

- Set a password for the **cluster**:

```bash
Copy code
sudo pcs cluster auth node1 node2
```

You will be prompted to enter the password for each node.

- **Verify the cluster status**:

```bash
Copy code
```

```
sudo pcs cluster status
```

6.5. CREATE THE CLUSTER

Once nodes are authenticated, you can create and configure the cluster.

- On any node, run:

```bash
Copy code
sudo pcs cluster setup --name my_cluster node1 node2
```
- Start the cluster:

```bash
Copy code
sudo pcs cluster start –all
```

6.6. CONFIGURE RESOURCES

Now you can configure resources (e.g., an application like SAP HANA, Apache, MySQL) to run on the cluster.

Example of configuring an Apache HTTP service:

- **Add the Apache resource**:

```bash
Copy code
sudo pcs resource create apache_service ocf:heartbeat:apache
configfile=/etc/httpd/conf/httpd.conf op monitor interval=30s
```
This command creates a resource named apache_service using the OCF (Open Cluster Framework) resource agent for Apache. The monitor operation ensures that the service is regularly checked.

- **Check the resource status**:

```bash
Copy code
sudo pcs status
```
You should now see the Apache service listed as running on one of the nodes.

6.7. CONFIGURE RESOURCE CONSTRAINTS (OPTIONAL)

Pacemaker allows you to configure constraints, which dictate where and when resources should run. For example, if you want to ensure that a service runs only on specific nodes:

- **Configure location constraints** to specify where the resource should run:

```bash
Copy code
sudo pcs constraint location apache_service prefers node1=INFINITY
```
This means the Apache service will prefer to run on node1 but can failover to node2 if necessary.

1. **Enable High Availability for Failover**

To enable automatic failover, ensure that you have set up **monitoring** for your resources, such as web servers, databases, or applications. Pacemaker will move the resources to another node in case of failure.

- **Example of setting up MySQL HA**: If you have a MySQL database, you can set up MySQL high availability with Pacemaker by using a MySQL resource agent:

```bash
Copy code
sudo pcs resource create mysql_service ocf:heartbeat:mysql
configfile=/etc/my.cnf op monitor interval=30s
```

- Pacemaker will automatically monitor the health of the resource and perform failover if necessary.

7. APPLICATION FAILOVER TEST CASES

After Pacemaker setup we'll run multiple Test Cases scenarios, with each different failure type

We'll iterate below failover scenarios in

1. Simulate ASCS node crash where ASCS is running
2. CRASH of VM or reboot VM situation
3. REBOOT VM WHERE ERS IS RUNNING
4. KILL MESSAGE SERVER PROCESS
5. KILL GATEWAY PROCESS
6. KILL ENQUEUE SERVER PROCESS
7. KILL STONITH PROCESS
8. KILL WD PROCESS

7.1. PRE-STEPS

After migration to Azure and DNS switch deleted all entries from /etc/hosts keeping only self-entry.

Check if replication status is green under smenq tcode.

7.2. TEST CASE 1 – SIMULATE ASCS CRASH

Simulate ASCS node crash where ASCS is running.

Resource state before starting the test:

```
sa______m> sudo pcs status
Cluster name: sapecqapp
Cluster Summary:
  * Stack: corosync
  * Current DC: sapecqacs (version 2.0.5-9.el8_4.3-ba59be7122) - partition with quorum
  * Last updated: Thu Jun  2 12:07:47 2022
  * Last change:  Thu Jun  2 12:05:42 2022 by root via crm_resource on sapecqacs
  * 2 nodes configured
  * 9 resource instances configured

Node List:
  * Online: [ sapecqacs sapecqber ]

Full List of Resources:
  * rsc_st_azure           (stonith:fence_azure_arm):      Started sapec
  * Resource Group: g-ECQ_ASCS:
    * fs_E__ASCS           (ocf::heartbeat:Filesystem):    Started sapec
    * vip_Q_ASCS           (ocf::heartbeat:IPaddr2):       Started sapec
    * nc_E_ASCS            (ocf::heartbeat:azure-lb):      Started sapec
    * rsc_sap_ECQ_ASCS60       (ocf::heartbeat:SAPInstance):   Start
  * Resource Group: g-ECQ_AERS:
    * fs_E__AERS           (ocf::heartbeat:Filesystem):    Started sapec
    * vip_Q_AERS           (ocf::heartbeat:IPaddr2):       Started sapec
    * nc_E_AERS            (ocf::heartbeat:azure-lb):      Started sapec
    * rsc_sap_E__ERS70 (ocf::heartbeat:SAPInstance):       Started sapec

Daemon Status:
  corosync: active/disabled
  pacemaker: active/disabled
  pcsd: active/enabled
sa______:ecqadm>
```

```
sap______:ecqadm> ps -ef | grep __adm
qadm     29377       1  0 May27 ?        00:01:02 /usr/lib/systemd/systemd --user
qadm     29382   29377  0 May27 ?        00:00:00 (sd-pam)
ot      233413    2040  0 11:38 ?        00:00:00 sshd: ecqadm [priv]
qadm    233581  233413  0 11:39 ?        00:00:00 sshd: ecqadm@pts/0
ot      233582    2040  0 11:39 ?        00:00:00 sshd: ecqadm [priv]
qadm    233585  233582  0 11:39 ?        00:00:00 sshd: ecqadm@notty
qadm    233586  233585  0 11:39 ?        00:00:00 /usr/libexec/openssh/sftp-server
qadm    233593  233581  0 11:39 pts/0    00:00:00 -ksh
qadm    280131       1  0 12:03 ?        00:00:01 /usr/sap/ECQ/ASCS60/exe/sapstartsrv pf=/sapmnt/ECQ/profile/ECQ_ASCS60_s    qcs
qadm    280401       1  0 12:03 ?        00:00:00 sapstart pf=/sapmnt/ECQ/profile/ECQ_ASCS60_sapecqcs
qadm    280457  280401  0 12:03 ?        00:00:00 ms.s                                              560_sapecqcs
qadm    280458  280401  3 12:03 ?        00:00:11 enq.                                              CS60_sapecqcs
qadm    280459  280401  0 12:03 ?        00:00:00 /usr                                              file/ECQ_ASCS60_
qadm    280460  280401  0 12:03 ?        00:00:02 wd.s                                              560_sap
qadm    294411  233593  0 12:08 pts/0    00:00:00 ps -ef
qadm    294412  233593  0 12:08 pts/0    00:00:00 grep --color=auto ecqadm
sapec__s:__m>
```

Before executing Node crash, edit the test user and it would create a lock in sm12

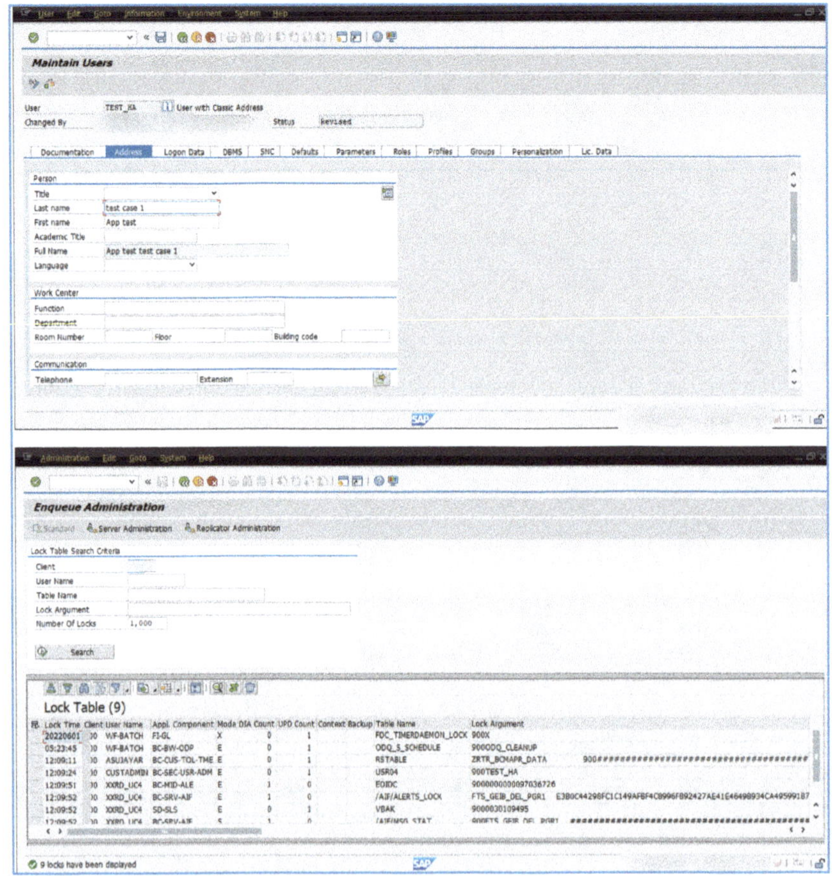

Run the following command as root on the node where the ASCS instance is running, here ASCS is running on node sapecqacs.

echo b > /proc/sysrq-trigger

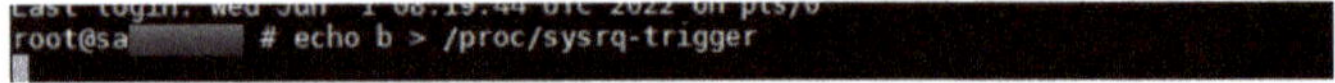

After executing the above command, save the changes to the user

The changes are saved successfully within **2 mins**.

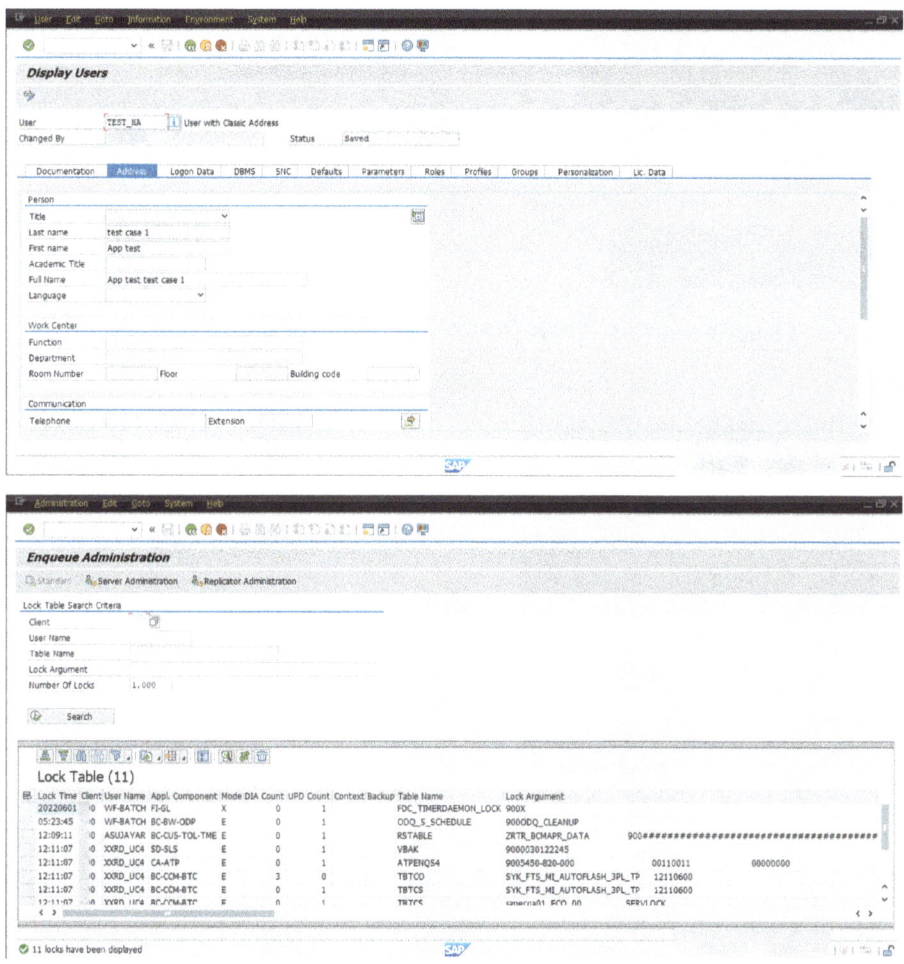

Check the pcs status: ASCS resources moved to sapecqber node and ERS resources remain to sapecqber node as sapecqacs node is crashed.

```
sapecqber:ecqadm> sudo pcs status
Cluster name: sap   app
Cluster Summary:
  * Stack: corosync
  * Current DC: sa    ber (version 2.0.5-9.el8_4.3-ba59be7122) - partition with quorum
  * Last updated: Thu Jun  2 12:11:59 2
  * Last change:  Thu Jun  2 12:05:42 2    by root via crm_resource on sapecqacs
  * 2 nodes configured
  * 9 resource instances configured

Node List:
  * Online: [ sape    r ]
  * OFFLINE: [ sape   cs ]

Full List of Resources:
  * rsc_st_azure          (stonith:fence_azure_arm):        Started sap    r
  * Resource Group: g-E   _ASCS:
    * fs_E   ASCS         (ocf::heartbeat:Filesystem):      Started sap   er
    * vip_   )_ASCS       (ocf::heartbeat:IPaddr2):         Started sap   er
    * nc_E   ASCS         (ocf::heartbeat:azure-lb):        Started sap   er
    * rsc_sap_ECQ_ASCS60          (ocf::heartbeat:SAPInstance):     Started sap    ber
  * Resource Group: g-E   _AERS:
    * fs_E   AERS         (ocf::heartbeat:Filesystem):      Started sap   ber
    * vip_   _AERS        (ocf::heartbeat:IPaddr2):         Started sap   ber
    * nc_E   AERS         (ocf::heartbeat:azure-lb):        Started sap   ber
    * rsc_   _E   ERS70 (ocf::heartbeat:SAPInstance):       Started sap   ber

Daemon Status:
  corosync: active/disabled
  pacemaker: active/disabled
  pcsd: active/enabled
sapecqber:ecqadm>
```

Check cluster status in ERS node: sap<SID>acs (which was crashed), cluster is not started automatically.

```
sap[  ]cs:ecqadm> uptime
 12:12:48 up 1 min,  1 user,  load average: 3.42, 1.22, 0.44
sap[    ]s:ecqadm> sudo pcs status
Error: error running crm_mon, is pacemaker running?
  crm_mon: Error: cluster is not available on this node
sap[   ]cs:e[ ]adm>
```

Start cluster in ASCS node: sap<sid>acs

```
  crm_mon: Error: cluster is not available on this node
sapecqacs:ecqadm> sudo pcs cluster start
Starting Cluster...
sapecqacs:ecqadm>
```

Check pcs status, **once cluster on ASCS node started, ERS resource will move to ASCS node: sapecqacs automatically.**

```
sapecqacs:ecqadm> sudo pcs status
Cluster name: sapecqapp
Cluster Summary:
  * Stack: corosync
  * Current DC: sapecqber (version 2.0.5-9.el8_4.3-ba59be7122) - partition with quorum
  * Last updated: Thu Jun  2 12:14:40 2022
  * Last change:  Thu Jun  2 12:05:42 2022 by root via crm_resource on sapecqacs
  * 2 nodes configured
  * 9 resource instances configured

Node List:
  * Online: [ sapecqacs sapecqber ]

Full List of Resources:
  * rsc_st_azure       (stonith:fence_azure_arm):       Started sapecqber
  * Resource Group: g-ECQ_ASCS:
    * fs_ECQ_ASCS      (ocf::heartbeat:Filesystem):     Started sapecqber
    * vip_ECQ_ASCS     (ocf::heartbeat:IPaddr2):        Started sapecqber
    * nc_ECQ_ASCS      (ocf::heartbeat:azure-lb):       Started sapecqber
    * rsc_sap_ECQ_ASCS60       (ocf::heartbeat:SAPInstance):    Started sapecqber
  * Resource Group: g-ECQ_AERS:
    * fs_ECQ_AERS      (ocf::heartbeat:Filesystem):     Started sapecqacs
    * vip_ECQ_AERS     (ocf::heartbeat:IPaddr2):        Started sapecqacs
    * nc_ECQ_AERS      (ocf::heartbeat:azure-lb):       Started sapecqacs
    * rsc_sap_ECQ_ERS70 (ocf::heartbeat:SAPInstance):   Started sapecqacs

Daemon Status:
  corosync: active/disabled
  pacemaker: active/disabled
  pcsd: active/enabled
sapecqacs:ecqadm>
```

Remove failed Resource actions if any
pcs resource cleanup <resource name >
eg pcs resource cleanup rsc_sap_ECQ_ERS70

Check location constraint if any. If exist clear it.
pcs constraint list
No location constraint found.

Resource state after executing Test case

```
sapecqacs:ecqadm> sudo pcs status
Cluster name: sapecqapp
Cluster Summary:
  * Stack: corosync
  * Current DC: sapecqber (version 2.0.5-9.el8_4.3-ba59be7122) - partition with quorum
  * Last updated: Thu Jun  2 12:15:15 2022
  * Last change:  Thu Jun  2 12:05:42 2022 by root via crm_resource on sapecqacs
  * 2 nodes configured
  * 9 resource instances configured

Node List:
  * Online: [ sapecqacs sapecqber ]

Full List of Resources:
  * rsc_st_azure:      (stonith:fence_azure_arm):       Started sapecqber
  * Resource Group: g-ECQ_ASCS:
    * fs_ECQ_ASCS      (ocf::heartbeat:Filesystem):     Started sapecqber
    * vip_ECQ_ASCS     (ocf::heartbeat:IPaddr2):        Started sapecqber
    * nc_ECQ_ASCS      (ocf::heartbeat:azure-lb):       Started sapecqber
    * rsc_sap_ECQ_ASCS60       (ocf::heartbeat:SAPInstance):    Started sapecqber
  * Resource Group: g-ECQ_AERS:
    * fs_ECQ_AERS      (ocf::heartbeat:Filesystem):     Started sapecqacs
    * vip_ECQ_AERS     (ocf::heartbeat:IPaddr2):        Started sapecqacs
    * nc_ECQ_AERS      (ocf::heartbeat:azure-lb):       Started sapecqacs
    * rsc_sap_ECQ_ERS70 (ocf::heartbeat:SAPInstance):   Started sapecqacs

Daemon Status:
  corosync: active/disabled
  pacemaker: active/disabled
  pcsd: active/enabled
sapecqacs:ecqadm>
```

Check the sap services on both ASCS and ERS nodes

```
sapecqacs:ecqadm> ps -ef | grep ecqadm
root        4774    2008  0 12:12 ?        00:00:00 sshd: ecqadm [priv]
ecqadm      4841       1  0 12:12 ?        00:00:00 /usr/lib/systemd/systemd --user
ecqadm      4842    4841  0 12:12 ?        00:00:00 (sd-pam)
root        4843    2008  0 12:12 ?        00:00:00 sshd: ecqadm [priv]
ecqadm      4851    4774  0 12:12 ?        00:00:00 sshd: ecqadm@pts/0
ecqadm      4852    4843  0 12:12 ?        00:00:00 sshd: ecqadm@notty
ecqadm      4853    4852  0 12:12 ?        00:00:00 /usr/libexec/openssh/sftp-server
ecqadm      4854    4851  0 12:12 pts/0    00:00:00 -ksh
ecqadm      7731       1  1 12:13 ?        00:00:01 /usr/sap/ECQ/ERS70/exe/sapstartsrv pf=/sapmnt/ECQ/profile/ECQ_ERS70_sapecqer -
ecqadm      8063       1  0 12:13 ?        00:00:00 sapstart pf=/sapmnt/ECQ/profile/ECQ_ERS70_sapecqer
ecqadm      8074    8063  4 12:13 ?        00:00:04 enqr.sapECQ_ERS70 pf=/usr/sap/ECQ/SYS/profile/ECQ_ERS70_sapecqer
ecqadm     11632    4854  0 12:15 pts/0    00:00:00 ps -ef
ecqadm     11633    4854  0 12:15 pts/0    00:00:00 grep --color=auto ecqadm
sapecqacs:ecqadm>
```

```
sapecqber:ecqadm> ps -ef | grep ecqadm
ecqadm      4461       1  0 Jun01 ?        00:00:09 /usr/lib/systemd/systemd --user
ecqadm      4462    4461  0 Jun01 ?        00:00:00 (sd-pam)
root     3679793    1778  0 11:39 ?        00:00:00 sshd: ecqadm [priv]
ecqadm   3680386 3679793  0 11:39 ?        00:00:00 sshd: ecqadm@pts/0
root     3680387    1778  0 11:39 ?        00:00:00 sshd: ecqadm [priv]
ecqadm   3680390 3680387  0 11:39 ?        00:00:00 sshd: ecqadm@notty
ecqadm   3680391 3680390  0 11:39 ?        00:00:00 /usr/libexec/openssh/sftp-server
ecqadm   3680437 3680386  0 11:39 pts/0    00:00:00 -ksh
ecqadm   3752295       1  0 12:10 ?        00:00:00 /usr/sap/ECQ/ASCS60/exe/sapstartsrv pf=/sapmnt/ECQ/profile/ECQ_ASCS60_sapecqcs
ecqadm   3752979       1  0 12:10 ?        00:00:00 sapstart pf=/sapmnt/ECQ/profile/ECQ_ASCS60_sapecqcs
ecqadm   3752993 3752979  0 12:11 ?        00:00:00 ms.sapECQ_ASCS60 pf=/usr/sap/ECQ/SYS/profile/ECQ_ASCS60_sapecqcs
ecqadm   3752994 3752979  3 12:11 ?        00:00:09 enq.sapECQ_ASCS60 pf=/usr/sap/ECQ/SYS/profile/ECQ_ASCS60_sapecqcs
ecqadm   3752995 3752979  0 12:11 ?        00:00:00 /usr/sap/ECQ/ASCS60/exe/gwrd pf=/usr/sap/ECQ/SYS/profile/ECQ_ASCS60_sapecqcs -
ecqadm   3752996 3752979  0 12:11 ?        00:00:02 wd.sapECQ_ASCS60 pf=/usr/sap/ECQ/SYS/profile/ECQ_ASCS60_sapecqcs
ecqadm   3767795 3680437  0 12:15 pts/0    00:00:00 ps -ef
ecqadm   3767796 3680437  0 12:15 pts/0    00:00:00 grep --color=auto ecqadm
sapecqber:ecqadm>
```

7.3. TEST CASE 2 – REBOOT VM WHERE ASCS IS RUNNING

In this scenario CRASH of VM or reboot VM situation

Resource state before starting the test:

```
sapecqber:ecqadm> sudo pcs status
Cluster name: sapecqapp
Cluster Summary:
  * Stack: corosync
  * Current DC: sapecqber (version 2.0.5-9.el8_4.3-ba59be7122) - partition with quorum
  * Last updated: Thu Jun  2 12:16:58 2022
  * Last change:  Thu Jun  2 12:05:42 2022 by root via crm_resource on sapecqacs
  * 2 nodes configured
  * 9 resource instances configured

Node List:
  * Online: [ sapecqacs sapecqber ]

Full List of Resources:
  * rsc_st_azure          (stonith:fence_azure_arm):       Started sapecqber
  * Resource Group: g-ECQ_ASCS:
    * fs_ECQ_ASCS         (ocf::heartbeat:Filesystem):     Started sapecqber
    * vip_ECQ_ASCS        (ocf::heartbeat:IPaddr2):        Started sapecqber
    * nc_ECQ_ASCS         (ocf::heartbeat:azure-lb):       Started sapecqber
    * rsc_sap_ECQ_ASCS60      (ocf::heartbeat:SAPInstance):      Started sapecqber
  * Resource Group: g-ECQ_AERS:
    * fs_ECQ_AERS         (ocf::heartbeat:Filesystem):     Started sapecqacs
    * vip_ECQ_AERS        (ocf::heartbeat:IPaddr2):        Started sapecqacs
    * nc_ECQ_AERS         (ocf::heartbeat:azure-lb):       Started sapecqacs
    * rsc_sap_ECQ_ERS70 (ocf::heartbeat:SAPInstance):      Started sapecqacs

Daemon Status:
  corosync: active/disabled
  pacemaker: active/disabled
  pcsd: active/enabled
sapecqber:ecqadm>
```

Before reboot of ASCS VM, edit the test user and it would create a lock in sm12

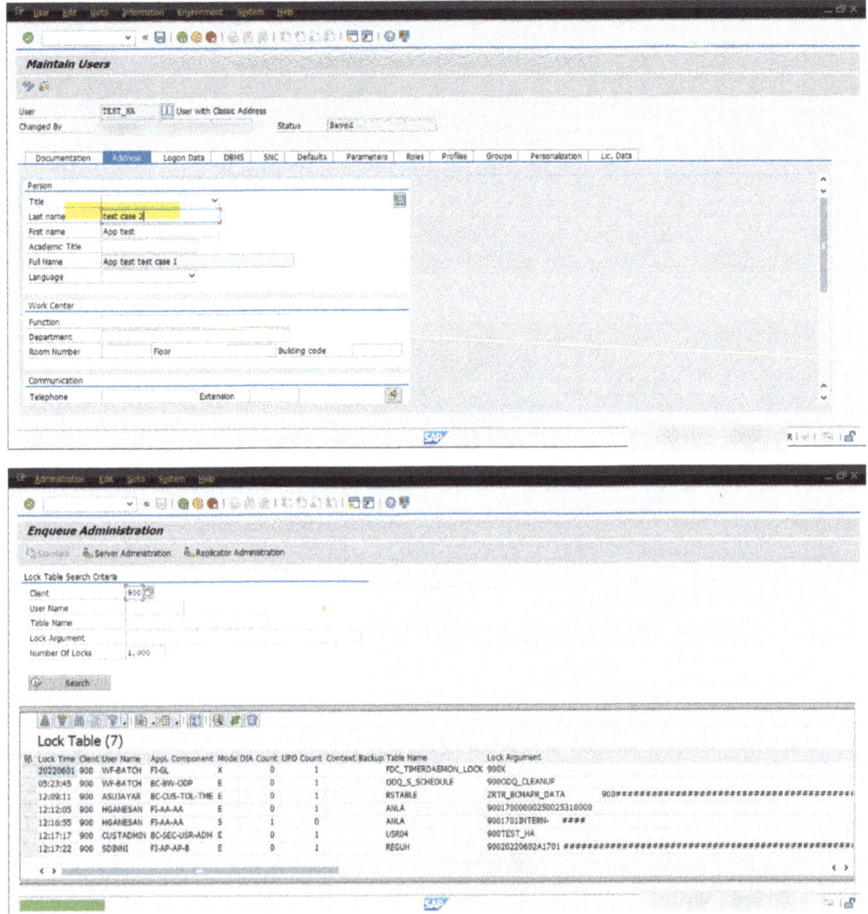

Check the sap services on both ASCS and ERS nodes

ASCS Services are running on sapecqber Node.

```
sapecqber:ecqadm> ps -ef | grep ecqadm
ecqadm      4461       1  0 Jun01 ?        00:00:09 /usr/lib/systemd/systemd --user
ecqadm      4462    4461  0 Jun01 ?        00:00:00 (sd-pam)
root     3679793    1778  0 11:39 ?        00:00:00 sshd: ecqadm [priv]
ecqadm   3680386 3679793  0 11:39 ?        00:00:00 sshd: ecqadm@pts/0
root     3680387    1778  0 11:39 ?        00:00:00 sshd: ecqadm [priv]
ecqadm   3680390 3680387  0 11:39 ?        00:00:00 sshd: ecqadm@notty
ecqadm   3680391 3680390  0 11:39 ?        00:00:00 /usr/libexec/openssh/sftp-server
ecqadm   3680437 3680386  0 11:39 pts/0    00:00:00 -ksh
ecqadm   3752295       1  0 12:10 ?        00:00:00 /usr/sap/ECQ/ASCS60/exe/sapstartsrv pf=/sapmnt/ECQ/profile/ECQ_ASCS60_sapecqcs
ecqadm   3752979       1  0 12:10 ?        00:00:00 sapstart pf=/sapmnt/ECQ/profile/ECQ_ASCS60_sapecqcs
ecqadm   3752993 3752979  0 12:11 ?        00:00:00 ms.sapECQ_ASCS60 pf=/usr/sap/ECQ/SYS/profile/ECQ_ASCS60_sapecqcs
ecqadm   3752994 3752979  2 12:11 ?        00:00:11 enq.sapECQ_ASCS60 pf=/usr/sap/ECQ/SYS/profile/ECQ_ASCS60_sapecqcs
ecqadm   3752995 3752979  0 12:11 ?        00:00:00 /usr/sap/ECQ/ASCS60/exe/gwrd pf=/usr/sap/ECQ/SYS/profile/ECQ_ASCS60_sapecqcs -
ecqadm   3752996 3752979  0 12:11 ?        00:00:02 wd.sapECQ_ASCS60 pf=/usr/sap/ECQ/SYS/profile/ECQ_ASCS60_sapecqcs
ecqadm   3774265 3680437  0 12:18 pts/0    00:00:00 ps -ef
ecqadm   3774266 3680437  0 12:18 pts/0    00:00:00 grep --color=auto ecqadm
sapecqber:ecqadm>
```

ERS Service is running on sapecqacs Node.

```
sapecqacs:ecqadm> ps -ef | grep ecqadm
root        4774    2008  0 12:12 ?        00:00:00 sshd: ecqadm [priv]
ecqadm      4841       1  0 12:12 ?        00:00:00 /usr/lib/systemd/systemd --user
ecqadm      4842    4841  0 12:12 ?        00:00:00 (sd-pam)
root        4843    2008  0 12:12 ?        00:00:00 sshd: ecqadm [priv]
ecqadm      4851    4774  0 12:12 ?        00:00:00 sshd: ecqadm@pts/0
ecqadm      4852    4843  0 12:12 ?        00:00:00 sshd: ecqadm@notty
ecqadm      4853    4852  0 12:12 ?        00:00:00 /usr/libexec/openssh/sftp-server
ecqadm      4854    4851  0 12:12 pts/0    00:00:00 -ksh
ecqadm      7731       1  0 12:13 ?        00:00:01 /usr/sap/ECQ/ERS70/exe/sapstartsrv pf=/sapmnt/ECQ/profile/ECQ_ERS70_sapecqer -
ecqadm      8063       1  0 12:13 ?        00:00:00 sapstart pf=/sapmnt/ECQ/profile/ECQ_ERS70_sapecqer
ecqadm      8074    8063  2 12:13 ?        00:00:08 enqr.sapECQ_ERS70 pf=/usr/sap/ECQ/SYS/profile/ECQ_ERS70_sapecqer
ecqadm     19728    4854  0 12:19 pts/0    00:00:00 ps -ef
ecqadm     19729    4854  0 12:19 pts/0    00:00:00 grep --color=auto ecqadm
sapecqacs:ecqadm>
```

Reboot sapecqber VM with root user.

After executing the above command, save the changes to the user.

The changes are saved successfully **within a mins**.

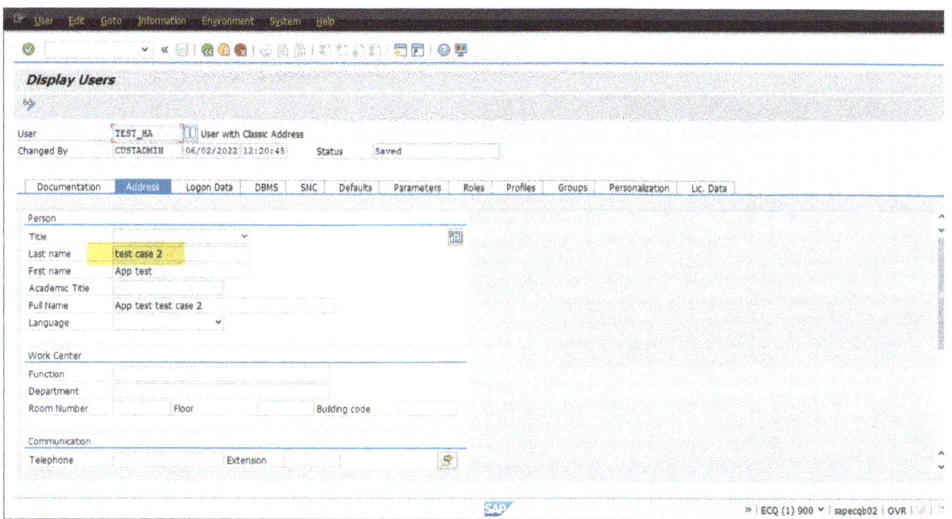

Check the pcs status: ASCS resources moved to sapecqacs node and ERS resource also remain on sapecqacs node.

```
sapecqacs:ecqadm> sudo pcs status
Cluster name: sapecqapp
Cluster Summary:
  * Stack: corosync
  * Current DC: sapecqacs (version 2.0.5-9.el8_4.3-ba59be7122) - partition with quorum
  * Last updated: Thu Jun  2 12:23:35 2022
  * Last change:  Thu Jun  2 12:05:42 2022 by root via crm_resource on sapecqacs
  * 2 nodes configured
  * 9 resource instances configured

Node List:
  * Online: [ sapecqacs ]
  * OFFLINE: [ sapecqber ]

Full List of Resources:
  * rsc_st_azure          (stonith:fence_azure_arm):      Started sapecqacs
  * Resource Group: g-ECQ_ASCS:
    * fs_ECQ_ASCS         (ocf::heartbeat:Filesystem):    Started sapecqacs
    * vip_ECQ_ASCS        (ocf::heartbeat:IPaddr2):       Started sapecqacs
    * nc_ECQ_ASCS         (ocf::heartbeat:azure-lb):      Started sapecqacs
    * rsc_sap_ECQ_ASCS60      (ocf::heartbeat:SAPInstance):   Started sapecqacs
  * Resource Group: g-ECQ_AERS:
    * fs_ECQ_AERS         (ocf::heartbeat:Filesystem):    Started sapecqacs
    * vip_ECQ_AERS        (ocf::heartbeat:IPaddr2):       Started sapecqacs
    * nc_ECQ_AERS         (ocf::heartbeat:azure-lb):      Started sapecqacs
    * rsc_sap_ECQ_ERS70 (ocf::heartbeat:SAPInstance):     Started sapecqacs

Daemon Status:
  corosync: active/disabled
  pacemaker: active/disabled
  pcsd: active/enabled
sapecqacs:ecqadm>
```

Check cluster status on ASCS node: sapecqber (which was rebooted), cluster is not started automatically.

```
sapecqber:ecqadm> uptime
 12:24:00 up 1 min,  1 user,  load average: 0.84, 0.51, 0.20
sapecqber:ecqadm> sudo pcs status
Error: error running crm_mon, is pacemaker running?
  crm_mon: Error: cluster is not available on this node
sapecqber:ecqadm>
```

Start cluster on ASCS node: sapecqber

```
sapecqber:ecqadm> sudo pcs cluster start
Starting Cluster...
sapecqber:ecqadm>
```

Check pcs status, **once cluster on ASCS node started, ERS resource will move to ASCS node: sapecqber automatically.**

```
sapecqber:ecqadm> sudo pcs status
Cluster name: sapecqapp
Cluster Summary:
  * Stack: corosync
  * Current DC: sapecqacs (version 2.0.5-9.el8_4.3-ba59be7122) - partition with quorum
  * Last updated: Thu Jun  2 12:25:05 2022
  * Last change:  Thu Jun  2 12:05:42 2022 by root via crm_resource on sapecqacs
  * 2 nodes configured
  * 9 resource instances configured

Node List:
  * Online: [ sapecqacs sapecqber ]

Full List of Resources:
  * rsc_st_azure          (stonith:fence_azure_arm):      Started sapecqacs
  * Resource Group: g-ECQ_ASCS:
    * fs_ECQ_ASCS         (ocf::heartbeat:Filesystem):    Started sapecqacs
    * vip_ECQ_ASCS        (ocf::heartbeat:IPaddr2):       Started sapecqacs
    * nc_ECQ_ASCS         (ocf::heartbeat:azure-lb):      Started sapecqacs
    * rsc_sap_ECQ_ASCS60      (ocf::heartbeat:SAPInstance):   Started sapecqacs
  * Resource Group: g-ECQ_AERS:
    * fs_ECQ_AERS         (ocf::heartbeat:Filesystem):    Started sapecqber
    * vip_ECQ_AERS        (ocf::heartbeat:IPaddr2):       Started sapecqber
    * nc_ECQ_AERS         (ocf::heartbeat:azure-lb):      Started sapecqber
    * rsc_sap_ECQ_ERS70 (ocf::heartbeat:SAPInstance):     Started sapecqber

Daemon Status:
  corosync: active/disabled
  pacemaker: active/disabled
  pcsd: active/enabled
sapecqber:ecqadm>
```

Remove failed Resource actions if any
pcs resource cleanup <resource name >
e.g pcs resource cleanup rsc_sap_ECQ_ERS70

Check location constraint if any. If exist clear it.
pcs constraint list
No location constraint found.
Resource state after executing Test case

```
sapecqber:ecqadm> sudo pcs status
Cluster name: sapecqapp
Cluster Summary:
  * Stack: corosync
  * Current DC: sapecqacs (version 2.0.5-9.el8_4.3-ba59be7122) - partition with quorum
  * Last updated: Thu Jun  2 12:25:05 2022
  * Last change:  Thu Jun  2 12:05:42 2022 by root via crm_resource on sapecqacs
  * 2 nodes configured
  * 9 resource instances configured

Node List:
  * Online: [ sapecqacs sapecqber ]

Full List of Resources:
  * rsc_st_azure        (stonith:fence_azure_arm):      Started sapecqacs
  * Resource Group: g-ECQ_ASCS:
    * fs_ECQ_ASCS       (ocf::heartbeat:Filesystem):    Started sapecqacs
    * vip_ECQ_ASCS      (ocf::heartbeat:IPaddr2):       Started sapecqacs
    * nc_ECQ_ASCS       (ocf::heartbeat:azure-lb):      Started sapecqacs
    * rsc_sap_ECQ_ASCS60        (ocf::heartbeat:SAPInstance):   Started sapecqacs
  * Resource Group: g-ECQ_AERS:
    * fs_ECQ_AERS       (ocf::heartbeat:Filesystem):    Started sapecqber
    * vip_ECQ_AERS      (ocf::heartbeat:IPaddr2):       Started sapecqber
    * nc_ECQ_AERS       (ocf::heartbeat:azure-lb):      Started sapecqber
    * rsc_sap_ECQ_ERS70 (ocf::heartbeat:SAPInstance):   Started sapecqber

Daemon Status:
  corosync: active/disabled
  pacemaker: active/disabled
  pcsd: active/enabled
sapecqber:ecqadm>
```

7.4.   TEST CASE 3 – REBOOT VM WHERE ERS IS RUNNING

Resource state before starting the test: ERS is running on sapecqber VM.

```
sapecqber:ecqadm> sudo pcs status
Cluster name: sapecqapp
Cluster Summary:
  * Stack: corosync
  * Current DC: sapecqacs (version 2.0.5-9.el8_4.3-ba59be7122) - partition with quorum
  * Last updated: Thu Jun  2 12:25:48 2022
  * Last change:  Thu Jun  2 12:05:42 2022 by root via crm_resource on sapecqacs
  * 2 nodes configured
  * 9 resource instances configured

Node List:
  * Online: [ sapecqacs sapecqber ]

Full List of Resources:
  * rsc_st_azure        (stonith:fence_azure_arm):      Started sapecqacs
  * Resource Group: g-ECQ_ASCS:
    * fs_ECQ_ASCS       (ocf::heartbeat:Filesystem):    Started sapecqacs
    * vip_ECQ_ASCS      (ocf::heartbeat:IPaddr2):       Started sapecqacs
    * nc_ECQ_ASCS       (ocf::heartbeat:azure-lb):      Started sapecqacs
    * rsc_sap_ECQ_ASCS60        (ocf::heartbeat:SAPInstance):   Started sapecqacs
  * Resource Group: g-ECQ_AERS:
    * fs_ECQ_AERS       (ocf::heartbeat:Filesystem):    Started sapecqber
    * vip_ECQ_AERS      (ocf::heartbeat:IPaddr2):       Started sapecqber
    * nc_ECQ_AERS       (ocf::heartbeat:azure-lb):      Started sapecqber
    * rsc_sap_ECQ_ERS70 (ocf::heartbeat:SAPInstance):   Started sapecqber

Daemon Status:
  corosync: active/disabled
  pacemaker: active/disabled
  pcsd: active/enabled
sapecqber:ecqadm>
```

Check ERS service. The ERS Service is running on sapecqber Node.

```
sapecqber:ecqadm> ps -ef | grep ecqadm
root      3798   1761  0 12:23 ?        00:00:00 sshd: ecqadm [priv]
ecqadm    3863      1  0 12:23 ?        00:00:00 /usr/lib/systemd/systemd --user
ecqadm    3864   3863  0 12:23 ?        00:00:00 (sd-pam)
root      3868   1761  0 12:23 ?        00:00:00 sshd: ecqadm [priv]
ecqadm    3873   3798  0 12:23 ?        00:00:00 sshd: ecqadm@pts/0
ecqadm    3877   3868  0 12:23 ?        00:00:00 sshd: ecqadm@notty
ecqadm    3878   3877  0 12:23 ?        00:00:00 /usr/libexec/openssh/sftp-server
ecqadm    3879   3873  0 12:23 pts/0    00:00:00 -ksh
ecqadm    6630      1  1 12:24 ?        00:00:01 /usr/sap/ECQ/ERS70/exe/sapstartsrv pf=/sapmnt/ECQ/profile/ECQ_ERS70_sapecqer
ecqadm    6913      1  0 12:24 ?        00:00:00 sapstart pf=/sapmnt/ECQ/profile/ECQ_ERS70_sapecqer
ecqadm    6924   6913  2 12:24 ?        00:00:02 enqr.sapECQ_ERS70 pf=/usr/sap/ECQ/SYS/profile/ECQ_ERS70_sapecqer
ecqadm    9775   3879  0 12:26 pts/0    00:00:00 ps -ef
ecqadm    9776   3879  0 12:26 pts/0    00:00:00 grep --color=auto ecqadm
sapecqber:ecqadm>
```

Check ASCS service is running on sapecqacs Node.

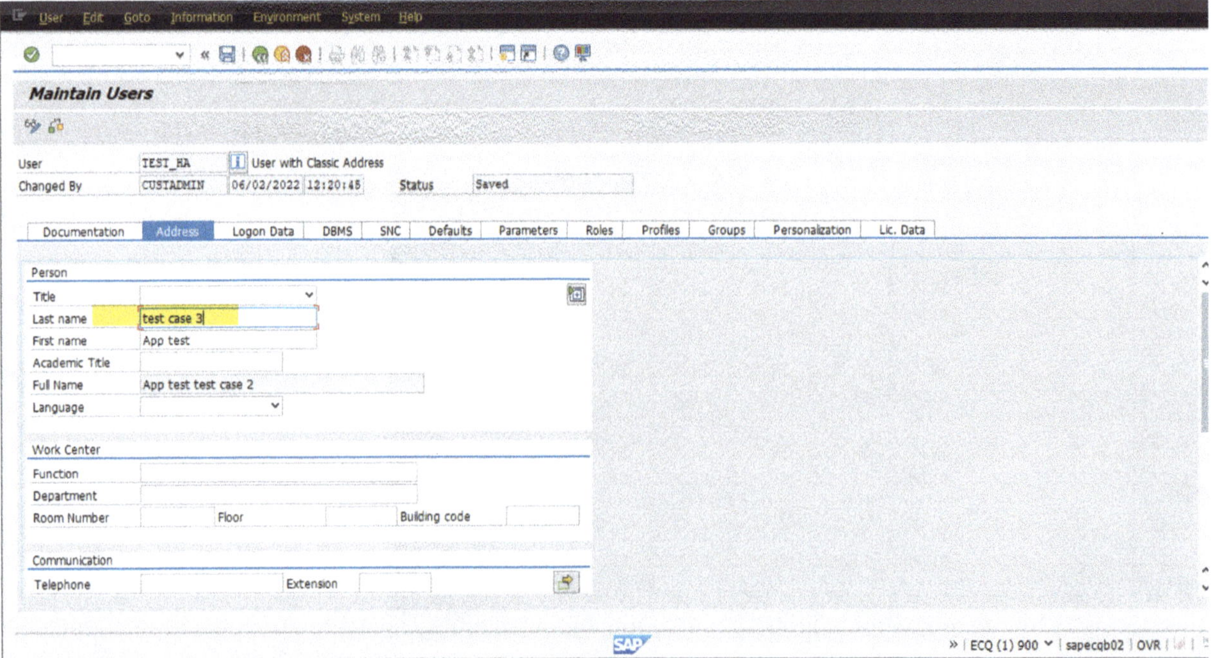

Before reboot of ERS VM, edit the test user and it would create a lock in sm12

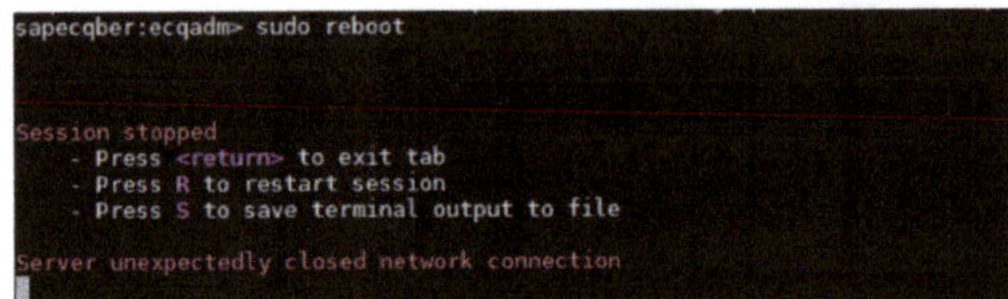

Reboot sapecqber VM with root user.

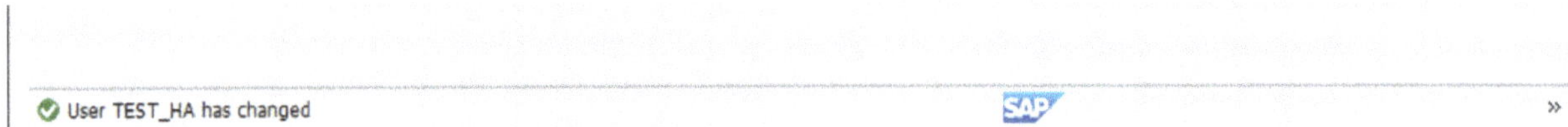

After executing the above command, save the changes to the user.

User TEST_HA has changed

The changes are saved successfully and **immediately.**

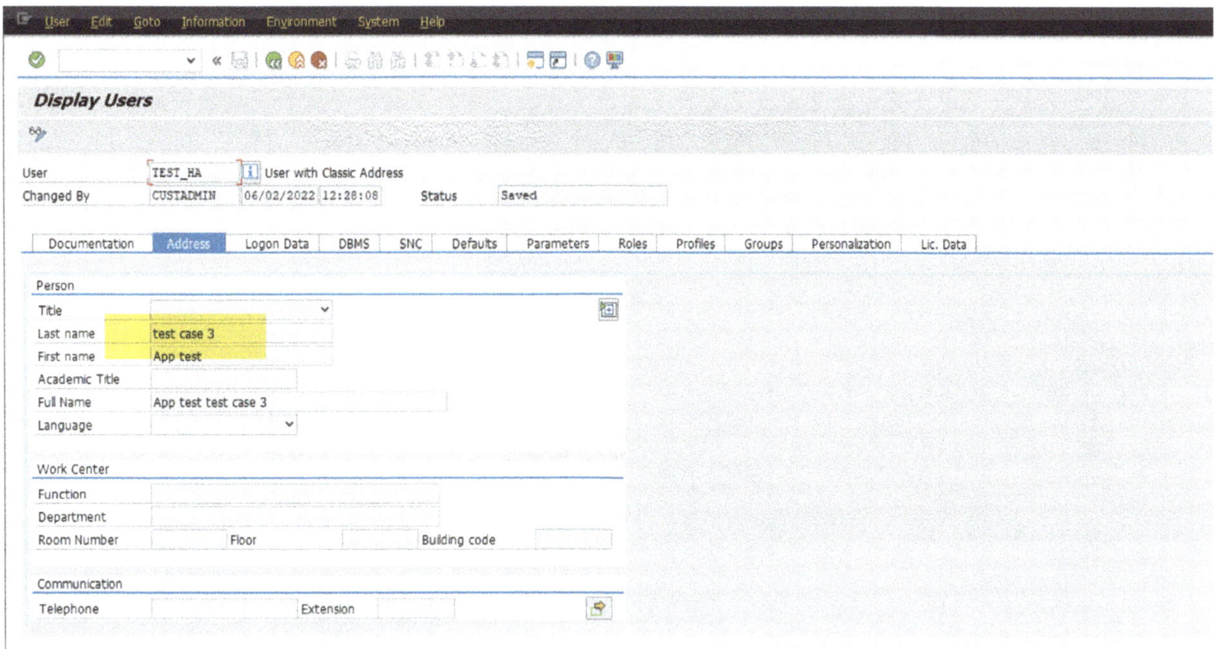

Check the pcs status: ASCS resources remain on sapecqacs node and ERS resource will move to sapecqacs node.

```
sapecqacs:ecqadm> sudo pcs status
Cluster name: sapecqapp
Cluster Summary:
  * Stack: corosync
  * Current DC: sapecqacs (version 2.0.5-9.el8_4.3-ba59be7122) - partition with quorum
  * Last updated: Thu Jun  2 12:28:43 2022
  * Last change:  Thu Jun  2 12:05:42 2022 by root via crm_resource on sapecqacs
  * 2 nodes configured
  * 9 resource instances configured

Node List:
  * Online: [ sapecqacs ]
  * OFFLINE: [ sapecqber ]

Full List of Resources:
  * rsc_st_azure        (stonith:fence_azure_arm):       Started sapecqacs
  * Resource Group: g-ECQ_ASCS:
    * fs_ECQ_ASCS       (ocf::heartbeat:Filesystem):     Started sapecqacs
    * vip_ECQ_ASCS      (ocf::heartbeat:IPaddr2):         Started sapecqacs
    * nc_ECQ_ASCS       (ocf::heartbeat:azure-lb):        Started sapecqacs
    * rsc_sap_ECQ_ASCS60        (ocf::heartbeat:SAPInstance):       Started sapecqacs
  * Resource Group: g-ECQ_AERS:
    * fs_ECQ_AERS       (ocf::heartbeat:Filesystem):     Started sapecqacs
    * vip_ECQ_AERS      (ocf::heartbeat:IPaddr2):         Started sapecqacs
    * nc_ECQ_AERS       (ocf::heartbeat:azure-lb):        Started sapecqacs
    * rsc_sap_ECQ_ERS70 (ocf::heartbeat:SAPInstance):     Starting sapecqacs

Daemon Status:
  corosync: active/disabled
  pacemaker: active/disabled
  pcsd: active/enabled
sapecqacs:ecqadm>
```

Check cluster status on ASCS node: sapecqber (which was rebooted), cluster is not started automatically.Start cluster on ASCS node: sapecqber

```
sapecqber:ecqadm> uptime
 12:29:58 up 1 min,  1 user,  load average: 1.03, 0.53, 0.20
sapecqber:ecqadm> sudo pcs status
Error: error running crm_mon, is pacemaker running?
  crm_mon: Error: cluster is not available on this node
sapecqber:ecqadm>
```

```
sapecqber:ecqadm> sudo pcs status
Error: error running crm_mon, is pacemaker running?
  crm_mon: Error: cluster is not available on this node
sapecqber:ecqadm> sudo pcs cluster start
Starting Cluster...
sapecqber:ecqadm>
```

Check pcs status, **once cluster on ERS node started, ERS resource will move to ERS node: sapecqber automatically.**

```
Starting Cluster...
sapecqber:ecqadm> sudo pcs status
Cluster name: sapecqapp
Cluster Summary:
  * Stack: corosync
  * Current DC: sapecqacs (version 2.0.5-9.el8_4.3-ba59be7122) - partition with quorum
  * Last updated: Thu Jun  2 12:31:03 2022
  * Last change:  Thu Jun  2 12:05:42 2022 by root via crm_resource on sapecqacs
  * 2 nodes configured
  * 9 resource instances configured

Node List:
  * Online: [ sapecqacs sapecqber ]

Full List of Resources:
  * rsc_st_azure          (stonith:fence_azure_arm):      Started sapecqacs
  * Resource Group: g-ECQ_ASCS:
    * fs_ECQ_ASCS         (ocf::heartbeat:Filesystem):    Started sapecqacs
    * vip_ECQ_ASCS        (ocf::heartbeat:IPaddr2):       Started sapecqacs
    * nc_ECQ_ASCS         (ocf::heartbeat:azure-lb):      Started sapecqacs
    * rsc_sap_ECQ_ASCS60         (ocf::heartbeat:SAPInstance):   Started sapecqacs
  * Resource Group: g-ECQ_AERS:
    * fs_ECQ_AERS         (ocf::heartbeat:Filesystem):    Started sapecqber
    * vip_ECQ_AERS        (ocf::heartbeat:IPaddr2):       Started sapecqber
    * nc_ECQ_AERS         (ocf::heartbeat:azure-lb):      Started sapecqber
    * rsc_sap_ECQ_ERS70 (ocf::heartbeat:SAPInstance):     Started sapecqber

Daemon Status:
  corosync: active/disabled
  pacemaker: active/disabled
  pcsd: active/enabled
sapecqber:ecqadm>
```

7.5. TEST CASE 4 – KILL MESSAGE SERVER PROCESS

Resource state before starting the test:

```
sapecqber:ecqadm> sudo pcs status
Cluster name: sapecqapp
Cluster Summary:
  * Stack: corosync
  * Current DC: sapecqber (version 2.0.5-9.el8_4.3-ba59be7122) - partition with quorum
  * Last updated: Fri Jun  3 09:06:44 2022
  * Last change:  Fri Jun  3 09:05:30 2022 by root via crm_resource on sapecqber
  * 2 nodes configured
  * 9 resource instances configured

Node List:
  * Online: [ sapecqacs sapecqber ]

Full List of Resources:
  * rsc_st_azure          (stonith:fence_azure_arm):      Started sapecqber
  * Resource Group: g-ECQ_ASCS:
    * fs_ECQ_ASCS         (ocf::heartbeat:Filesystem):    Started sapecqber
    * vip_ECQ_ASCS        (ocf::heartbeat:IPaddr2):       Started sapecqber
    * nc_ECQ_ASCS         (ocf::heartbeat:azure-lb):      Started sapecqber
    * rsc_sap_ECQ_ASCS60         (ocf::heartbeat:SAPInstance):   Started sapecqber
  * Resource Group: g-ECQ_AERS:
    * fs_ECQ_AERS         (ocf::heartbeat:Filesystem):    Started sapecqacs
    * vip_ECQ_AERS        (ocf::heartbeat:IPaddr2):       Started sapecqacs
    * nc_ECQ_AERS         (ocf::heartbeat:azure-lb):      Started sapecqacs
    * rsc_sap_ECQ_ERS70 (ocf::heartbeat:SAPInstance):     Started sapecqacs

Daemon Status:
  corosync: active/disabled
  pacemaker: active/disabled
  pcsd: active/enabled
sapecqber:ecqadm>
```

Here ms.sap service is running on sapecqber Node.

```
sapecqber:ecqadm> ps -ef | grep ecqadm
root        4308    1802  0 08:25 ?        00:00:00 sshd: ecqadm [priv]
ecqadm      4314       1  0 08:25 ?        00:00:00 /usr/lib/systemd/systemd --user
ecqadm      4315    4314  0 08:25 ?        00:00:00 (sd-pam)
root        4318    1802  0 08:25 ?        00:00:00 sshd: ecqadm [priv]
ecqadm      4324    4308  0 08:25 ?        00:00:00 sshd: ecqadm@pts/0
ecqadm      4325    4318  0 08:25 ?        00:00:00 sshd: ecqadm@notty
ecqadm      4326    4325  0 08:25 ?        00:00:00 /usr/libexec/openssh/sftp-server
ecqadm      4327    4324  0 08:25 pts/0    00:00:00 -ksh
ecqadm     96214       1  0 09:04 ?        00:00:00 /usr/sap/ECQ/ASCS60/exe/sapstartsrv pf=/sapmnt/ECQ/profile/ECQ_ASCS60_sapecqcs
ecqadm     96514       1  0 09:04 ?        00:00:00 sapstart pf=/sapmnt/ECQ/profile/ECQ_ASCS60_sapecqcs
ecqadm     96527   96514  0 09:04 ?        00:00:00 ms.sapECQ_ASCS60 pf=/usr/sap/ECQ/SYS/profile/ECQ_ASCS60_sapecqcs
ecqadm     96528   96514  1 09:04 ?        00:00:04 enq.sapECQ_ASCS60 pf=/usr/sap/ECQ/SYS/profile/ECQ_ASCS60_sapecqcs
ecqadm     96529   96514  0 09:04 ?        00:00:00 /usr/sap/ECQ/ASCS60/exe/gwrd pf=/usr/sap/ECQ/SYS/profile/ECQ_ASCS60_sapecqcs
ecqadm     96530   96514  0 09:04 ?        00:00:01 wd.sapECQ_ASCS60 pf=/usr/sap/ECQ/SYS/profile/ECQ_ASCS60_sapecqcs
ecqadm    106465    4327  0 09:08 pts/0    00:00:00 ps -ef
ecqadm    106466    4327  0 09:08 pts/0    00:00:00 grep --color=auto ecqadm
sapecqber:ecqadm>
```

Before killing the message server process, edit the test user and it would create a lock in sm12

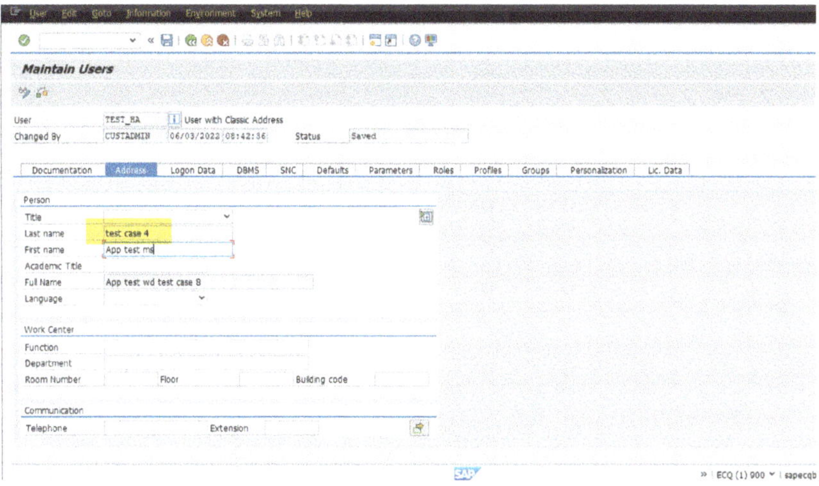

Run the following commands as root to identify the process of the message server and kill it.

If you only kill the message server once, it will be restarted by sapstart. If you kill it often enough, Pacemaker will eventually move the ASCS instance to the other node. Run the following commands as root to clean up the resource state of the ASCS and ERS instance after the test.

pgrep -f ms.sapECQ | xargs kill -9

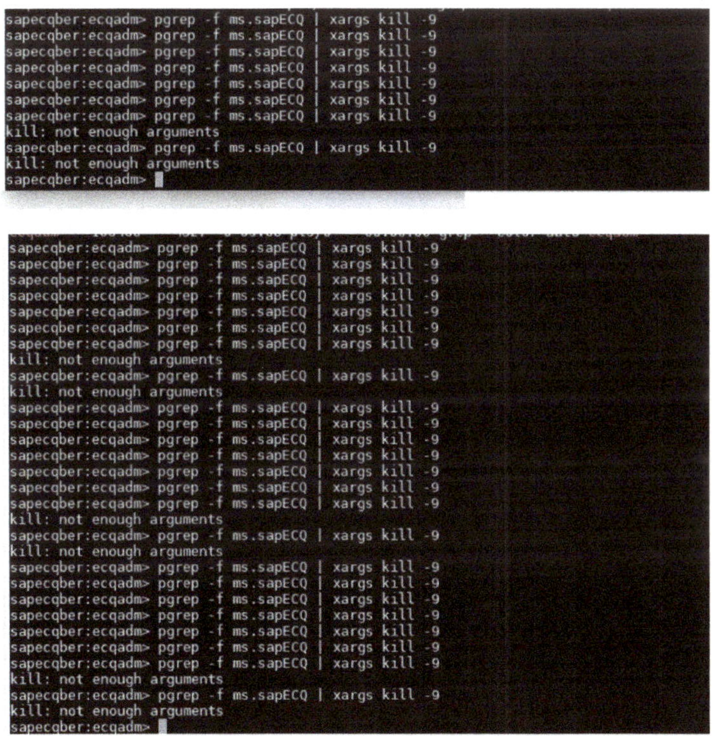

After executing the above command, save the changes to the user.

The changes are saved successfully

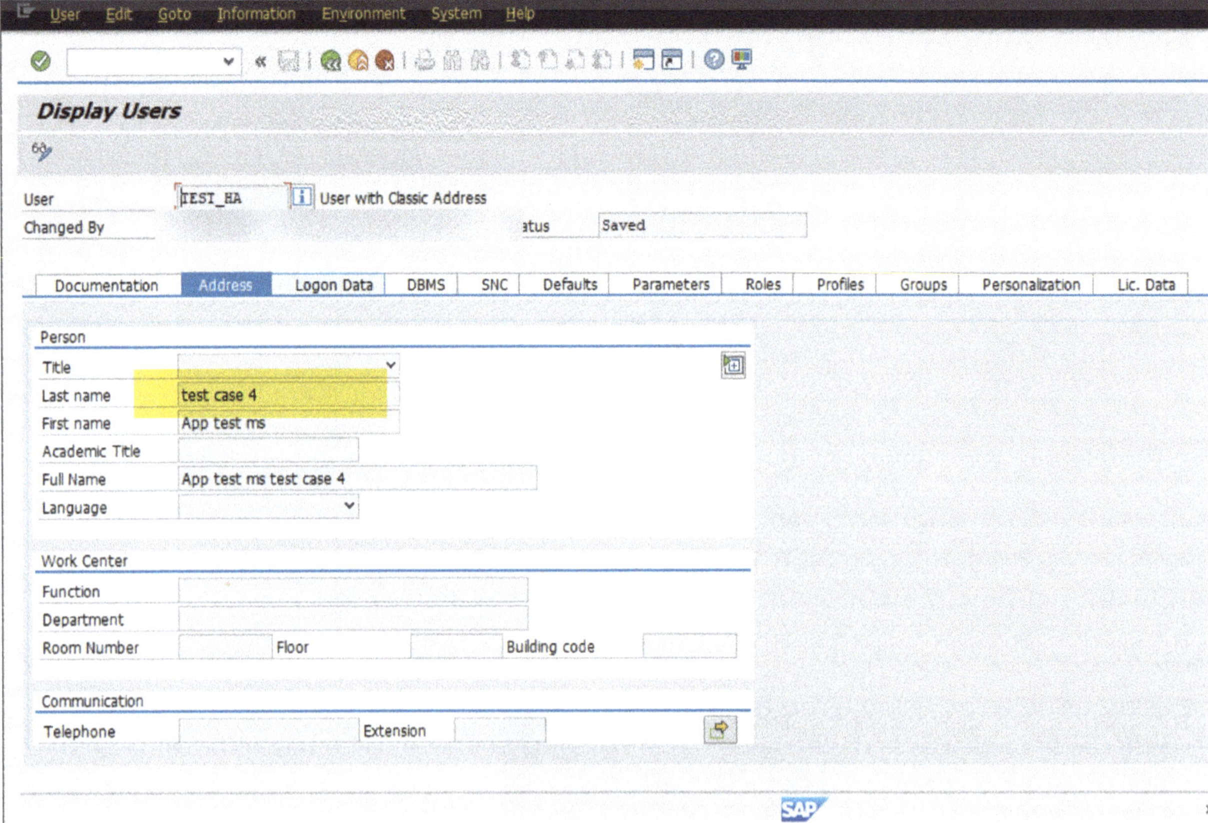

Check the pcs status: ASCS resources moved to sapmdacs node and ERS resources moved to sapecqber node.

ASCS Is running in sapecqacs Node

Remove failed Resource actions if any

pcs resource cleanup <resource name >

e.g pcs resource cleanup rsc_sap_ECQ_ASCS60

```
sapecqacs:ecqadm> sudo pcs resource cleanup rsc_sap_ECQ_ASCS60
Cleaned up fs_ECQ_ASCS on sapecqber
Cleaned up fs_ECQ_ASCS on sapecqacs
Cleaned up vip_ECQ_ASCS on sapecqber
Cleaned up vip_ECQ_ASCS on sapecqacs
Cleaned up nc_ECQ_ASCS on sapecqber
Cleaned up nc_ECQ_ASCS on sapecqacs
Cleaned up rsc_sap_ECQ_ASCS60 on sapecqber
Cleaned up rsc_sap_ECQ_ASCS60 on sapecqacs
Waiting for 1 reply from the controller
... got reply (done)
sapecqacs:ecqadm>
```

Check location constraint if any. If exist clear it.

pcs constraint list

No location constraint found.

Resource state after executing Test case

```
Cleaned up rsc_sap_ECQ_ASCS60 on sapecqacs
Waiting for 1 reply from the controller
... got reply (done)
sapecqacs:ecqadm> sudo pcs status
Cluster name: sapecqapp
Cluster Summary:
  * Stack: corosync
  * Current DC: sapecqber (version 2.0.5-9.el8_4.3-ba59be7122)  partition with quorum
  * Last updated: Fri Jun  3 09:18:26 2022
  * Last change:  Fri Jun  3 09:18:06 2022 by hacluster via crmd on sapecqber
  * 2 nodes configured
  * 9 resource instances configured

Node List:
  * Online: [ sapecqacs sapecqber ]

Full List of Resources:
  * rsc_st_azure          (stonith:fence_azure_arm):      Started sapecqber
  * Resource Group: g-ECQ_ASCS:
    * fs_ECQ_ASCS         (ocf::heartbeat:Filesystem):    Started sapecqacs
    * vip_ECQ_ASCS        (ocf::heartbeat:IPaddr2):       Started sapecqacs
    * nc_ECQ_ASCS         (ocf::heartbeat:azure-lb):      Started sapecqacs
    * rsc_sap_ECQ_ASCS60    (ocf::heartbeat:SAPInstance):   Started sapecqacs
  * Resource Group: g-ECQ_AERS:
    * fs_ECQ_AERS         (ocf::heartbeat:Filesystem):    Started sapecqber
    * vip_ECQ_AERS        (ocf::heartbeat:IPaddr2):       Started sapecqber
    * nc_ECQ_AERS         (ocf::heartbeat:azure-lb):      Started sapecqber
    * rsc_sap_ECQ_ERS70 (ocf::heartbeat:SAPInstance):   Started sapecqber

Daemon Status:
  corosync: active/disabled
  pacemaker: active/disabled
  pcsd: active/enabled
sapecqacs:ecqadm>
```

7.6. TEST CASE 5 – KILL GATEWAY PROCESS

Gateway service is running on A node

```
sapecqacs:ecqadm> /usr/sap/ECQ/SYS/exe/uc/linuxx86_64/sapcontrol -nr 60 -function GetProcessList

02.06.2022 12:32:38
GetProcessList
OK
name, description, dispstatus, textstatus, starttime, elapsedtime, pid
msg_server, MessageServer, GREEN, Running, 2022 06 02 12:20:57, 0:11:41, 23325
enq_server, Enqueue Server 2, GREEN, Running, 2022 06 02 12:20:57, 0:11:41, 23326
gwrd, Gateway, GREEN, Running, 2022 06 02 12:20:57, 0:11:41, 23327
sapwebdisp, Web Dispatcher, GREEN, Running, 2022 06 02 12:20:57, 0:11:41, 23328
sapecqacs:ecqadm>
```

Edit user in su01

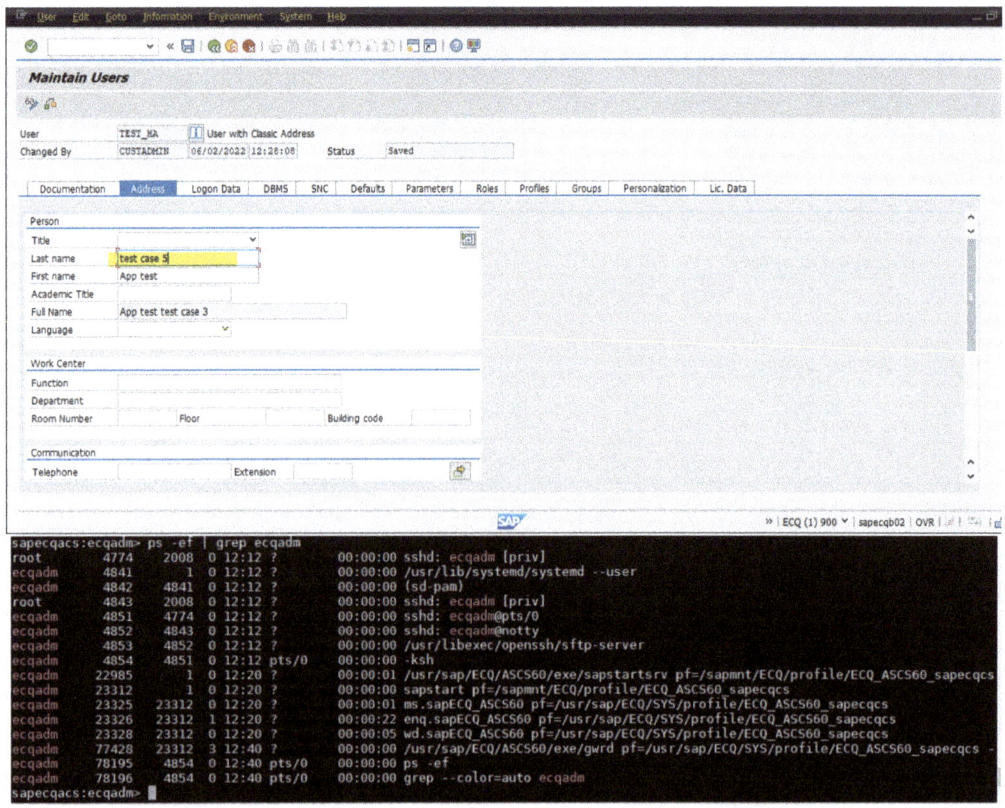

Gateway service started automatically once killed

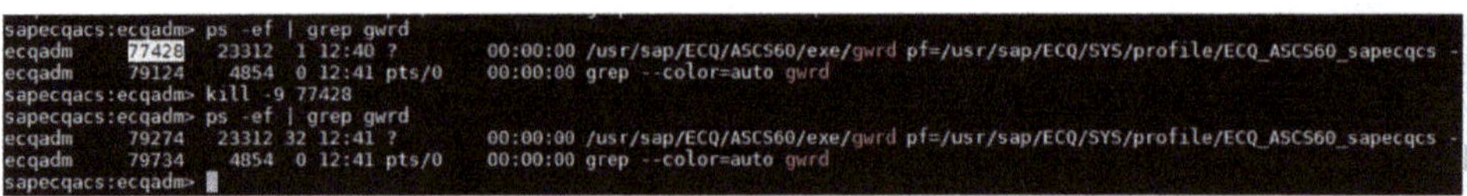

User saved

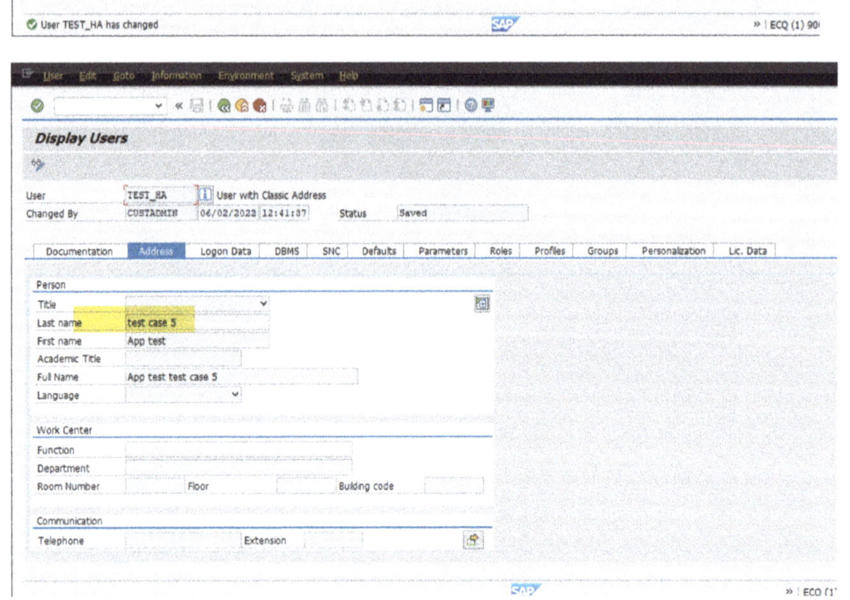

7.7. TEST CASE 6 – KILL ENQUEUE SERVER PROCESS

Resource state before Test

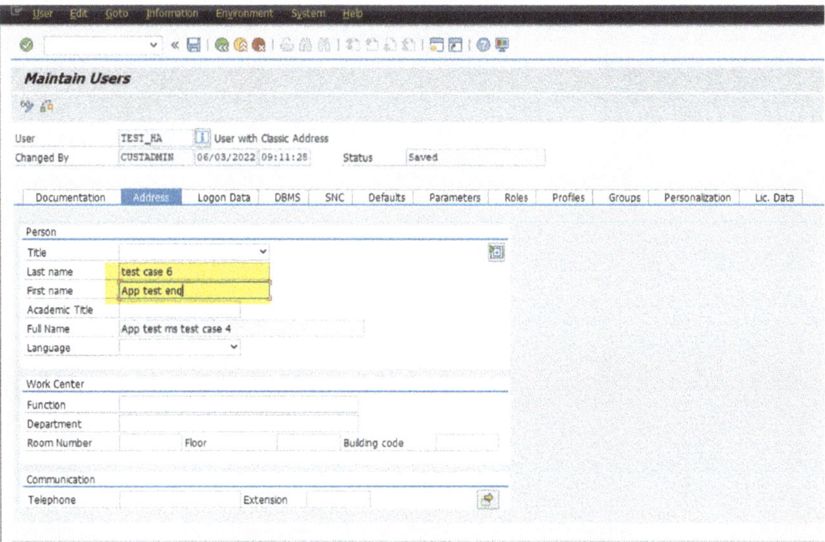

Here enq.sap service is running on sapecqacs Node.

Before killing the enqueue server process, edit the test user and it would create a lock in sm12

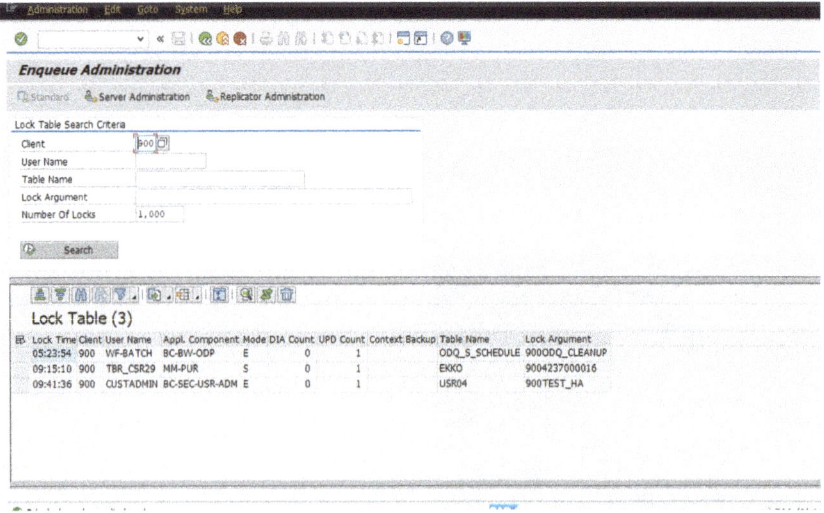

Run the following commands as root on the node where the ASCS instance is running to kill the enqueue server. Here ASCS Services are running on sapecqacs Node.

For ENSA2, Enqueue Server 2 will be there.

```
sapecqacs:ecqadm> /usr/sap/ECQ/SYS/exe/uc/linuxx86_64/sapcontrol -nr 60 -function GetProcessList

03.06.2022 09:43:20
GetProcessList
OK
name, description, dispstatus, textstatus, starttime, elapsedtime, pid
msg_server, MessageServer, GREEN, Running, 2022 06 03 09:15:32, 0:27:48, 93601
enq_server, Enqueue Server 2, GREEN, Running, 2022 06 03 09:15:32, 0:27:48, 93602
gwrd, Gateway, GREEN, Running, 2022 06 03 09:15:32, 0:27:48, 93603
sapwebdisp, Web Dispatcher, GREEN, Running, 2022 06 03 09:15:32, 0:27:48, 93609
sapecqacs:ecqadm>
```

```
#If using ENSA1
 pgrep -f en.sapECQ | xargs kill -9
#If using ENSA2
 pgrep -f enq.sapECQ | xargs kill -9
```

Run pgrep -f enq.sapECQ | xargs kill -9 on sapecqacs node:

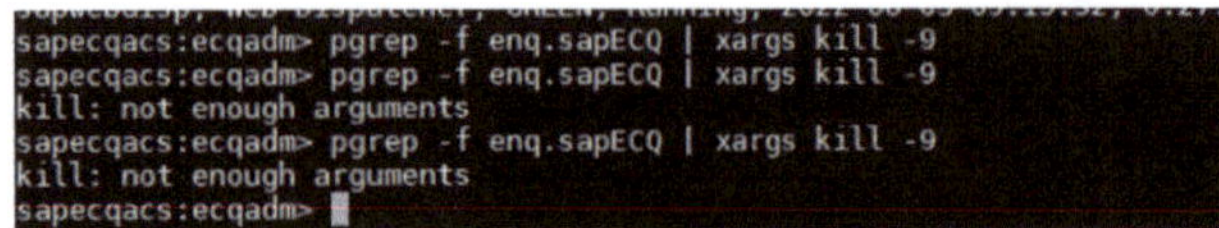

After executing the above command, save the changes to the user.

The changes are saved successfully

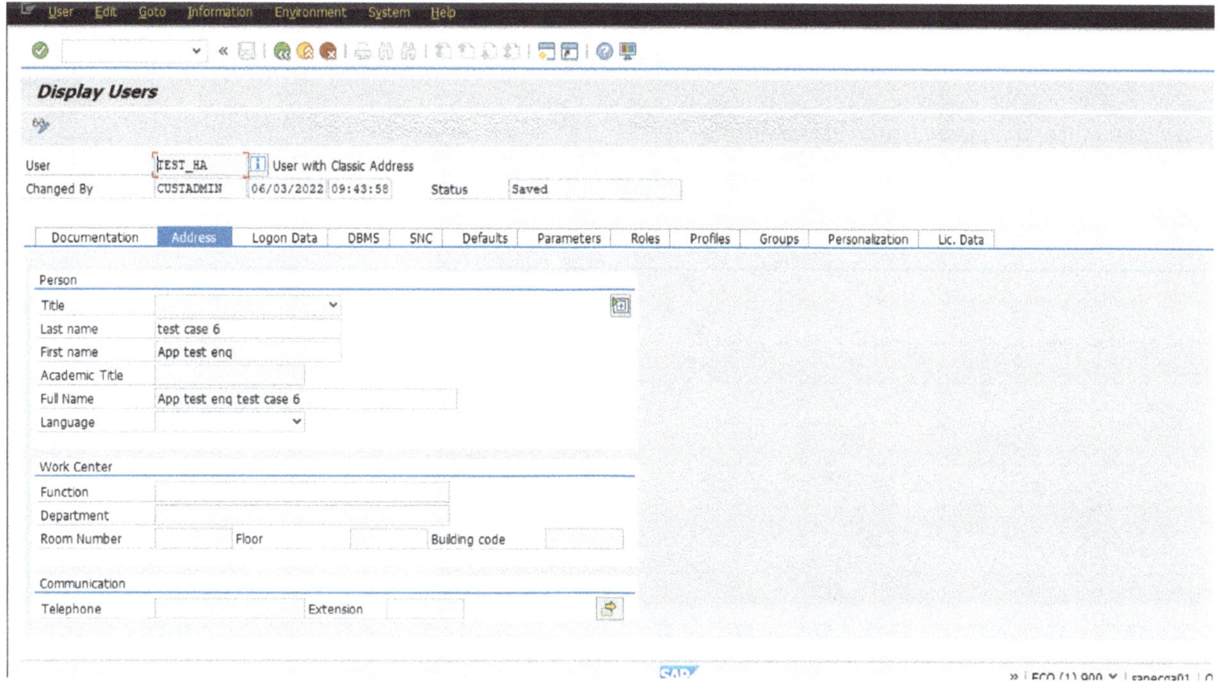

The ASCS instance should immediately fail over to the other node, in the case of ENSA1/ENSA2. The ERS instance should also fail over after the ASCS instance is started.

Check the pcs status: ASCS resources moved to sapecqber node and ERS resources moved to sapecqacs node.

```
Cluster name: sapecqapp
Cluster Summary:
  * Stack: corosync
  * Current DC: sapecqber (version 2.0.5-9.el8_4.3-ba59be7122) - partition with quorum
  * Last updated: Fri Jun  3 09:48:21 2022
  * Last change:  Fri Jun  3 09:18:06 2022 by hacluster via crmd on sapecqber
  * 2 nodes configured
  * 9 resource instances configured

Node List:
  * Online: [ sapecqacs sapecqber ]

Full List of Resources:
  * rsc_st_azure         (stonith:fence_azure_arm):       Started sapecqber
  * Resource Group: g-ECQ_ASCS:
    * fs_ECQ_ASCS        (ocf::heartbeat:Filesystem):     Started sapecqber
    * vip_ECQ_ASCS       (ocf::heartbeat:IPaddr2):        Started sapecqber
    * nc_ECQ_ASCS        (ocf::heartbeat:azure-lb):       Started sapecqber
    * rsc_sap_ECQ_ASCS60 (ocf::heartbeat:SAPInstance):    Started sapecqber
  * Resource Group: g-ECQ_AERS:
    * fs_ECQ_AERS        (ocf::heartbeat:Filesystem):     Started sapecqacs
    * vip_ECQ_AERS       (ocf::heartbeat:IPaddr2):        Started sapecqacs
    * nc_ECQ_AERS        (ocf::heartbeat:azure-lb):       Started sapecqacs
    * rsc_sap_ECQ_ERS70 (ocf::heartbeat:SAPInstance):     Started sapecqacs

Failed Resource Actions:
  * rsc_sap_ECQ_ASCS60_monitor_20000 on sapecqacs 'not running' (7): call=101, status='complete', exitreason='', last-rc-change='2
022-06-03 09:46:45Z', queued=0ms, exec=0ms

Daemon Status:
  corosync: active/disabled
  pacemaker: active/disabled
  pcsd: active/enabled
sapecqber:ecqadm>
```

Remove failed Resource actions for the ASCS.
pcs resource cleanup rsc_sap_ECQ_ASCS60

```
sapecqacs:ecqadm> sudo pcs resource cleanup rsc_sap_ECQ_ASCS60
Cleaned up fs_ECQ_ASCS on sapecqber
Cleaned up fs_ECQ_ASCS on sapecqacs
Cleaned up vip_ECQ_ASCS on sapecqber
Cleaned up vip_ECQ_ASCS on sapecqacs
Cleaned up nc_ECQ_ASCS on sapecqber
Cleaned up nc_ECQ_ASCS on sapecqacs
Cleaned up rsc_sap_ECQ_ASCS60 on sapecqber
Cleaned up rsc_sap_ECQ_ASCS60 on sapecqacs
Waiting for 1 reply from the controller
... got reply (done)
```

Check location constraint if any. If exist clear it.

pcs constraint list
No location constraint found.

Resource state after executing Test case.

```
sapecqacs:ecqadm> sudo pcs status
Cluster name: sapecqapp
Cluster Summary:
  * Stack: corosync
  * Current DC: sapecqber (version 2.0.5-9.el8_4.3-ba59be7122) - partition with quorum
  * Last updated: Fri Jun  3 09:52:19 2022
  * Last change:  Fri Jun  3 09:52:12 2022 by hacluster via crmd on sapecqacs
  * 2 nodes configured
  * 9 resource instances configured

Node List:
  * Online: [ sapecqacs sapecqber ]

Full List of Resources:
  * rsc_st_azure          (stonith:fence_azure_arm):      Started sapecqber
  * Resource Group: g-ECQ_ASCS:
    * fs_ECQ_ASCS          (ocf::heartbeat:Filesystem):   Started sapecqber
    * vip_ECQ_ASCS         (ocf::heartbeat:IPaddr2):       Started sapecqber
    * nc_ECQ_ASCS          (ocf::heartbeat:azure-lb):      Started sapecqber
    * rsc_sap_ECQ_ASCS60        (ocf::heartbeat:SAPInstance):    Started sapecqber
  * Resource Group: g-ECQ_AERS:
    * fs_ECQ_AERS          (ocf::heartbeat:Filesystem):   Started sapecqacs
    * vip_ECQ_AERS         (ocf::heartbeat:IPaddr2):       Started sapecqacs
    * nc_ECQ_AERS          (ocf::heartbeat:azure-lb):      Started sapecqacs
    * rsc_sap_ECQ_ERS70 (ocf::heartbeat:SAPInstance):     Started sapecqacs

Daemon Status:
  corosync: active/disabled
  pacemaker: active/disabled
  pcsd: active/enabled
sapecqacs:ecqadm>
```

7.8.   TEST CASE 7 – KILL STONITH PROCESS

1.   Execute Stonith script on sapecqacs Node to reboot sapecqber node where MS is running

Resource state before starting the test:

```
sapecqacs:ecqadm> sudo pcs status
Cluster name: sapecqapp
Cluster Summary:
  * Stack: corosync
  * Current DC: sapecqacs (version 2.0.5-9.el8_4.3-ba59be7122) - partition with quorum
  * Last updated: Fri Jun  3 08:15:18 2022
  * Last change:  Fri Jun  3 08:13:59 2022 by root via crm_resource on sapecqacs
  * 2 nodes configured
  * 9 resource instances configured

Node List:
  * Online: [ sapecqacs sapecqber ]

Full List of Resources:
  * rsc_st_azure          (stonith:fence_azure_arm):      Started sapecqacs
  * Resource Group: g-ECQ_ASCS:
    * fs_ECQ_ASCS          (ocf::heartbeat:Filesystem):   Started sapecqber
    * vip_ECQ_ASCS         (ocf::heartbeat:IPaddr2):       Started sapecqber
    * nc_ECQ_ASCS          (ocf::heartbeat:azure-lb):      Started sapecqber
    * rsc_sap_ECQ_ASCS60        (ocf::heartbeat:SAPInstance):    Started sapecqber
  * Resource Group: g-ECQ_AERS:
    * fs_ECQ_AERS          (ocf::heartbeat:Filesystem):   Started sapecqacs
    * vip_ECQ_AERS         (ocf::heartbeat:IPaddr2):       Started sapecqacs
    * nc_ECQ_AERS          (ocf::heartbeat:azure-lb):      Started sapecqacs
    * rsc_sap_ECQ_ERS70 (ocf::heartbeat:SAPInstance):     Started sapecqacs

Daemon Status:
  corosync: active/disabled
  pacemaker: active/disabled
  pcsd: active/enabled
sapecqacs:ecqadm>
```

Check the sap services on both ASCS and ERS nodes

ASCS Services are running on sapecqber Node.

```
sapecqber:ecqadm> ps -ef | grep ecqadm
root       3601   1804  0 08:09 ?        00:00:00 sshd: ecqadm [priv]
ecqadm     4064      1  0 08:10 ?        00:00:00 /usr/lib/systemd/systemd --user
ecqadm     4065   4064  0 08:10 ?        00:00:00 (sd-pam)
root       4069   1804  0 08:10 ?        00:00:00 sshd: ecqadm [priv]
ecqadm     4074   3601  0 08:10 ?        00:00:00 sshd: ecqadm@pts/0
ecqadm     4075   4069  0 08:10 ?        00:00:00 sshd: ecqadm@notty
ecqadm     4076   4075  0 08:10 ?        00:00:00 /usr/libexec/openssh/sftp-server
ecqadm     4083   4074  0 08:10 pts/0    00:00:00 -ksh
ecqadm     9110      1  0 08:12 ?        00:00:01 /usr/sap/ECQ/ASCS60/exe/sapstartsrv pf=/sapmnt/ECQ/profile/ECQ_ASCS60_sapecqcs
ecqadm     9901      1  0 08:12 ?        00:00:00 sapstart pf=/sapmnt/ECQ/profile/ECQ_ASCS60_sapecqcs
ecqadm     9914   9901  0 08:12 ?        00:00:00 ms.sapECQ_ASCS60 pf=/usr/sap/ECQ/SYS/profile/ECQ_ASCS60_sapecqcs
ecqadm     9915   9901  2 08:12 ?        00:00:10 enq.sapECQ_ASCS60 pf=/usr/sap/ECQ/SYS/profile/ECQ_ASCS60_sapecqcs
ecqadm     9916   9901  0 08:12 ?        00:00:00 /usr/sap/ECQ/ASCS60/exe/gwrd pf=/usr/sap/ECQ/SYS/profile/ECQ_ASCS60_sapecqcs -
ecqadm     9917   9901  0 08:12 ?        00:00:01 wd.sapECQ_ASCS60 pf=/usr/sap/ECQ/SYS/profile/ECQ_ASCS60_sapecqcs
ecqadm    25147   4083  0 08:18 pts/0    00:00:00 ps -ef
ecqadm    25148   4083  0 08:18 pts/0    00:00:00 grep --color=auto ecqadm
sapecqber:ecqadm>
```

ERS Service is running on sapecqacs Node.

Before killing the Stonith process, edit the test user and it would create a lock in sm12

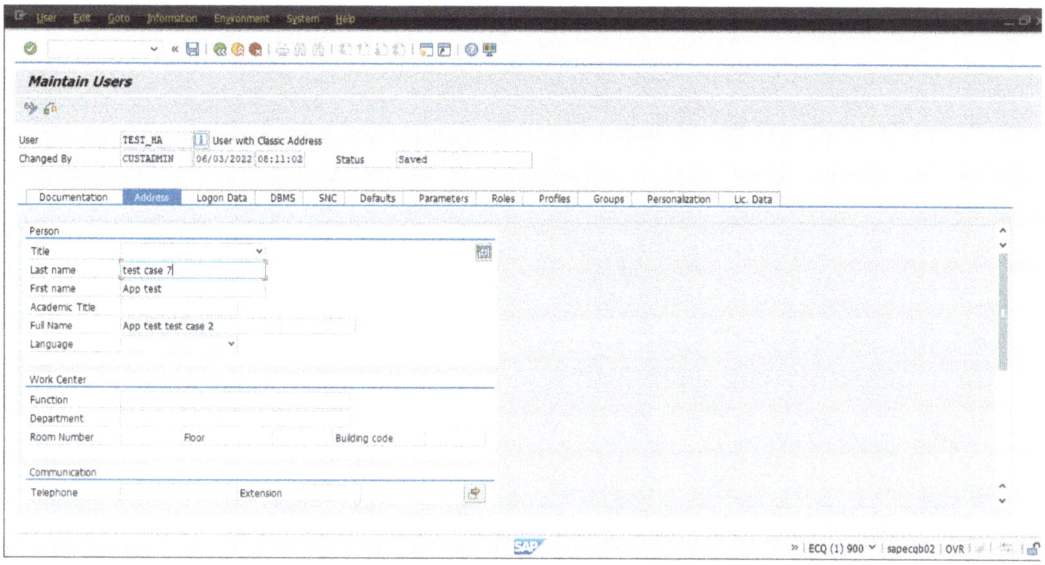

Maintain Users

User	TEST_HA
Changed By	CUSTADMIN	06/03/2022 08:11:02	Status	Saved

Documentation | Address | Logon Data | DBMS | SNC | Defaults | Parameters | Roles | Profiles | Groups | Personalization | Lic. Data

Person

Title	
Last name	test case 7
First name	App test
Academic Title	
Full Name	App test test case 2
Language	

Work Center

Function	
Department	
Room Number	Floor	Building code

Communication

Telephone	Extension

» | ECQ (1) 900 ∨ | sapecqb02 | OVR

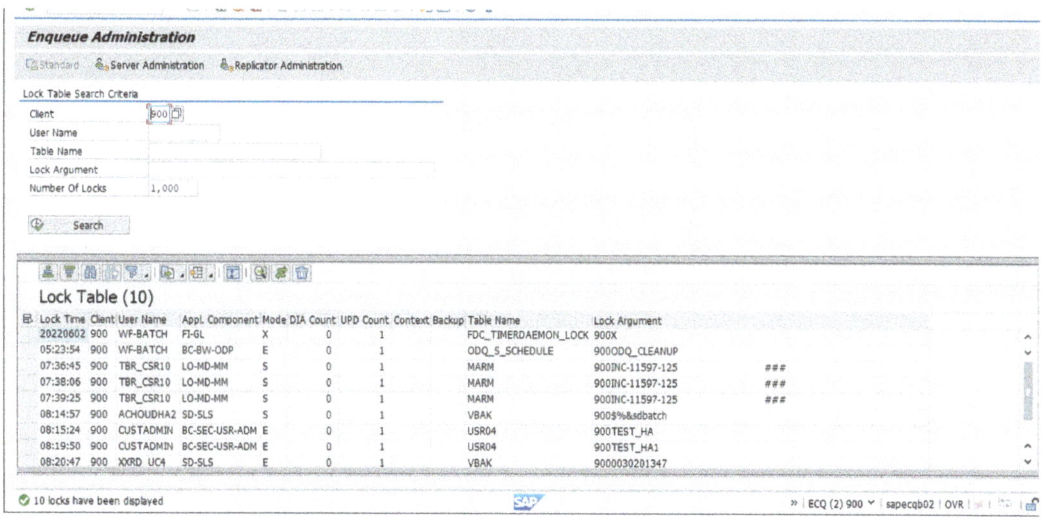

Enqueue Administration

Standard | Server Administration | Replicator Administration

Lock Table Search Criteria

Client	900
User Name	
Table Name	
Lock Argument	
Number Of Locks	1,000

Search

Lock Table (10)

Lock Time	Client	User Name	Appl. Component	Mode	DIA Count	UPD Count	Context Backup	Table Name	Lock Argument	
20220602	900	WF-BATCH	FI-GL	X	0	1		FDC_TIMERDAEMON_LOCK	900X	
05:23:54	900	WF-BATCH	BC-BW-ODP	E	0	1		ODQ_S_SCHEDULE	900ODQ_CLEANUP	
07:36:45	900	TBR_CSR10	LO-MD-MM	S	0	1		MARM	900INC-11597-125	###
07:38:06	900	TBR_CSR10	LO-MD-MM	S	0	1		MARM	900INC-11597-125	###
07:39:25	900	TBR_CSR10	LO-MD-MM	S	0	1		MARM	900INC-11597-125	###
08:14:57	900	ACHOUDHA2	SD-SLS	S	0	1		VBAK	900$%&sdbatch	
08:15:24	900	CUSTADMIN	BC-SEC-USR-ADM	E	0	1		USR04	900TEST_HA	
08:19:50	900	CUSTADMIN	BC-SEC-USR-ADM	E	0	1		USR04	900TEST_HA1	
08:20:47	900	XXRD UC4	SD-SLS	E	0	1		VBAK	9000030201347	

✓ 10 locks have been displayed

» | ECQ (2) 900 ∨ | sapecqb02 | OVR

Run the stonith.sh script as root on the node where the ERS service is running, here on sapecqacs node.
As per the stonith.sh file, plug =sapecqber, so sapecqber will be rebooted.

```
sapecqacs:ecqadm> cd /backup/
sapecqacs:ecqadm> cat Stonith_fencing_script.sh
#!/bin/bash
action=reboot
login="b1e5bbbf-3c38-4125-8c3f-c00b5fa4a457"
passwd="wAu7Q~14p.EhseZkR6A5t.opV~1VvHv5gz2jm"
pcmk_reboot_timeout=900
power_timeout=240
resourceGroup=RSG-SAP-PreProd

subscriptionId=91cbd599-d354-48e3-b7b9-380006e84af6
tenantId=4e9dbbfb-394a-4583-8810-53f81f819e3b
verbose=1
plug=azusapecqber


fence_azure_arm --action=$action --username=$login --password="$passwd" \
--resourceGroup=$resourceGroup --tenantId=$tenantId --subscriptionId=$subscriptionId \
--power-timeout=$power_timeout --verbose --plug=$plug
echo "Return Value $?"
sapecqacs:ecqadm>
```

```
':'...'}
2022-06-03 08:21:43,041 DEBUG: 2cce4b53-5f3e-4ce1-a3dd-96ade0228a65 - CacheDriver:Found 1 potential entries.
2022-06-03 08:21:43,041 DEBUG: 2cce4b53-5f3e-4ce1-a3dd-96ade0228a65 - CacheDriver:Resource specific token found.
2022-06-03 08:21:43,041 DEBUG: 2cce4b53-5f3e-4ce1-a3dd-96ade0228a65 - CacheDriver:Returning token from cache lookup, AccessTokenId
: b'QETx9fvBLvZD5TJOGICG7yr/OrRku9kmkI6jXVo7qbU='
2022-06-03 08:21:43,042 DEBUG: Configuring redirects: allow=True, max=30
2022-06-03 08:21:43,042 DEBUG: Configuring request: timeout=100, verify=True, cert=None
2022-06-03 08:21:43,042 DEBUG: Configuring proxies: ''
2022-06-03 08:21:43,043 DEBUG: Evaluate proxies against ENV settings: True
2022-06-03 08:21:43,044 DEBUG: Starting new HTTPS connection (1): management.azure.com:443
2022-06-03 08:21:43,980 DEBUG: https://management.azure.com:443 "GET /subscriptions/91cbd599-d354-48e3-b7b9-380006e84af6/resourceG
roups/RSG-SAP-PreProd/providers/Microsoft.Compute/virtualMachines/azusapecqber?$expand=instanceView&api-version=2019-03-01 HTTP/1.
1" 200 None
2022-06-03 08:21:43,989 INFO: Found power state of VM: on (running)
2022-06-03 08:21:43,989 INFO: setting power status for VM azusapecqber to off
2022-06-03 08:21:43,989 INFO: Poweroff azusapecqber in resource group RSG-SAP-PreProd
2022-06-03 08:21:43,990 DEBUG: Accept header absent and forced to application/json
2022-06-03 08:21:43,990 DEBUG: 361c32bc-93d1-49da-ba4f-5184d1325e0b - Authority:Instance discovery/validation has either already b
een completed or is turned off: ...
2022-06-03 08:21:43,990 INFO: 361c32bc-93d1-49da-ba4f-5184d1325e0b - TokenRequest:Getting token with client credentials.
2022-06-03 08:21:43,991 DEBUG: 361c32bc-93d1-49da-ba4f-5184d1325e0b - TokenRequest:No user_id passed for cache query
2022-06-03 08:21:43,991 DEBUG: 361c32bc-93d1-49da-ba4f-5184d1325e0b - CacheDriver:finding with query keys: {'_clientId': '...'}
2022-06-03 08:21:43,991 DEBUG: 361c32bc-93d1-49da-ba4f-5184d1325e0b - CacheDriver:Looking for potential cache entries: {'_clientId
': '...'}
2022-06-03 08:21:43,991 DEBUG: 361c32bc-93d1-49da-ba4f-5184d1325e0b - CacheDriver:Found 1 potential entries.
2022-06-03 08:21:43,991 DEBUG: 361c32bc-93d1-49da-ba4f-5184d1325e0b - CacheDriver:Resource specific token found.
2022-06-03 08:21:43,991 DEBUG: 361c32bc-93d1-49da-ba4f-5184d1325e0b - CacheDriver:Returning token from cache lookup, AccessTokenId
: b'QETx9fvBLvZD5TJOGICG7yr/OrRku9kmkI6jXVo7qbU='
2022-06-03 08:21:43,992 DEBUG: Configuring redirects: allow=True, max=30
2022-06-03 08:21:43,992 DEBUG: Configuring request: timeout=100, verify=True, cert=None
2022-06-03 08:21:43,992 DEBUG: Configuring proxies: ''
2022-06-03 08:21:43,992 DEBUG: Evaluate proxies against ENV settings: True
2022-06-03 08:21:43,993 DEBUG: Starting new HTTPS connection (1): management.azure.com:443
```

After executing the above command, save the changes to the user.

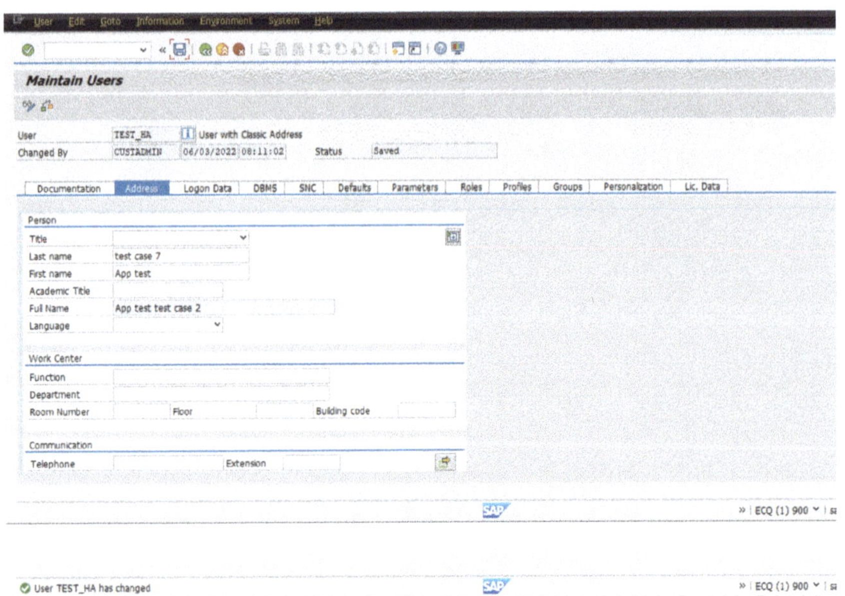

The changes are saved successfully

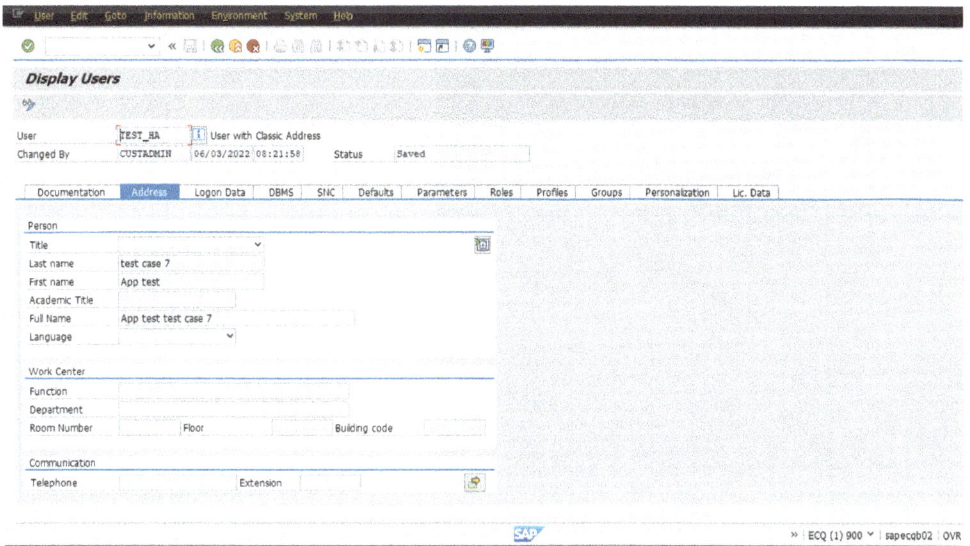

Check the pcs status: ASCS resources moved on sapecqacs node. ERS remain on sapecqacs as sapecqber is rebooted and cluster not started automatically.

```
sapecqacs:ecqadm> sudo pcs status
Cluster name: sapecqapp
Cluster Summary:
  * Stack: corosync
  * Current DC: sapecqacs (version 2.0.5-9.el8_4.3-ba59be7122) - partition with quorum
  * Last updated: Fri Jun  3 08:24:30 2022
  * Last change:  Fri Jun  3 08:13:59 2022 by root via crm_resource on sapecqacs
  * 2 nodes configured
  * 9 resource instances configured

Node List:
  * Online: [ sapecqacs ]
  * OFFLINE: [ sapecqber ]

Full List of Resources:
  * rsc_st_azure          (stonith:fence_azure_arm):       Started sapecqacs
  * Resource Group: g-ECQ_ASCS:
    * fs_ECQ_ASCS         (ocf::heartbeat:Filesystem):     Started sapecqacs
    * vip_ECQ_ASCS        (ocf::heartbeat:IPaddr2):        Started sapecqacs
    * nc_ECQ_ASCS         (ocf::heartbeat:azure-lb):       Started sapecqacs
    * rsc_sap_ECQ_ASCS60      (ocf::heartbeat:SAPInstance):    Started sapecqacs
  * Resource Group: g-ECQ_AERS:
    * fs_ECQ_AERS         (ocf::heartbeat:Filesystem):     Started sapecqacs
    * vip_ECQ_AERS        (ocf::heartbeat:IPaddr2):        Started sapecqacs
    * nc_ECQ_AERS         (ocf::heartbeat:azure-lb):       Started sapecqacs
    * rsc_sap_ECQ_ERS70 (ocf::heartbeat:SAPInstance):      Started sapecqacs

Daemon Status:
  corosync: active/disabled
  pacemaker: active/disabled
  pcsd: active/enabled
sapecqacs:ecqadm>
```

Check cluster status on sapecqber Node and start cluster.

```
sapecqber:ecqadm> sudo pcs status
Error: error running crm_mon, is pacemaker running?
  crm_mon: Error: cluster is not available on this node
sapecqber:ecqadm> sudo pcs cluster start
Starting Cluster...
sapecqber:ecqadm>
```

Check pcs status, **once cluster on sapecqber node started, ERS resource will move to sapecqber node automatically.**

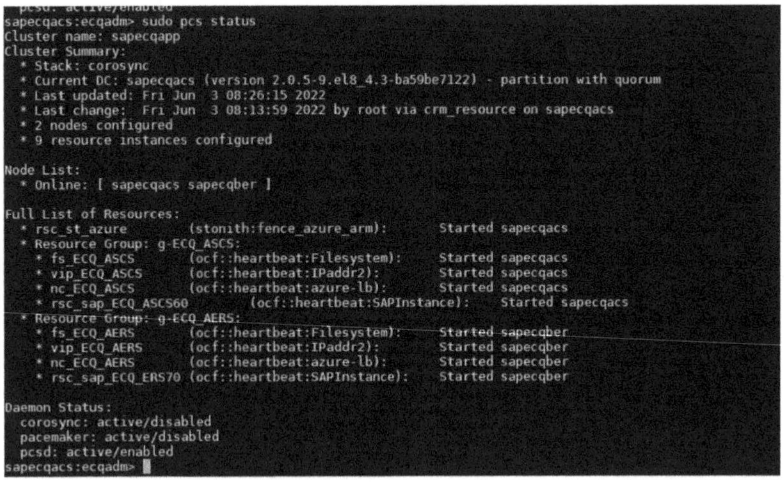

```
pcsd: active/enabled
sapecqacs:ecqadm> sudo pcs status
Cluster name: sapecqapp
Cluster Summary:
  * Stack: corosync
  * Current DC: sapecqacs (version 2.0.5-9.el8_4.3-ba59be7122) - partition with quorum
  * Last updated: Fri Jun  3 08:26:15 2022
  * Last change:  Fri Jun  3 08:13:59 2022 by root via crm_resource on sapecqacs
  * 2 nodes configured
  * 9 resource instances configured

Node List:
  * Online: [ sapecqacs sapecqber ]

Full List of Resources:
  * rsc_st_azure          (stonith:fence_azure_arm):      Started sapecqacs
  * Resource Group: g-ECQ_ASCS:
    * fs_ECQ_ASCS         (ocf::heartbeat:Filesystem):    Started sapecqacs
    * vip_ECQ_ASCS        (ocf::heartbeat:IPaddr2):       Started sapecqacs
    * nc_ECQ_ASCS         (ocf::heartbeat:azure-lb):      Started sapecqacs
    * rsc_sap_ECQ_ASCS60       (ocf::heartbeat:SAPInstance):   Started sapecqacs
  * Resource Group: g-ECQ_AERS:
    * fs_ECQ_AERS         (ocf::heartbeat:Filesystem):    Started sapecqber
    * vip_ECQ_AERS        (ocf::heartbeat:IPaddr2):       Started sapecqber
    * nc_ECQ_AERS         (ocf::heartbeat:azure-lb):      Started sapecqber
    * rsc_sap_ECQ_ERS70 (ocf::heartbeat:SAPInstance):     Started sapecqber

Daemon Status:
  corosync: active/disabled
  pacemaker: active/disabled
  pcsd: active/enabled
sapecqacs:ecqadm> 
```

Remove failed Resource actions if any

pcs resource cleanup <resource name >

e.g pcs resource cleanup rsc_sap_ECQ_ERS70

Check location constraint if any. If exist clear it.

pcs constraint list

No location constraint found.

Resource state after executing Test case

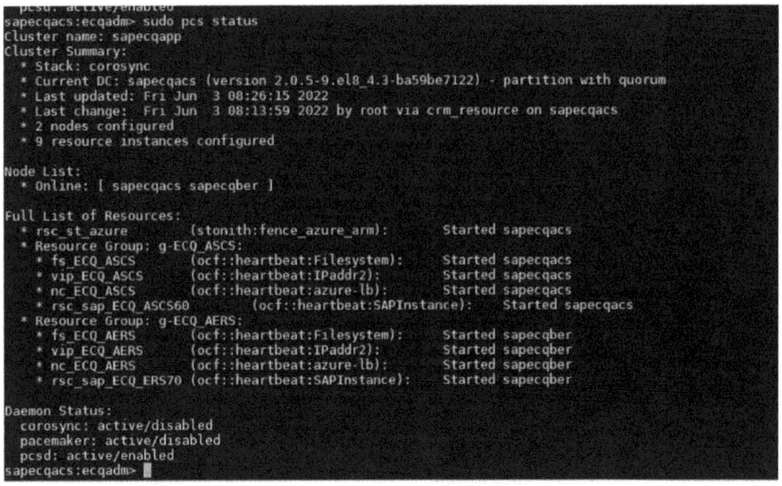

```
pcsd: active/enabled
sapecqacs:ecqadm> sudo pcs status
Cluster name: sapecqapp
Cluster Summary:
  * Stack: corosync
  * Current DC: sapecqacs (version 2.0.5-9.el8_4.3-ba59be7122) - partition with quorum
  * Last updated: Fri Jun  3 08:26:15 2022
  * Last change:  Fri Jun  3 08:13:59 2022 by root via crm_resource on sapecqacs
  * 2 nodes configured
  * 9 resource instances configured

Node List:
  * Online: [ sapecqacs sapecqber ]

Full List of Resources:
  * rsc_st_azure          (stonith:fence_azure_arm):      Started sapecqacs
  * Resource Group: g-ECQ_ASCS:
    * fs_ECQ_ASCS         (ocf::heartbeat:Filesystem):    Started sapecqacs
    * vip_ECQ_ASCS        (ocf::heartbeat:IPaddr2):       Started sapecqacs
    * nc_ECQ_ASCS         (ocf::heartbeat:azure-lb):      Started sapecqacs
    * rsc_sap_ECQ_ASCS60       (ocf::heartbeat:SAPInstance):   Started sapecqacs
  * Resource Group: g-ECQ_AERS:
    * fs_ECQ_AERS         (ocf::heartbeat:Filesystem):    Started sapecqber
    * vip_ECQ_AERS        (ocf::heartbeat:IPaddr2):       Started sapecqber
    * nc_ECQ_AERS         (ocf::heartbeat:azure-lb):      Started sapecqber
    * rsc_sap_ECQ_ERS70 (ocf::heartbeat:SAPInstance):     Started sapecqber

Daemon Status:
  corosync: active/disabled
  pacemaker: active/disabled
  pcsd: active/enabled
sapecqacs:ecqadm> 
```

2. Kill Stonith process on sapecqacs

Here Stonith/ASCS service/resource are running on sapecqacs node. ERS resource is on sapecqber node.

Run stonith.sh script on Node sapecqber to reboot sapecqacs Node.

```
pcsu: active/enabled
sapecqacs:ecqadm> sudo pcs status
Cluster name: sapecqapp
Cluster Summary:
  * Stack: corosync
  * Current DC: sapecqacs (version 2.0.5-9.el8_4.3-ba59be7122) - partition with quorum
  * Last updated: Fri Jun  3 08:26:15 2022
  * Last change:  Fri Jun  3 08:13:59 2022 by root via crm_resource on sapecqacs
  * 2 nodes configured
  * 9 resource instances configured

Node List:
  * Online: [ sapecqacs sapecqber ]

Full List of Resources:
  * rsc_st_azure        (stonith:fence_azure_arm):      Started sapecqacs
  * Resource Group: g-ECQ_ASCS:
    * fs_ECQ_ASCS       (ocf::heartbeat:Filesystem):    Started sapecqacs
    * vip_ECQ_ASCS      (ocf::heartbeat:IPaddr2):        Started sapecqacs
    * nc_ECQ_ASCS       (ocf::heartbeat:azure-lb):       Started sapecqacs
    * rsc_sap_ECQ_ASCS60        (ocf::heartbeat:SAPInstance):       Started sapecqacs
  * Resource Group: g-ECQ_AERS:
    * fs_ECQ_AERS       (ocf::heartbeat:Filesystem):    Started sapecqber
    * vip_ECQ_AERS      (ocf::heartbeat:IPaddr2):        Started sapecqber
    * nc_ECQ_AERS       (ocf::heartbeat:azure-lb):       Started sapecqber
    * rsc_sap_ECQ_ERS70 (ocf::heartbeat:SAPInstance):   Started sapecqber

Daemon Status:
  corosync: active/disabled
  pacemaker: active/disabled
  pcsd: active/enabled
sapecqacs:ecqadm> 
```

Before killing the Stonith process, edit the test user and it would create a lock in sm12

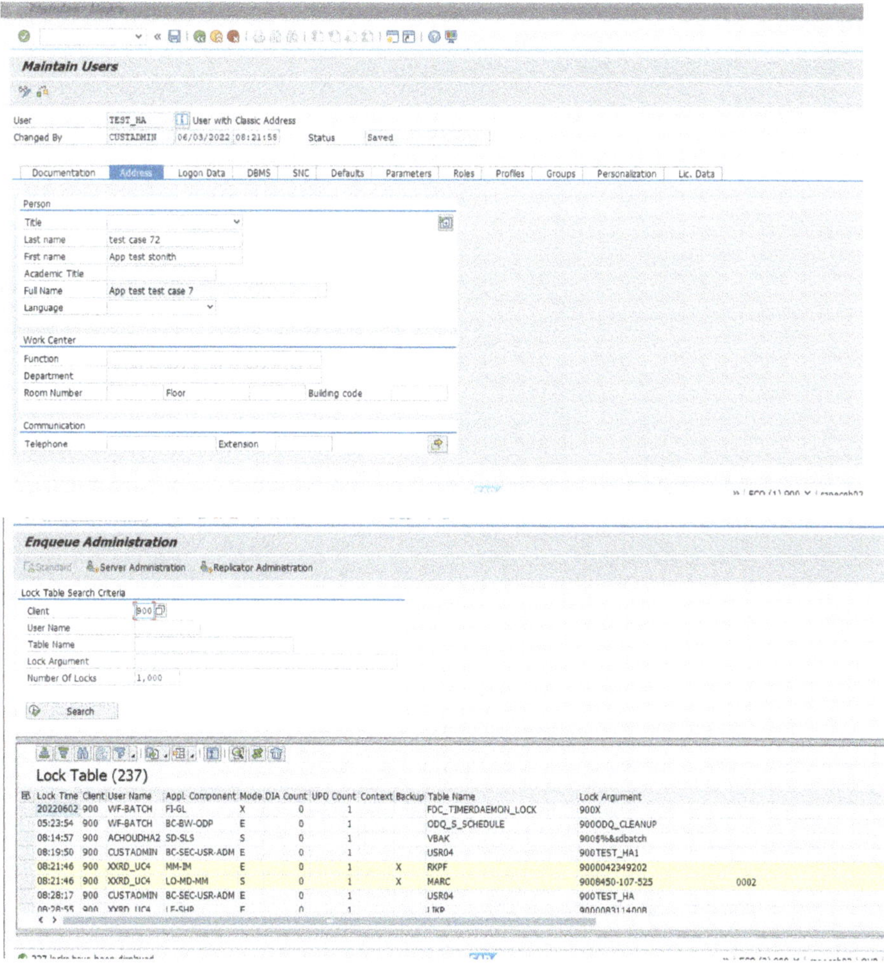

```
sapecqber:ecqadm> cat Stonith_fencing_script.sh
#!/bin/bash
action=reboot
login="b1e5bbbf-3c38-4125-8c3f-c00b5fa4a457"
passwd="wAu7Q~14p.EhseZkR6A5t.opV~1VvHv5gz2jm"
pcmk_reboot_timeout=900
power_timeout=240
resourceGroup=RSG-SAP-PreProd

subscriptionId=91cbd599-d354-48e3-b7b9-380006e84af6
tenantId=4e9dbbfb-394a-4583-8810-53f81f819e3b
verbose=1
plug=azusapecqacs


fence_azure_arm --action=$action --username=$login --password="$passwd" \
--resourceGroup=$resourceGroup --tenantId=$tenantId --subscriptionId=$subscriptionId \
--power-timeout=$power_timeout --verbose --plug=$plug
echo "Return Value $?"
sapecqber:ecqadm>
```

```
2022-06-03 08:30:21,501 DEBUG: 053a18c7-c437-4959-a03d-d132c7378454 - TokenRequest:No user_id passed for cache query
2022-06-03 08:30:21,501 DEBUG: 053a18c7-c437-4959-a03d-d132c7378454 - CacheDriver:finding with query keys: {'_clientId': '...'}
2022-06-03 08:30:21,501 DEBUG: 053a18c7-c437-4959-a03d-d132c7378454 - CacheDriver:Looking for potential cache entries: {'_clientId
': '...'}
2022-06-03 08:30:21,502 DEBUG: 053a18c7-c437-4959-a03d-d132c7378454 - CacheDriver:Found 1 potential entries.
2022-06-03 08:30:21,502 DEBUG: 053a18c7-c437-4959-a03d-d132c7378454 - CacheDriver:Resource specific token found.
2022-06-03 08:30:21,502 DEBUG: 053a18c7-c437-4959-a03d-d132c7378454 - CacheDriver:Returning token from cache lookup, AccessTokenId
: b'nis/oAQaeIxTyxvyu0MnVUuik0fEzc4MzWe0ETJNx6Y='
2022-06-03 08:30:21,502 DEBUG: Configuring redirects: allow=True, max=30
2022-06-03 08:30:21,502 DEBUG: Configuring request: timeout=100, verify=True, cert=None
2022-06-03 08:30:21,502 DEBUG: Configuring proxies: ''
2022-06-03 08:30:21,503 DEBUG: Evaluate proxies against ENV settings: True
2022-06-03 08:30:21,503 DEBUG: Starting new HTTPS connection (1): management.azure.com:443
2022-06-03 08:30:22,135 DEBUG: https://management.azure.com:443 "POST /subscriptions/91cbd599-d354-48e3-b7b9-380006e84af6/resource
Groups/RSG-SAP-PreProd/providers/Microsoft.Compute/virtualMachines/azusapecqacs/powerOff?skipShutdown=true&api-version=2019-03-01
HTTP/1.1" 202 0
2022-06-03 08:30:22,138 INFO: getting power status for VM azusapecqacs
2022-06-03 08:30:22,139 DEBUG: 7c70f37f-e5c6-4dac-9778-f68650988462 - Authority:Instance discovery/validation has either already b
een completed or is turned off: ...
2022-06-03 08:30:22,139 INFO: 7c70f37f-e5c6-4dac-9778-f68650988462 - TokenRequest:Getting token with client credentials.
2022-06-03 08:30:22,139 DEBUG: 7c70f37f-e5c6-4dac-9778-f68650988462 - TokenRequest:No user_id passed for cache query
2022-06-03 08:30:22,139 DEBUG: 7c70f37f-e5c6-4dac-9778-f68650988462 - CacheDriver:finding with query keys: {'_clientId': '...'}
2022-06-03 08:30:22,140 DEBUG: 7c70f37f-e5c6-4dac-9778-f68650988462 - CacheDriver:Looking for potential cache entries: {'_clientId
': '...'}
2022-06-03 08:30:22,140 DEBUG: 7c70f37f-e5c6-4dac-9778-f68650988462 - CacheDriver:Found 1 potential entries.
2022-06-03 08:30:22,140 DEBUG: 7c70f37f-e5c6-4dac-9778-f68650988462 - CacheDriver:Resource specific token found.
2022-06-03 08:30:22,140 DEBUG: 7c70f37f-e5c6-4dac-9778-f68650988462 - CacheDriver:Returning token from cache lookup, AccessTokenId
: b'nis/oAQaeIxTyxvyu0MnVUuik0fEzc4MzWe0ETJNx6Y='
2022-06-03 08:30:22,140 DEBUG: Configuring redirects: allow=True, max=30
2022-06-03 08:30:22,140 DEBUG: Configuring request: timeout=100, verify=True, cert=None
2022-06-03 08:30:22,141 DEBUG: Configuring proxies: ''
2022-06-03 08:30:22,141 DEBUG: Evaluate proxies against ENV settings: True
2022-06-03 08:30:22,142 DEBUG: Starting new HTTPS connection (1): management.azure.com:443
```

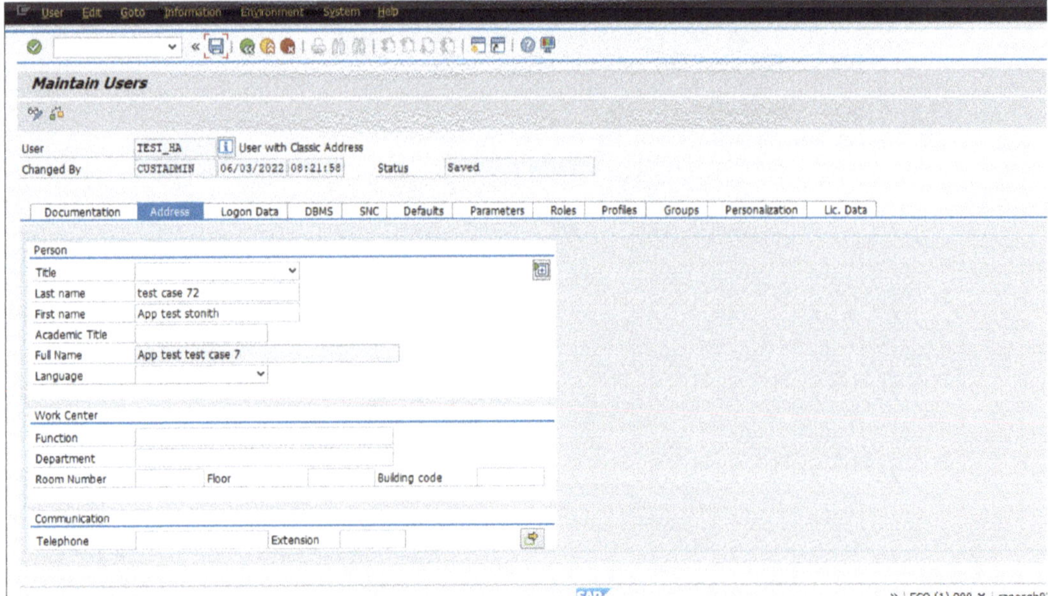

After executing the above command, save the changes to the user.

The changes are saved successfully

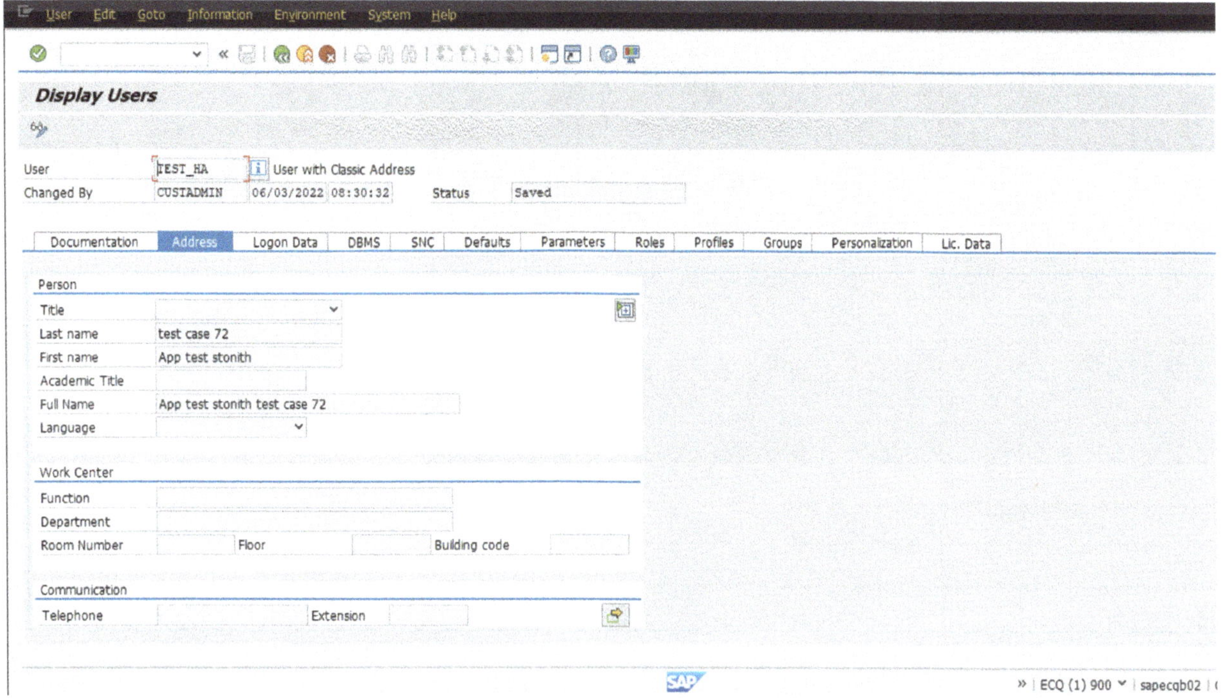

Check the pcs status: ASCS resources moved to sapecqber node, ERS remain on sapecqber as sapecqacs is rebooted and cluster not started automatically.

```
sapecqber:ecqadm> sudo pcs status
Cluster name: sapecqapp
Cluster Summary:
  * Stack: corosync
  * Current DC: sapecqber (version 2.0.5-9.el8_4.3-ba59be7122) - partition with quorum
  * Last updated: Fri Jun  3 08:33:02 2022
  * Last change:  Fri Jun  3 08:13:59 2022 by root via crm_resource on sapecqacs
  * 2 nodes configured
  * 9 resource instances configured

Node List:
  * Online: [ sapecqber ]
  * OFFLINE: [ sapecqacs ]

Full List of Resources:
  * rsc_st_azure      (stonith:fence_azure_arm):       Started sapecqber
  * Resource Group: g-ECQ_ASCS:
    * fs_ECQ_ASCS         (ocf::heartbeat:Filesystem):     Started sapecqber
    * vip_ECQ_ASCS        (ocf::heartbeat:IPaddr2):        Started sapecqber
    * nc_ECQ_ASCS         (ocf::heartbeat:azure-lb):       Started sapecqber
    * rsc_sap_ECQ_ASCS60      (ocf::heartbeat:SAPInstance):    Started sapecqber
  * Resource Group: g-ECQ_AERS:
    * fs_ECQ_AERS         (ocf::heartbeat:Filesystem):     Started sapecqber
    * vip_ECQ_AERS        (ocf::heartbeat:IPaddr2):        Started sapecqber
    * nc_ECQ_AERS         (ocf::heartbeat:azure-lb):       Started sapecqber
    * rsc_sap_ECQ_ERS70 (ocf::heartbeat:SAPInstance):    Started sapecqber

Daemon Status:
  corosync: active/disabled
  pacemaker: active/disabled
  pcsd: active/enabled
sapecqber:ecqadm>
```

Check cluster status on sapecqacs Node and start cluster.

```
sapecqacs:ecqadm> sudo pcs status
Error: error running crm_mon, is pacemaker running?
  crm_mon: Error: cluster is not available on this node
sapecqacs:ecqadm> sudo pcs cluster start
Starting Cluster...
sapecqacs:ecqadm>
```

Check pcs status, **once cluster on sapecqacs node started, ERS resource will move to sapecqacs node automatically.**

```
sapecqacs:ecqadm> sudo pcs status
Cluster name: sapecqapp
Cluster Summary:
  * Stack: corosync
  * Current DC: sapecqber (version 2.0.5-9.el8_4.3-ba59be7122) - partition with quorum
  * Last updated: Fri Jun  3 08:35:06 2022
  * Last change:  Fri Jun  3 08:13:59 2022 by root via crm_resource on sapecqacs
  * 2 nodes configured
  * 9 resource instances configured

Node List:
  * Online: [ sapecqacs sapecqber ]

Full List of Resources:
  * rsc_st_azure          (stonith:fence_azure_arm):      Started sapecqber
  * Resource Group: g-ECQ_ASCS:
    * fs_ECQ_ASCS          (ocf::heartbeat:Filesystem):    Started sapecqber
    * vip_ECQ_ASCS         (ocf::heartbeat:IPaddr2):       Started sapecqber
    * nc_ECQ_ASCS          (ocf::heartbeat:azure-lb):      Started sapecqber
    * rsc_sap_ECQ_ASCS60        (ocf::heartbeat:SAPInstance):   Started sapecqber
  * Resource Group: g-ECQ_AERS:
    * fs_ECQ_AERS          (ocf::heartbeat:Filesystem):    Started sapecqacs
    * vip_ECQ_AERS         (ocf::heartbeat:IPaddr2):       Started sapecqacs
    * nc_ECQ_AERS          (ocf::heartbeat:azure-lb):      Started sapecqacs
    * rsc_sap_ECQ_ERS70 (ocf::heartbeat:SAPInstance):      Started sapecqacs

Daemon Status:
  corosync: active/disabled
  pacemaker: active/disabled
  pcsd: active/enabled
sapecqacs:ecqadm>
```

Remove failed Resource actions if any
pcs resource cleanup <resource name >
e.g pcs resource cleanup rsc_sap_ECQ_ERS70

Check location constraint if any. If exist clear it.
pcs constraint list
No location constraint found.

Resource state after executing Test case

```
sapecqacs:ecqadm> sudo pcs status
Cluster name: sapecqapp
Cluster Summary:
  * Stack: corosync
  * Current DC: sapecqber (version 2.0.5-9.el8_4.3-ba59be7122) - partition with quorum
  * Last updated: Fri Jun  3 08:35:06 2022
  * Last change:  Fri Jun  3 08:13:59 2022 by root via crm_resource on sapecqacs
  * 2 nodes configured
  * 9 resource instances configured

Node List:
  * Online: [ sapecqacs sapecqber ]

Full List of Resources:
  * rsc_st_azure          (stonith:fence_azure_arm):      Started sapecqber
  * Resource Group: g-ECQ_ASCS:
    * fs_ECQ_ASCS          (ocf::heartbeat:Filesystem):    Started sapecqber
    * vip_ECQ_ASCS         (ocf::heartbeat:IPaddr2):       Started sapecqber
    * nc_ECQ_ASCS          (ocf::heartbeat:azure-lb):      Started sapecqber
    * rsc_sap_ECQ_ASCS60        (ocf::heartbeat:SAPInstance):   Started sapecqber
  * Resource Group: g-ECQ_AERS:
    * fs_ECQ_AERS          (ocf::heartbeat:Filesystem):    Started sapecqacs
    * vip_ECQ_AERS         (ocf::heartbeat:IPaddr2):       Started sapecqacs
    * nc_ECQ_AERS          (ocf::heartbeat:azure-lb):      Started sapecqacs
    * rsc_sap_ECQ_ERS70 (ocf::heartbeat:SAPInstance):      Started sapecqacs

Daemon Status:
  corosync: active/disabled
  pacemaker: active/disabled
  pcsd: active/enabled
sapecqacs:ecqadm>
```

7.9.   TEST CASE 8 – KILL WD PROCESS

Resource state before Test

```
pcsd: active/enabled
sapecqacs:ecqadm> sudo pcs status
Cluster name: sapecqapp
Cluster Summary:
  * Stack: corosync
  * Current DC: sapecqber (version 2.0.5-9.el8_4.3-ba59be7122) - partition with quorum
  * Last updated: Fri Jun  3 08:39:30 2022
  * Last change:  Fri Jun  3 08:13:59 2022 by root via crm_resource on sapecqacs
  * 2 nodes configured
  * 9 resource instances configured

Node List:
  * Online: [ sapecqacs sapecqber ]

Full List of Resources:
  * rsc_st_azure            (stonith:fence_azure_arm):       Started sapecqber
  * Resource Group: g-ECQ_ASCS:
    * fs_ECQ_ASCS           (ocf::heartbeat:Filesystem):     Started sapecqber
    * vip_ECQ_ASCS          (ocf::heartbeat:IPaddr2):        Started sapecqber
    * nc_ECQ_ASCS           (ocf::heartbeat:azure-lb):       Started sapecqber
    * rsc_sap_ECQ_ASCS60            (ocf::heartbeat:SAPInstance):     Started sapecqber
  * Resource Group: g-ECQ_AERS:
    * fs_ECQ_AERS           (ocf::heartbeat:Filesystem):     Started sapecqacs
    * vip_ECQ_AERS          (ocf::heartbeat:IPaddr2):        Started sapecqacs
    * nc_ECQ_AERS           (ocf::heartbeat:azure-lb):       Started sapecqacs
    * rsc_sap_ECQ_ERS70 (ocf::heartbeat:SAPInstance):       Started sapecqacs

Daemon Status:
  corosync: active/disabled
  pacemaker: active/disabled
  pcsd: active/enabled
sapecqacs:ecqadm>
```

Check WD service is running on sapecqber Node.

```
sapecqber:ecqadm> ps -ef | grep ecqadm
root         4308    1802  0 08:25 ?        00:00:00 sshd: ecqadm [priv]
ecqadm       4314       1  0 08:25 ?        00:00:00 /usr/lib/systemd/systemd --user
ecqadm       4315    4314  0 08:25 ?        00:00:00 (sd-pam)
root         4318    1802  0 08:25 ?        00:00:00 sshd: ecqadm [priv]
ecqadm       4324    4308  0 08:25 ?        00:00:00 sshd: ecqadm@pts/0
ecqadm       4325    4318  0 08:25 ?        00:00:00 sshd: ecqadm@notty
ecqadm       4326    4325  0 08:25 ?        00:00:00 /usr/libexec/openssh/sftp-server
ecqadm       4327    4324  0 08:25 pts/0    00:00:00 -ksh
ecqadm      17490       1  0 08:30 ?        00:00:01 /usr/sap/ECQ/ASCS60/exe/sapstartsrv pf=/sapmnt/ECQ/profile/ECQ_ASCS60_sapecqcs
ecqadm      17787       1  0 08:31 ?        00:00:00 sapstart pf=/sapmnt/ECQ/profile/ECQ_ASCS60_sapecqcs
ecqadm      17824   17787  0 08:31 ?        00:00:00 ms.sapECQ_ASCS60 pf=/usr/sap/ECQ/SYS/profile/ECQ_ASCS60_sapecqcs
ecqadm      17828   17787  2 08:31 ?        00:00:12 enq.sapECQ_ASCS60 pf=/usr/sap/ECQ/SYS/profile/ECQ_ASCS60_sapecqcs
ecqadm      17834   17787  0 08:31 ?        00:00:00 /usr/sap/ECQ/ASCS60/exe/gwrd pf=/usr/sap/ECQ/SYS/profile/ECQ_ASCS60_sapecqcs
ecqadm      17838   17787  0 08:31 ?        00:00:01 wd.sapECQ_ASCS60 pf=/usr/sap/ECQ/SYS/profile/ECQ_ASCS60_sapecqcs
ecqadm      43666    4327  0 08:40 pts/0    00:00:00 ps -ef
ecqadm      43667    4327  0 08:40 pts/0    00:00:00 grep --color=auto ecqadm
sapecqber:ecqadm>
```

Before killing the WD process, edit the test user and it would create a lock in sm12

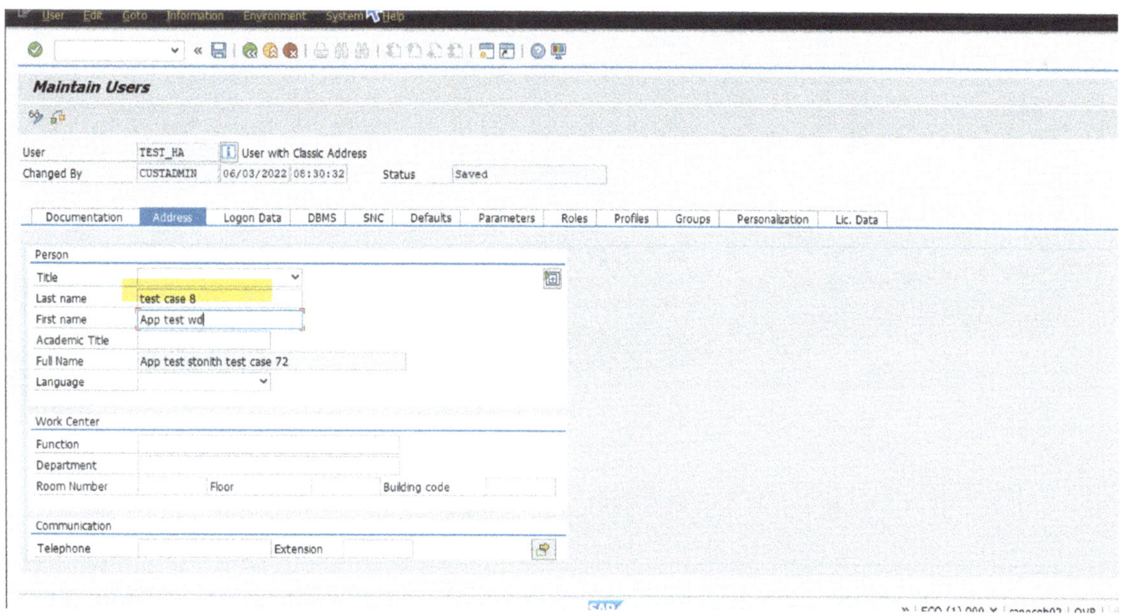

Check webgui

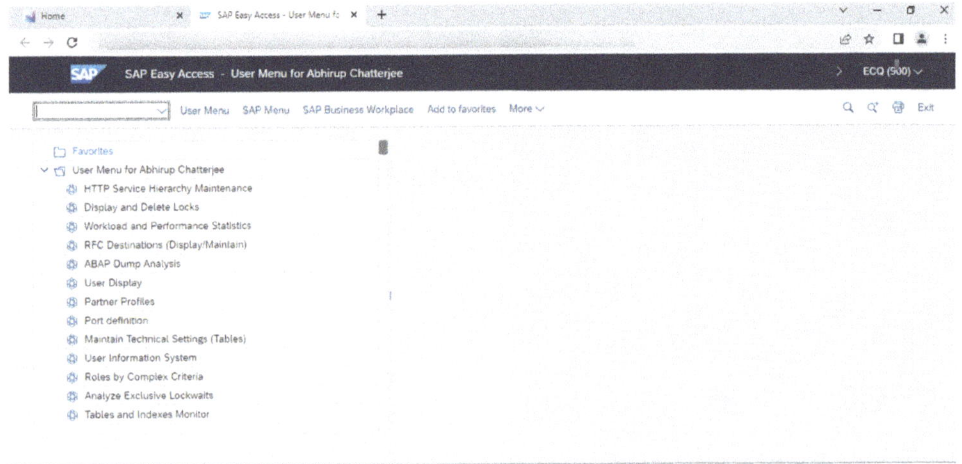

Run the following commands as root on the node where the ASCS instance is running to kill the WD process.

Kill WD process

pgrep -f wd.sapECQ | xargs kill -9

```
sapecqber:ecqadm> pgrep -f wd.sapECQ | xargs kill -9
sapecqber:ecqadm> pgrep -f wd.sapECQ
48013
sapecqber:ecqadm> pgrep -f wd.sapECQ | xargs kill -9
sapecqber:ecqadm> pgrep -f wd.sapECQ
48700
sapecqber:ecqadm> pgrep -f wd.sapECQ | xargs kill -9
sapecqber:ecqadm> pgrep -f wd.sapECQ
48855
sapecqber:ecqadm> pgrep -f wd.sapECQ | xargs kill -9
sapecqber:ecqadm> pgrep -f wd.sapECQ
49518
sapecqber:ecqadm> ps -ef | grep ecqadm
root       4308   1802  0 08:25 ?        00:00:00 sshd: ecqadm [priv]
ecqadm     4314      1  0 08:25 ?        00:00:00 /usr/lib/systemd/systemd --user
ecqadm     4315   4314  0 08:25 ?        00:00:00 (sd-pam)
root       4318   1802  0 08:25 ?        00:00:00 sshd: ecqadm [priv]
ecqadm     4324   4308  0 08:25 ?        00:00:00 sshd: ecqadm@pts/0
ecqadm     4325   4318  0 08:25 ?        00:00:00 sshd: ecqadm@notty
ecqadm     4326   4325  0 08:25 ?        00:00:00 /usr/libexec/openssh/sftp-server
ecqadm     4327   4324  0 08:25 pts/0    00:00:00 -ksh
ecqadm    17490      1  0 08:30 ?        00:00:01 /usr/sap/ECQ/ASCS60/exe/sapstartsrv pf=/sapmnt/ECQ/profile/ECQ_ASCS60_sapecqcs
ecqadm    17787      1  0 08:31 ?        00:00:00 sapstart pf=/sapmnt/ECQ/profile/ECQ_ASCS60_sapecqcs
ecqadm    17824  17787  0 08:31 ?        00:00:00 ms.sapECQ_ASCS60 pf=/usr/sap/ECQ/SYS/profile/ECQ_ASCS60_sapecqcs
ecqadm    17828  17787  2 08:31 ?        00:00:15 enq.sapECQ_ASCS60 pf=/usr/sap/ECQ/SYS/profile/ECQ_ASCS60_sapecqcs
ecqadm    17834  17787  0 08:31 ?        00:00:00 /usr/sap/ECQ/ASCS60/exe/gwrd pf=/usr/sap/ECQ/SYS/profile/ECQ_ASCS60_sapecqcs -
ecqadm    49518  17787  2 08:42 ?        00:00:01 wd.sapECQ_ASCS60 pf=/usr/sap/ECQ/SYS/profile/ECQ_ASCS60_sapecqcs
ecqadm    51315   4327  0 08:43 pts/0    00:00:00 ps -ef
ecqadm    51316   4327  0 08:43 pts/0    00:00:00 grep --color=auto ecqadm
sapecqber:ecqadm>
```

After executing the above command, save the changes to the user.

The changes are saved successfully

```
sapecqber:ecqadm> pgrep -f wd.sapECQ | xargs kill -9
sapecqber:ecqadm> pgrep -f wd.sapECQ
48013
sapecqber:ecqadm> pgrep -f wd.sapECQ | xargs kill -9
sapecqber:ecqadm> pgrep -f wd.sapECQ
48700
sapecqber:ecqadm> pgrep -f wd.sapECQ | xargs kill -9
sapecqber:ecqadm> pgrep -f wd.sapECQ
48855
sapecqber:ecqadm> pgrep -f wd.sapECQ | xargs kill -9
sapecqber:ecqadm> pgrep -f wd.sapECQ
49518
sapecqber:ecqadm> ps -ef | grep ecqadm
root        4308    1802  0 08:25 ?        00:00:00 sshd: ecqadm [priv]
ecqadm      4314       1  0 08:25 ?        00:00:00 /usr/lib/systemd/systemd --user
ecqadm      4315    4314  0 08:25 ?        00:00:00 (sd-pam)
root        4318    1802  0 08:25 ?        00:00:00 sshd: ecqadm [priv]
ecqadm      4324    4308  0 08:25 ?        00:00:00 sshd: ecqadm@pts/0
ecqadm      4325    4318  0 08:25 ?        00:00:00 sshd: ecqadm@notty
ecqadm      4326    4325  0 08:25 ?        00:00:00 /usr/libexec/openssh/sftp-server
ecqadm      4327    4324  0 08:25 pts/0    00:00:00 -ksh
ecqadm     17490       1  0 08:30 ?        00:00:01 /usr/sap/ECQ/ASCS60/exe/sapstartsrv pf=/sapmnt/ECQ/profile/ECQ_ASCS60_sapecqcs
ecqadm     17787       1  0 08:31 ?        00:00:00 sapstart pf=/sapmnt/ECQ/profile/ECQ_ASCS60_sapecqcs
ecqadm     17824   17787  0 08:31 ?        00:00:00 ms.sapECQ_ASCS60 pf=/usr/sap/ECQ/SYS/profile/ECQ_ASCS60_sapecqcs
ecqadm     17828   17787  2 08:31 ?        00:00:15 enq.sapECQ_ASCS60 pf=/usr/sap/ECQ/SYS/profile/ECQ_ASCS60_sapecqcs
ecqadm     17834   17787  0 08:31 ?        00:00:00 /usr/sap/ECQ/ASCS60/exe/gwrd pf=/usr/sap/ECQ/SYS/profile/ECQ_ASCS60_sapecqcs -
ecqadm     49518   17787  2 08:42 ?        00:00:01 wd.sapECQ_ASCS60 pf=/usr/sap/ECQ/SYS/profile/ECQ_ASCS60_sapecqcs
ecqadm     51315    4327  0 08:43 pts/0    00:00:00 ps -ef
ecqadm     51316    4327  0 08:43 pts/0    00:00:00 grep --color=auto ecqadm
sapecqber:ecqadm>
```

The WD process should always be restarted by the Pacemaker resource agent as part of the monitoring.
The ASCS resource will not move in this test case.

Check the pcs status: ASCS resources remain on sapecqber node and ERS resource remain on sapecqacs
node.

```
sapecqber:ecqadm> sudo pcs status
Cluster name: sapecqapp
Cluster Summary:
  * Stack: corosync
  * Current DC: sapecqber (version 2.0.5-9.el8_4.3-ba59be7122) - partition with quorum
  * Last updated: Fri Jun  3 08:44:25 2022
  * Last change:  Fri Jun  3 08:13:59 2022 by root via crm_resource on sapecqacs
  * 2 nodes configured
  * 9 resource instances configured

Node List:
  * Online: [ sapecqacs sapecqber ]

Full List of Resources:
  * rsc_st_azure        (stonith:fence_azure_arm):       Started sapecqber
  * Resource Group: g-ECQ_ASCS:
    * fs_ECQ_ASCS       (ocf::heartbeat:Filesystem):     Started sapecqber
    * vip_ECQ_ASCS      (ocf::heartbeat:IPaddr2):        Started sapecqber
    * nc_ECQ_ASCS       (ocf::heartbeat:azure-lb):       Started sapecqber
    * rsc_sap_ECQ_ASCS60        (ocf::heartbeat:SAPInstance):       Started sapecqber
  * Resource Group: g-ECQ_AERS:
    * fs_ECQ_AERS       (ocf::heartbeat:Filesystem):     Started sapecqacs
    * vip_ECQ_AERS      (ocf::heartbeat:IPaddr2):        Started sapecqacs
    * nc_ECQ_AERS       (ocf::heartbeat:azure-lb):       Started sapecqacs
    * rsc_sap_ECQ_ERS70 (ocf::heartbeat:SAPInstance):    Started sapecqacs

Daemon Status:
  corosync: active/disabled
  pacemaker: active/disabled
  pcsd: active/enabled
sapecqber:ecqadm>
```

Check webgui

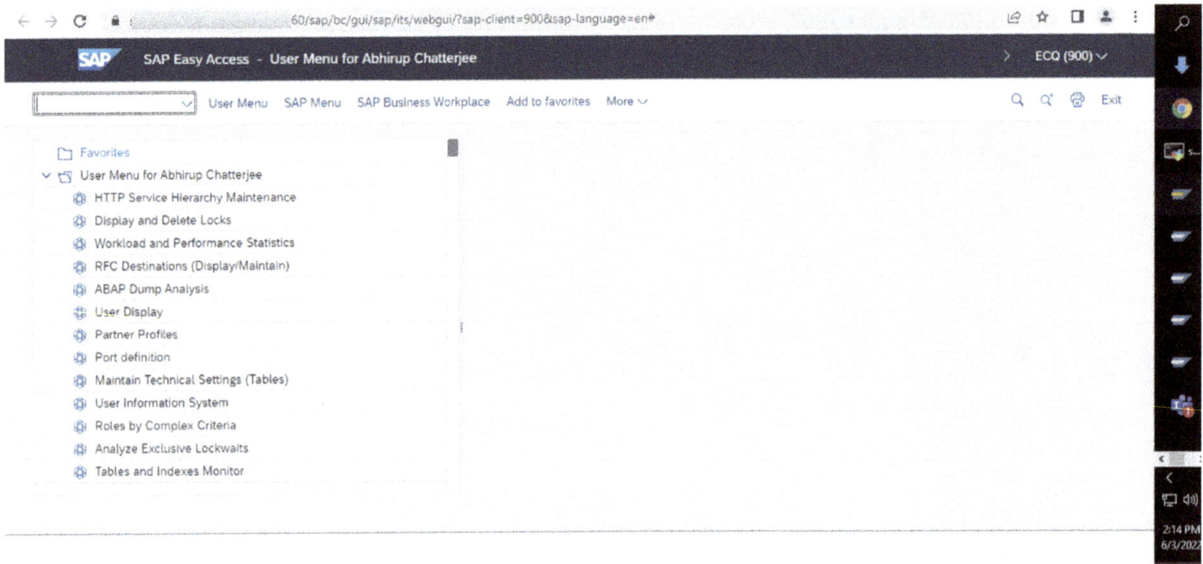

This is most critical scenarios across the platform, based on loads, however HANA database itself is a robust database column stored based, **SAP HANA System Replication** is a powerful feature that enhances the reliability and availability of SAP HANA databases. By leveraging different replication modes, organizations can tailor their strategies to meet their specific requirements for data integrity, performance, and disaster recovery. Proper planning and implementation of HSR can significantly improve operational resilience, ensuring that businesses can withstand disruptions and maintain continuous access to critical data.

SAP HANA System Replication (HSR) is a crucial feature that provides high availability and disaster recovery for SAP HANA databases. It enables the replication of data from a primary SAP HANA system (the source) to one or more secondary systems (the targets). This replication ensures that organizations can maintain continuous operations and minimize downtime in the event of hardware failures, outages, or planned maintenance.

Key Features of **SAP HANA System Replication (HSR)**

- **Data Replication Modes:**
  - Synchronous Replication:
    - Data is replicated to the secondary system in real-time. The primary system waits for the acknowledgment from the secondary system before committing a transaction.
    - Benefits: Provides the highest level of data consistency and ensures zero data loss.

- Use Case: Ideal for mission-critical applications where data integrity is paramount.

  - **Asynchronous Replication:**

    - Data is replicated with a delay, meaning the primary system does not wait for an acknowledgment from the secondary system before committing transactions.

    - Benefits: Reduces latency and improves performance on the primary system, but may lead to potential data loss in case of a failure.

    - Use Case: Suitable for scenarios where slight delays in data availability are acceptable.

- **Automatic Failover:**
  - In case the primary system fails, HSR can automatically switch operations to the secondary system, allowing for minimal disruption to business processes.

- **Flexible Configuration:**
  - Organizations can configure multiple secondary systems for replication, enabling various disaster recovery and load balancing strategies.

  - HSR supports both unidirectional and bidirectional replication setups.

- **Data Consistency:**
  - HSR ensures that the replicated data is consistent across systems, maintaining data integrity during replication processes.

- **Monitoring and Management:**
  - Administrators can monitor the health and status of the replication through tools like SAP HANA Studio and SAP HANA Cockpit, enabling proactive management of replication processes.

- **Support for Multi-Tenancy:**
  - HSR can be configured in multi-tenant scenarios, allowing different databases within a single SAP HANA system to replicate independently.

Implementation Considerations

- **Network Requirements:**
  - A reliable and low-latency network connection is essential for effective data replication, especially in synchronous modes.

- **Hardware Sizing:**
  - Secondary systems must be appropriately sized to handle the expected load and performance requirements, particularly during failover situations.

- **Backup and Recovery:**
  - While HSR provides high availability, it should be complemented with regular backup strategies to protect against data corruption or loss scenarios.

- **Testing Failover Procedures:**

- o Organizations should regularly test failover procedures to ensure that all components work correctly in case of a real disaster.

- **Licensing and Support:**
  - o Ensure compliance with SAP licensing agreements for additional systems and validate that necessary support agreements are in place.

Use Cases for SAP HANA System Replication

- Disaster Recovery: Organizations can quickly recover from site failures or disasters by switching to the secondary SAP HANA system.

- High Availability: Continuous operations are maintained during planned maintenance or unexpected outages of the primary system.

- Load Balancing: Secondary systems can be used for reporting and analytics, reducing the load on the primary transactional system.

Below FAILOVER scenarios from Section 8.1 to 8.13

- Shutdown HANA for maintenance
- Stop HANA on Primary A node
- Stop HANA on Primary
- Crash HANA on Primary side
- Crash HANA on Primary side
- Power off HANA server Primary (A) side
- Power off HANA server Primary (B) side
- Stop HANA on the 'Secondary' side (B)
- Kill HANA on the 'Secondary' side (B)
- Power off 'Secondary' HANA server (B)
- Stop the network interfaces on Secondary HANA node B
- Stop the network interfaces on Primary HANA node A
- INTENTIONAL FAIL OVER FROM PRIMARY HANA NODE (B)

8.1. Test case 1: Shutdown HANA for maintenance

Test Description	Shutdown HANA for maintenance	
Test action	Place Cluster on maintenance mode, shutdown HANA	
Result	Pass	
Expected results	HANA does not failover from sapecqahdb (Primary) to sapecqbhdb (Secondary). Virtual IP (VIP) does not failover from sapecqahdb (Primary) to sapecqbhdb (Secondary). Application connectivity to HANA is lost.	
Desired results	HANA does not failover from sapecqahdb (Primary) to sapecqbhdb (Secondary).	

	Virtual IP (VIP) does not failover from sapecqahdb (Primary) to sapecqbhdb (Secondary). Application connectivity to HANA is lost.	
Post-test execution steps	Place cluster out of maintenance mode Check system replication status Check cluster status	

Current status of RHEL cluster and HANA 'System replication' before making any changes

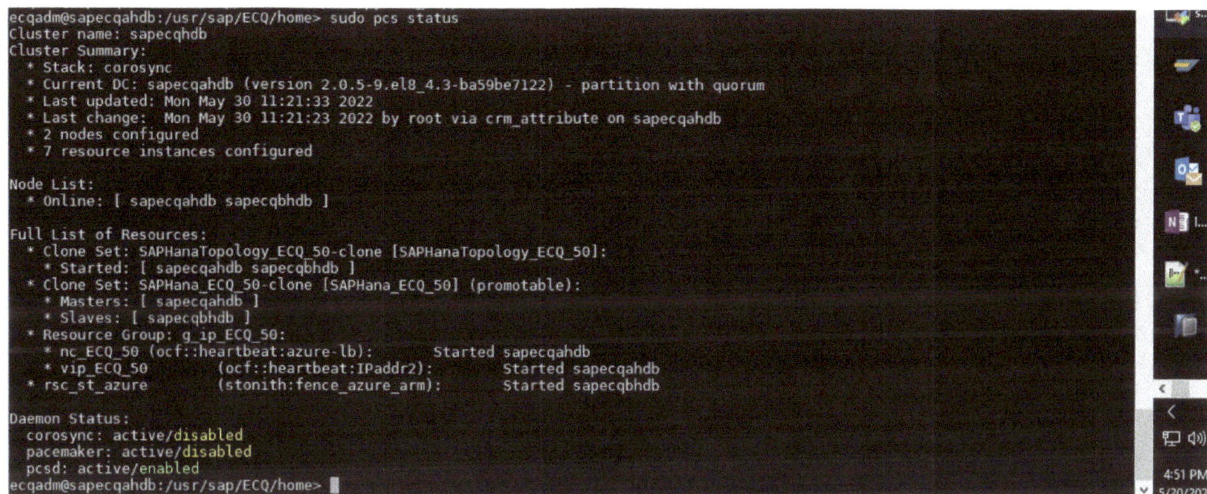

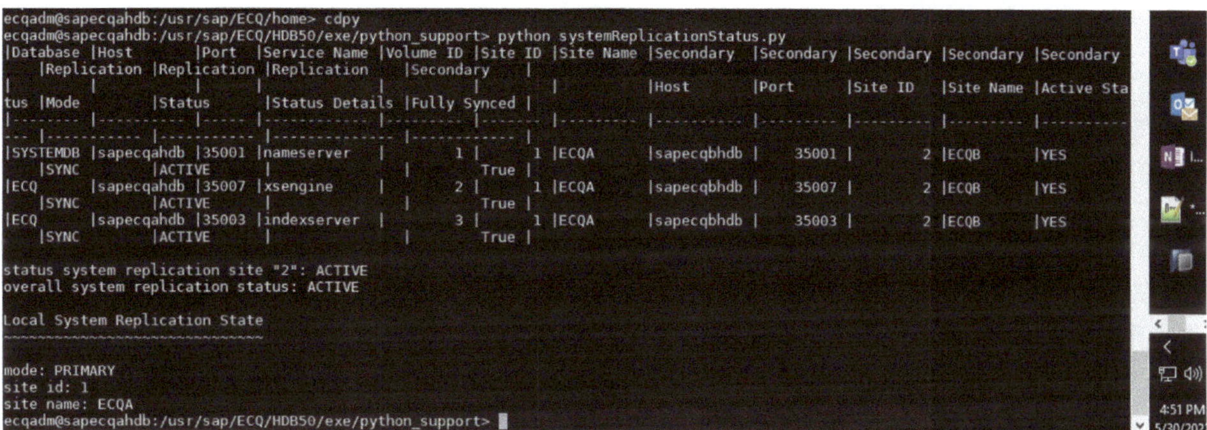

Put cluster in maintenance mode

sudo pcs property set maintenance-mode=true

```
ecqadm@sapecqahdb:/usr/sap/ECQ/HDB50/exe/python_support> sudo pcs status
Cluster name: sapecqhdb
Cluster Summary:
  * Stack: corosync
  * Current DC: sapecqahdb (version 2.0.5-9.el8_4.3-ba59be7122) - partition with quorum
  * Last updated: Mon May 30 11:22:15 2022
  * Last change:  Mon May 30 11:22:11 2022 by root via cibadmin on sapecqahdb
  * 2 nodes configured
  * 7 resource instances configured

            *** Resource management is DISABLED ***
  The cluster will not attempt to start, stop or recover services

Node List:
  * Online: [ sapecqahdb sapecqbhdb ]

Full List of Resources:
  * Clone Set: SAPHanaTopology_ECQ_50-clone [SAPHanaTopology_ECQ_50] (unmanaged):
    * SAPHanaTopology_ECQ_50    (ocf::heartbeat:SAPHanaTopology):      Started sapecqbhdb (unmanaged)
    * SAPHanaTopology_ECQ_50    (ocf::heartbeat:SAPHanaTopology):      Started sapecqahdb (unmanaged)
  * Clone Set: SAPHana_ECQ_50-clone [SAPHana_ECQ_50] (promotable) (unmanaged):
    * SAPHana_ECQ_50    (ocf::heartbeat:SAPHana):      Slave sapecqbhdb (unmanaged)
    * SAPHana_ECQ_50    (ocf::heartbeat:SAPHana):      Master sapecqahdb (unmanaged)
  * Resource Group: g_ip_ECQ_50 (unmanaged):
    * nc_ECQ_50 (ocf::heartbeat:azure-lb):      Started sapecqahdb (unmanaged)
    * vip_ECQ_50    (ocf::heartbeat:IPaddr2):      Started sapecqahdb (unmanaged)
  * rsc_st_azure    (stonith:fence_azure_arm):      Started sapecqbhdb (unmanaged)

Daemon Status:
  corosync: active/disabled
  pacemaker: active/disabled
  pcsd: active/enabled
ecqadm@sapecqahdb:/usr/sap/ECQ/HDB50/exe/python_support>
```

Now, cluster is in "unmanaged" state.

Stop HANA on node A first (Primary), Wait until ALL HANA services are stopped before stopping HANA on other node

Stop A node:

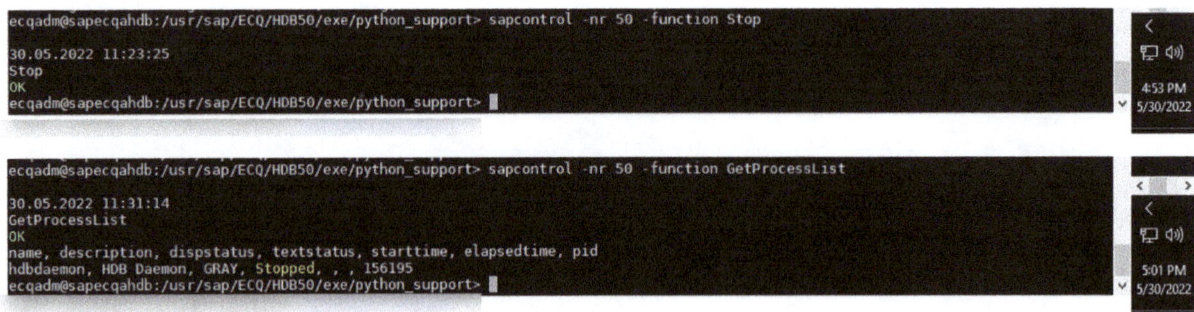

```
ecqadm@sapecqahdb:/usr/sap/ECQ/HDB50/exe/python_support> sapcontrol -nr 50 -function Stop

30.05.2022 11:23:25
Stop
OK
ecqadm@sapecqahdb:/usr/sap/ECQ/HDB50/exe/python_support>
```

```
ecqadm@sapecqahdb:/usr/sap/ECQ/HDB50/exe/python_support> sapcontrol -nr 50 -function GetProcessList

30.05.2022 11:31:14
GetProcessList
OK
name, description, dispstatus, textstatus, starttime, elapsedtime, pid
hdbdaemon, HDB Daemon, GRAY, Stopped, , , 156195
ecqadm@sapecqahdb:/usr/sap/ECQ/HDB50/exe/python_support>
```

Check: hdbnsutil -sr_state

```
ecqadm@sapecqahdb:/usr/sap/ECQ/HDB50/exe/python_support> hdbnsutil -sr_state

System Replication State
~~~~~~~~~~~~~~~~~~~~~~~~~

online: false

mode: primary
operation mode: unknown
site id: 1
site name: ECQA

is source system: unknown
is secondary/consumer system: false
has secondaries/consumers attached: unknown
is a takeover active: false
is primary suspended: false
done.
ecqadm@sapecqahdb:/usr/sap/ECQ/HDB50/exe/python_support>
```

```
is secondary/consumer system: true
has secondaries/consumers attached: false
is a takeover active: false
is primary suspended: false
is timetravel enabled: false
replay mode: auto
active primary site: 1

primary masters: sapecqahdb

Host Mappings:
~~~~~~~~~~~~~~

sapecqbhdb -> [ECQB] sapecqbhdb
sapecqbhdb -> [ECQA] sapecqahdb


Site Mappings:
~~~~~~~~~~~~~~
ECQA (primary/primary)
    |---ECQB (sync/logreplay)

Tier of ECQA: 1
Tier of ECQB: 2

Replication mode of ECQA: primary
Replication mode of ECQB: sync

Operation mode of ECQA: primary
Operation mode of ECQB: logreplay

Mapping: ECQA -> ECQB
done.
ecqadm@sapecqbhdb:/usr/sap/ECQ/HDB50/exe/python_support>
```

Application not able to connect to DB

```
sapecqa01:ecqadm> R3trans -d
This is R3trans version 6.26 (release 781 - 24.06.21 - 18:50:42).
unicode enabled version
2EETW169 no connect possible: "DBMS = HDB                    --- SERVER = '' PORT = ''"
R3trans finished (0012).
sapecqa01:ecqadm>
```

Start A node:

```
ecqadm@sapecqahdb:/usr/sap/ECQ/HDB50/exe/python_support> sapcontrol -nr 50 -function Start

30.05.2022 11:33:10
Start
OK
ecqadm@sapecqahdb:/usr/sap/ECQ/HDB50/exe/python_support>
```

Once DB is started

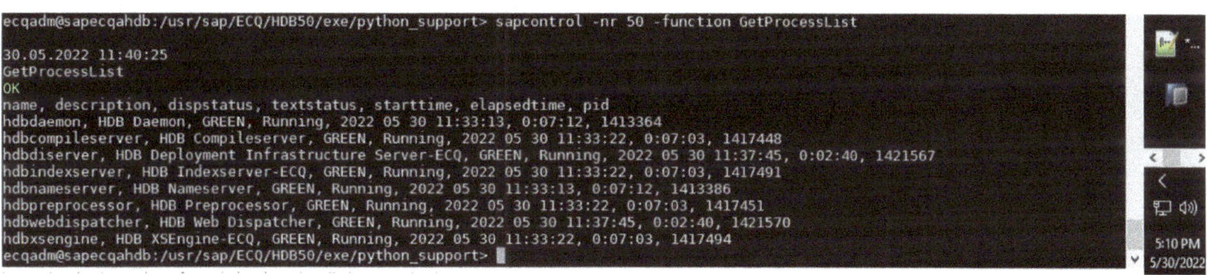

```
ecqadm@sapecqahdb:/usr/sap/ECQ/HDB50/exe/python_support> sapcontrol -nr 50 -function GetProcessList

30.05.2022 11:40:25
GetProcessList
OK
name, description, dispstatus, textstatus, starttime, elapsedtime, pid
hdbdaemon, HDB Daemon, GREEN, Running, 2022 05 30 11:33:13, 0:07:12, 1413364
hdbcompileserver, HDB Compileserver, GREEN, Running, 2022 05 30 11:33:22, 0:07:03, 1417448
hdbdiserver, HDB Deployment Infrastructure Server-ECQ, GREEN, Running, 2022 05 30 11:37:45, 0:02:40, 1421567
hdbindexserver, HDB Indexserver-ECQ, GREEN, Running, 2022 05 30 11:33:22, 0:07:03, 1417491
hdbnameserver, HDB Nameserver, GREEN, Running, 2022 05 30 11:33:13, 0:07:12, 1413386
hdbpreprocessor, HDB Preprocessor, GREEN, Running, 2022 05 30 11:33:22, 0:07:03, 1417451
hdbwebdispatcher, HDB Web Dispatcher, GREEN, Running, 2022 05 30 11:37:45, 0:02:40, 1421570
hdbxsengine, HDB XSEngine-ECQ, GREEN, Running, 2022 05 30 11:33:22, 0:07:03, 1417494
ecqadm@sapecqahdb:/usr/sap/ECQ/HDB50/exe/python_support>
```

Check application status:

```
sapecqa01:ecqadm> R3trans -d
This is R3trans version 6.26 (release 781 - 24.06.21 - 18:50:42).
unicode enabled version
R3trans finished (0000).
sapecqa01:ecqadm>
```

Check replication status

```
ecqadm@sapecqahdb:/usr/sap/ECQ/HDB50/exe/python_support> python systemReplicationStatus.py
|Database |Host         |Port  |Service Name |Volume ID |Site ID |Site Name |Secondary   |Secondary |Secondary |Secondary  |Secondary
    |Replication |Replication |Replication    |Secondary    |
|            |            |            |             |          |        |          |Host        |Port      |Site ID   |Site Name |Active Sta
tus |Mode        |Status      |Status Details |Fully Synced |
|-------- |---------- |---------- |----- |---------- |--------- |-------- |---------- |---------- |--------- |---------- |--------- |----------
--- |---------- |---------- |---------- |---------- |---------- |
|SYSTEMDB |sapecqahdb |35001 |nameserver   |    1 |     1 |ECQA     |sapecqbhdb |   35001 |     2 |ECQB     |YES
    |SYNC       |ACTIVE     |             |        True |
|ECQ      |sapecqahdb |35007 |xsengine     |    2 |     1 |ECQA     |sapecqbhdb |   35007 |     2 |ECQB     |YES
    |SYNC       |ACTIVE     |             |        True |
|ECQ      |sapecqahdb |35003 |indexserver  |    3 |     1 |ECQA     |sapecqbhdb |   35003 |     2 |ECQB     |YES
    |SYNC       |ACTIVE     |             |        True |

status system replication site "2": ACTIVE
overall system replication status: ACTIVE

Local System Replication State
~~~~~~~~~~~~~~~~~~~~~~~~~~~~~~~~~~~~~~~~~~~~~~~~~~~~~~~~~~~~~~~~~~

mode: PRIMARY
site id: 1
site name: ECQA
ecqadm@sapecqahdb:/usr/sap/ECQ/HDB50/exe/python_support>
```

Remove cluster from Maintenance mode:

sudo pcs property set maintenance-mode=false

```
ecqadm@sapecqahdb:/usr/sap/ECQ/HDB50/exe/python_support> sudo pcs status
Cluster name: sapecqhdb
Cluster Summary:
  * Stack: corosync
  * Current DC: sapecqahdb (version 2.0.5-9.el8_4.3-ba59be7122) - partition with quorum
  * Last updated: Mon May 30 15:31:16 2022
  * Last change:  Mon May 30 15:30:33 2022 by root via crm_attribute on sapecqahdb
  * 2 nodes configured
  * 7 resource instances configured

Node List:
  * Online: [ sapecqahdb sapecqbhdb ]

Full List of Resources:
  * Clone Set: SAPHanaTopology_ECQ_50-clone [SAPHanaTopology_ECQ_50]:
    * Started: [ sapecqahdb sapecqbhdb ]
  * Clone Set: SAPHana_ECQ_50-clone [SAPHana_ECQ_50] (promotable):
    * Masters: [ sapecqahdb ]
    * Slaves: [ sapecqbhdb ]
  * Resource Group: g_ip_ECQ_50:
    * nc_ECQ_50 (ocf::heartbeat:azure-lb):          Started sapecqahdb
    * vip_ECQ_50        (ocf::heartbeat:IPaddr2):        Started sapecqahdb
  * rsc_st_azure        (stonith:fence_azure_arm):       Started sapecqbhdb

Daemon Status:
  corosync: active/disabled
  pacemaker: active/disabled
  pcsd: active/enabled
ecqadm@sapecqahdb:/usr/sap/ECQ/HDB50/exe/python_support>
```

8.2. Test case 2: Stop HANA on Primary A node

Test Description	Stop HANA on Primary
Test action	Shutdown HANA on sapecqahdb (Primary)
Result	Pass
Expected results	HANA fails over from sapecqahdb (Primary) to sapecqbhdb (Secondary). Virtual IP (VIP) fails over from sapecqahdb (Primary) to sapecqbhdb (Secondary). Application connectivity to HANA is lost during fail over and re-established.
Desired results	HANA fails over from sapecqahdb (Primary) to sapecqbhdb (Secondary). Virtual IP (VIP) fails over from sapecqahdb (Primary) to sapecqbhdb (Secondary). Application connectivity to HANA is lost during fail over and re-established.
Post-test execution steps	Clean up replication and re-configure system replication with sapecqbhdb as Primary and sapecqahdb as Secondary Restart pacemaker on failed node (sapecqahdb)

	Check system replication status Check cluster status

Test execution steps

Check status of cluster and HANA System replication before starting the test.

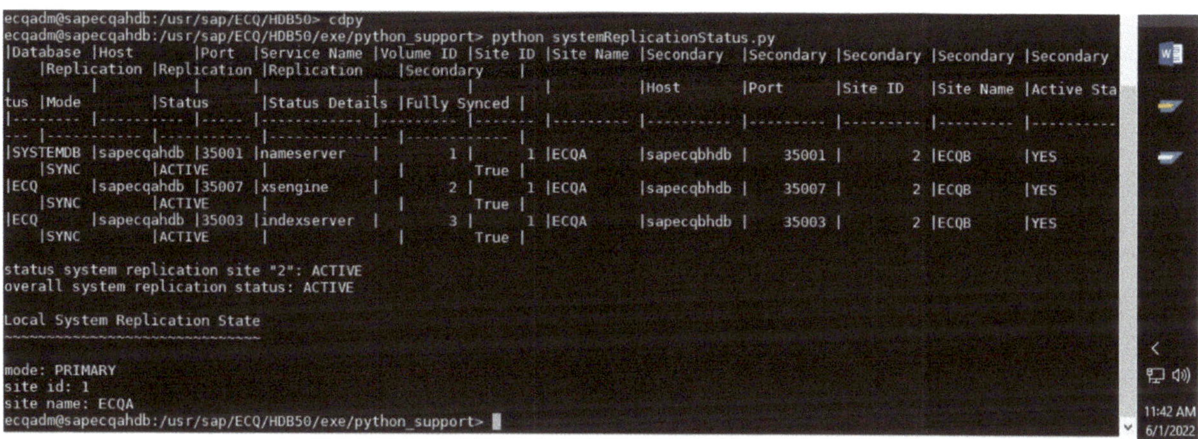

Check replication status:

Create user/edit (do not save) click save it after executing HDB stop command on A HDB node

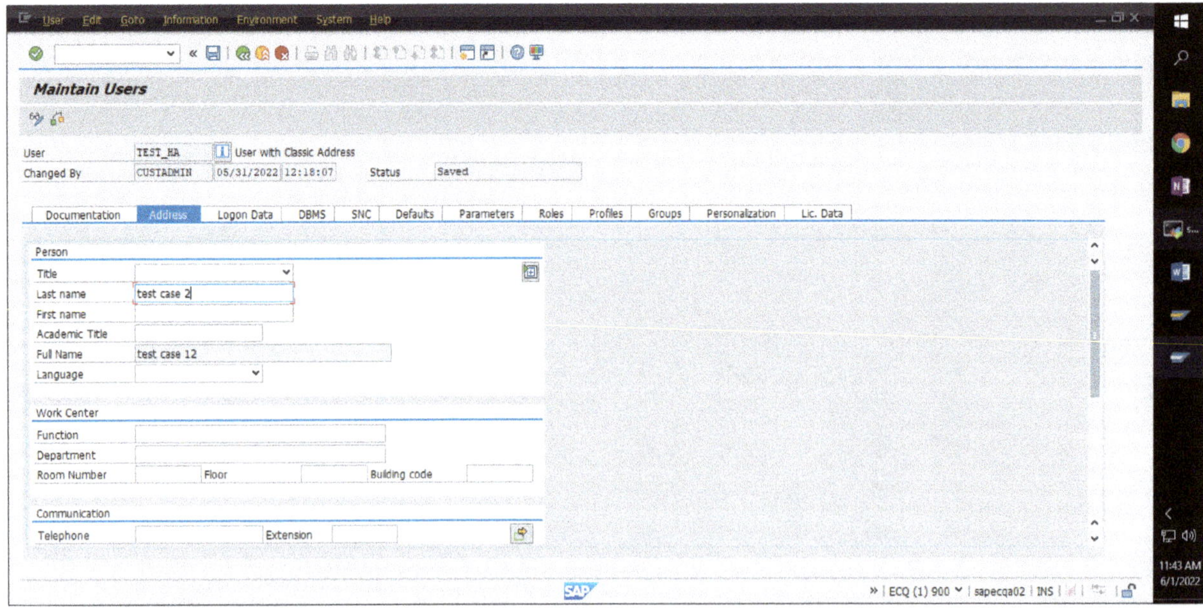

Stop DB in A node

baXterm by subscribing to the professional edition here: http://mobaxterm.mobatek.net

Try to save user

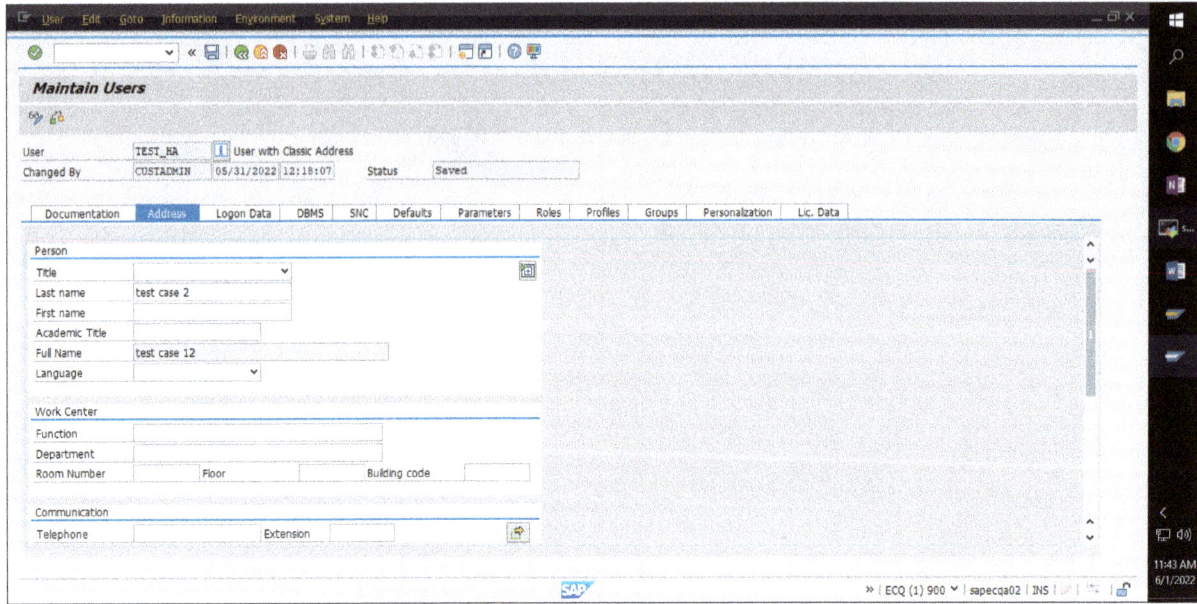

Took 6 mins to stop

```
ecqadm@sapecqahdb:/usr/sap/ECQ/HDB50/exe/python_support> HDB stop
hdbdaemon will wait maximal 300 seconds for NewDB services finishing.
Stopping instance using: /usr/sap/ECQ/SYS/exe/hdb/sapcontrol -prot NI_HTTP -nr 50 -function Stop 400

01.06.2022 06:13:33
Stop
OK
Waiting for stopped instance using: /usr/sap/ECQ/SYS/exe/hdb/sapcontrol -prot NI_HTTP -nr 50 -function WaitforStopped 600 2

01.06.2022 06:19:39
WaitforStopped
OK
hdbdaemon is stopped.
ecqadm@sapecqahdb:/usr/sap/ECQ/HDB50/exe/python_support>
```



```
ecqadm@sapecqbhdb:/usr/sap/ECQ/HDB50/exe/python_support> sudo pcs status
Cluster name: sapecqhdb
Cluster Summary:
  * Stack: corosync
  * Current DC: sapecqbhdb (version 2.0.5-9.el8_4.3-ba59be7122) - partition with quorum
  * Last updated: Wed Jun  1 06:22:02 2022
  * Last change:  Wed Jun  1 06:21:31 2022 by root via crm_attribute on sapecqbhdb
  * 2 nodes configured
  * 7 resource instances configured

Node List:
  * Online: [ sapecqahdb sapecqbhdb ]

Full List of Resources:
  * Clone Set: SAPHanaTopology_ECQ_50-clone [SAPHanaTopology_ECQ_50]:
    * Started: [ sapecqahdb sapecqbhdb ]
  * Clone Set: SAPHana_ECQ_50-clone [SAPHana_ECQ_50] (promotable):
    * Masters: [ sapecqbhdb ]
    * Stopped: [ sapecqahdb ]
  * Resource Group: g_ip_ECQ_50:
    * nc_ECQ_50  (ocf::heartbeat:azure-lb):        Started sapecqbhdb
    * vip_ECQ_50        (ocf::heartbeat:IPaddr2):        Started sapecqbhdb
  * rsc_st_azure         (stonith:fence_azure_arm):        Started sapecqahdb

Failed Resource Actions:
  * SAPHana_ECQ_50_start_0 on sapecqahdb 'not running' (7): call=60, status='complete', exitreason='', last-rc-change='2022-06-01
06:20:29Z', queued=0ms, exec=2560ms

Daemon Status:
  corosync: active/disabled
  pacemaker: active/disabled
  pcsd: active/enabled
ecqadm@sapecqbhdb:/usr/sap/ECQ/HDB50/exe/python_support>
```


A node: hdbnsutil -sr_state

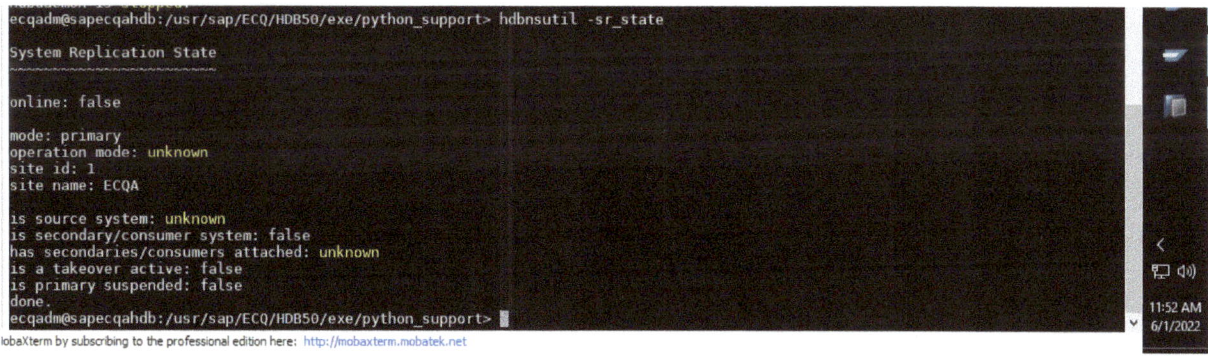

```
ecqadm@sapecqahdb:/usr/sap/ECQ/HDB50/exe/python_support> hdbnsutil -sr_state

System Replication State
~~~~~~~~~~~~~~~~~~~~~~~~~~

online: false

mode: primary
operation mode: unknown
site id: 1
site name: ECQA

is source system: unknown
is secondary/consumer system: false
has secondaries/consumers attached: unknown
is a takeover active: false
is primary suspended: false
done.
ecqadm@sapecqahdb:/usr/sap/ECQ/HDB50/exe/python_support>
```


B node: check hdbnsutil –sr_state

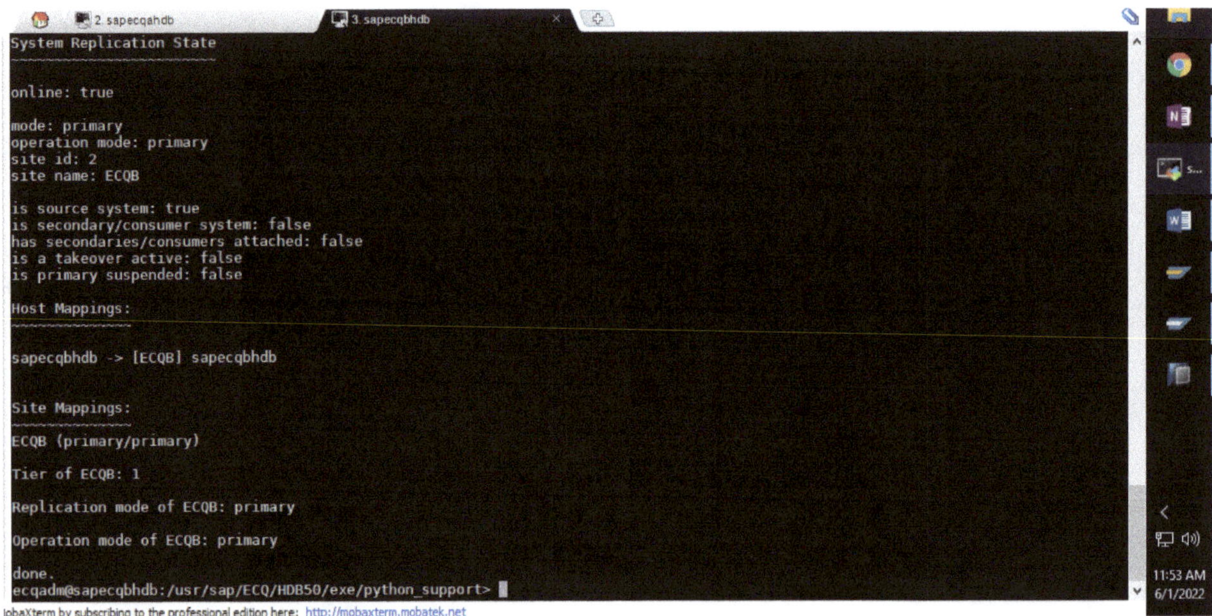

From: A node:

Now, register the failed 'Primary' as the NEW 'Secondary' and check replication is working fine

```
ecqadm@sapecqahdb:/usr/sap/ECQ/HDB50/exe/python_support> hdbnsutil -sr_register --remoteHost=sapecqbhdb --remoteInstance=50 --repl
icationMode=sync --name=ECQA --operationMode=logreplay
adding site ...
collecting information ...
registered at 10.197.42.19 (sapecqbhdb)
updating local ini files ...
done.
ecqadm@sapecqahdb:/usr/sap/ECQ/HDB50/exe/python_support>
```

Clear failed action of the cluster to start DB node A : pcs resource cleanup SAPHana_ECQ_50

```
ecqadm@sapecqahdb:/usr/sap/ECQ/HDB50/exe/python_support> sudo pcs resource cleanup SAPHana_ECQ_50
Cleaned up SAPHana_ECQ_50:0 on sapecqbhdb
Cleaned up SAPHana_ECQ_50:1 on sapecqahdb
Waiting for 1 reply from the controller
... got reply (done)
ecqadm@sapecqahdb:/usr/sap/ECQ/HDB50/exe/python_support>
```

Check: hsbnsutil –sr_state

Replication is working from B(primary) to A node

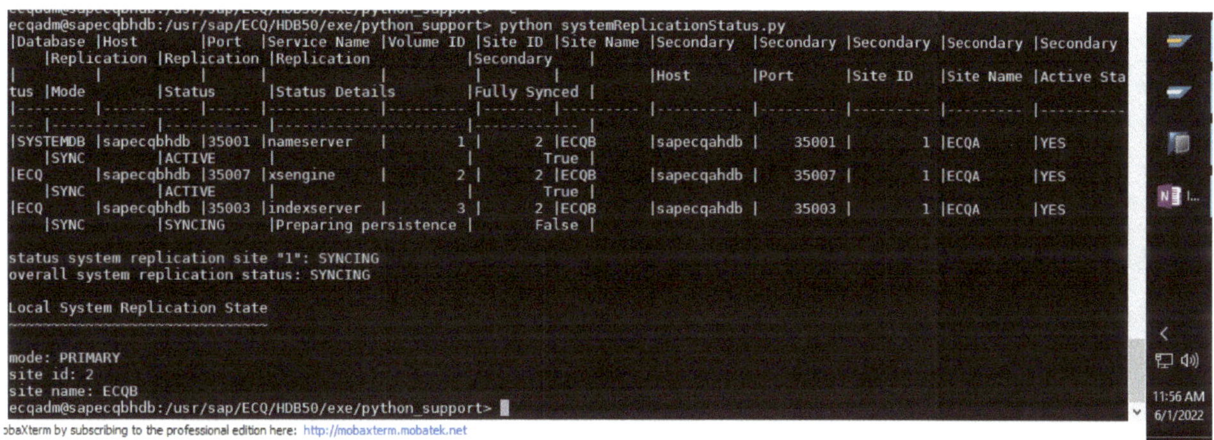

Check cluster status

```
ecqadm@sapecqbhdb:/usr/sap/ECQ/HDB50/exe/python_support> sudo pcs status
Cluster name: sapecqhdb
Cluster Summary:
  * Stack: corosync
  * Current DC: sapecqbhdb (version 2.0.5-9.el8_4.3-ba59be7122) - partition with quorum
  * Last updated: Wed Jun  1 06:27:37 2022
  * Last change:  Wed Jun  1 06:26:43 2022 by root via crm_attribute on sapecqbhdb
  * 2 nodes configured
  * 7 resource instances configured

Node List:
  * Online: [ sapecqahdb sapecqbhdb ]

Full List of Resources:
  * Clone Set: SAPHanaTopology_ECQ_50-clone [SAPHanaTopology_ECQ_50]:
    * Started: [ sapecqahdb sapecqbhdb ]
  * Clone Set: SAPHana_ECQ_50-clone [SAPHana_ECQ_50] (promotable):
    * Masters: [ sapecqbhdb ]
    * Slaves: [ sapecqahdb ]
  * Resource Group: g_ip_ECQ_50:
    * nc_ECQ_50    (ocf::heartbeat:azure-lb):       Started sapecqbhdb
    * vip_ECQ_50   (ocf::heartbeat:IPaddr2):        Started sapecqbhdb
  * rsc_st_azure   (stonith:fence_azure_arm):       Started sapecqahdb

Daemon Status:
  corosync: active/disabled
  pacemaker: active/disabled
  pcsd: active/enabled
ecqadm@sapecqbhdb:/usr/sap/ECQ/HDB50/exe/python_support>
```


8.3. Test case 3: Stop HANA on Primary

Test Description	Stop HANA on Primary (B node as primary)
Test action	Shutdown HANA on sapecqbhdb (Primary)
Result	Pass
Expected results	HANA fails over from sapecqbhdb (Primary) to sapecqahdb (Secondary). Virtual IP (VIP) fails over from sapecqbhdb (Primary) to sapecqahdb (Secondary). Application connectivity to HANA is lost during fail over and re-established.
Desired results	HANA fails over from sapecqbhdb (Primary) to sapecqahdb (Secondary). Virtual IP (VIP) fails over from sapecqbhdb (Primary) to sapecqahdb (Secondary). Application connectivity to HANA is lost during fail over and re-established.
Post-test execution steps	Clean up replication and re-configure system replication with sapecqahdb as Primary and sapecqbhdb as Secondary Restart pacemaker on failed node (sapecqbhdb) Check system replication status Check cluster status

Test execution steps

Check status of cluster and HANA System replication before starting the test.

Check cluster status

```
sapecqbhdb:ecqadm> sudo pcs status
Cluster name: sapecqhdb
Cluster Summary:
  * Stack: corosync
  * Current DC: sapecqbhdb (version 2.0.5-9.el8_4.3-ba59be7122) - partition with quorum
  * Last updated: Fri May 27 11:22:17 2022
  * Last change:  Fri May 27 11:21:21 2022 by root via crm_attribute on sapecqbhdb
  * 2 nodes configured
  * 7 resource instances configured

Node List:
  * Online: [ sapecqahdb sapecqbhdb ]

Full List of Resources:
  * Clone Set: SAPHanaTopology_ECQ_50-clone [SAPHanaTopology_ECQ_50]:
    * Started: [ sapecqahdb sapecqbhdb ]
  * Clone Set: SAPHana_ECQ_50-clone [SAPHana_ECQ_50] (promotable):
    * Masters: [ sapecqbhdb ]
    * Slaves: [ sapecqahdb ]
  * Resource Group: g_ip_ECQ_50:
    * nc_ECQ_50  (ocf::heartbeat:azure-lb):        Started sapecqbhdb
    * vip_ECQ_50        (ocf::heartbeat:IPaddr2):        Started sapecqbhdb
  * rsc_st_azure        (stonith:fence_azure_arm):        Started sapecqahdb

Daemon Status:
  corosync: active/disabled
  pacemaker: active/disabled
  pcsd: active/enabled
sapecqbhdb:ecqadm>
```

Replication is working

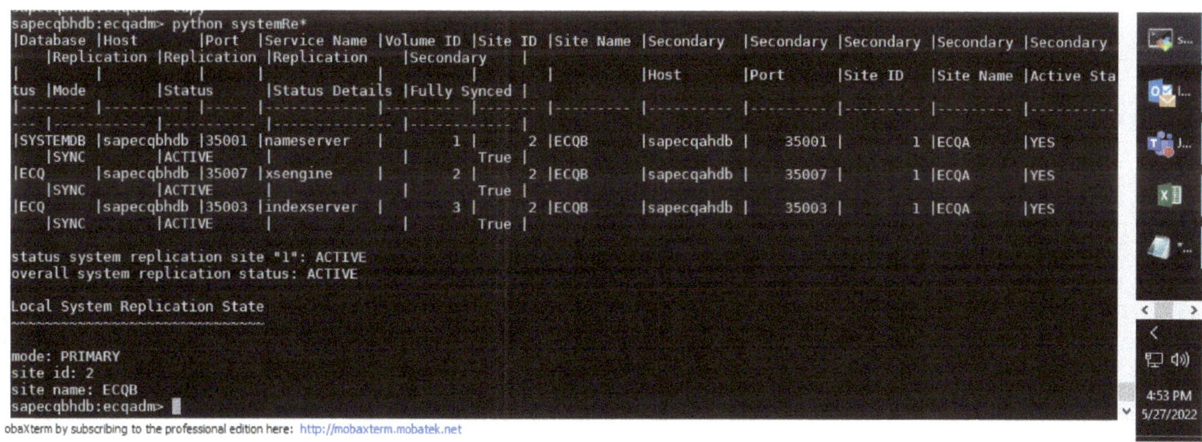

```
sapecqbhdb:ecqadm> python systemRe*
|Database |Host       |Port  |Service Name |Volume ID |Site ID |Site Name |Secondary  |Secondary |Secondary |Secondary |Secondary
   |Replication |Replication |Replication    |Secondary    |          |          |Host       |Port      |Site ID   |Site Name |Active Sta
|         |          |          |          |              |          |          |          |          |          |          |
tus |Mode         |Status         |Status Details |Fully Synced |
|-------- |--------- |------ |------------- |--------- |-------- |--------- |--------- |--------- |--------- |--------- |---------
--- |--------- |--------- |------------- |------------- |
|SYSTEMDB |sapecqbhdb |35001 |nameserver    |     1 |     2 |ECQB    |sapecqahdb |   35001 |     1 |ECQA     |YES
   |SYNC         |ACTIVE         |              |     True |
|ECQ     |sapecqbhdb |35007 |xsengine      |     2 |     2 |ECQB    |sapecqahdb |   35007 |     1 |ECQA     |YES
   |SYNC         |ACTIVE         |              |     True |
|ECQ     |sapecqbhdb |35003 |indexserver   |     3 |     2 |ECQB    |sapecqahdb |   35003 |     1 |ECQA     |YES
   |SYNC         |ACTIVE         |              |     True |

status system replication site "1": ACTIVE
overall system replication status: ACTIVE

Local System Replication State
~~~~~~~~~~~~~~~~~~~~~~~~~~~~~~~~

mode: PRIMARY
site id: 2
site name: ECQB
sapecqbhdb:ecqadm>
```

Check hdbnsutil –sr_state

```
operation mode: primary
site id: 2
site name: ECQB

is source system: true
is secondary/consumer system: false
has secondaries/consumers attached: true
is a takeover active: false
is primary suspended: false

Host Mappings:

sapecqbhdb -> [ECQB] sapecqbhdb
sapecqbhdb -> [ECQA] sapecqahdb


Site Mappings:

ECQB (primary/primary)
    |---ECQA (sync/logreplay)

Tier of ECQB: 1
Tier of ECQA: 2

Replication mode of ECQB: primary
Replication mode of ECQA: sync

Operation mode of ECQB: primary
Operation mode of ECQA: logreplay

Mapping: ECQB -> ECQA
done.
sapecqbhdb:ecqadm>
```


Change user and do not save, save it after stopping HDB on B (primary) node:

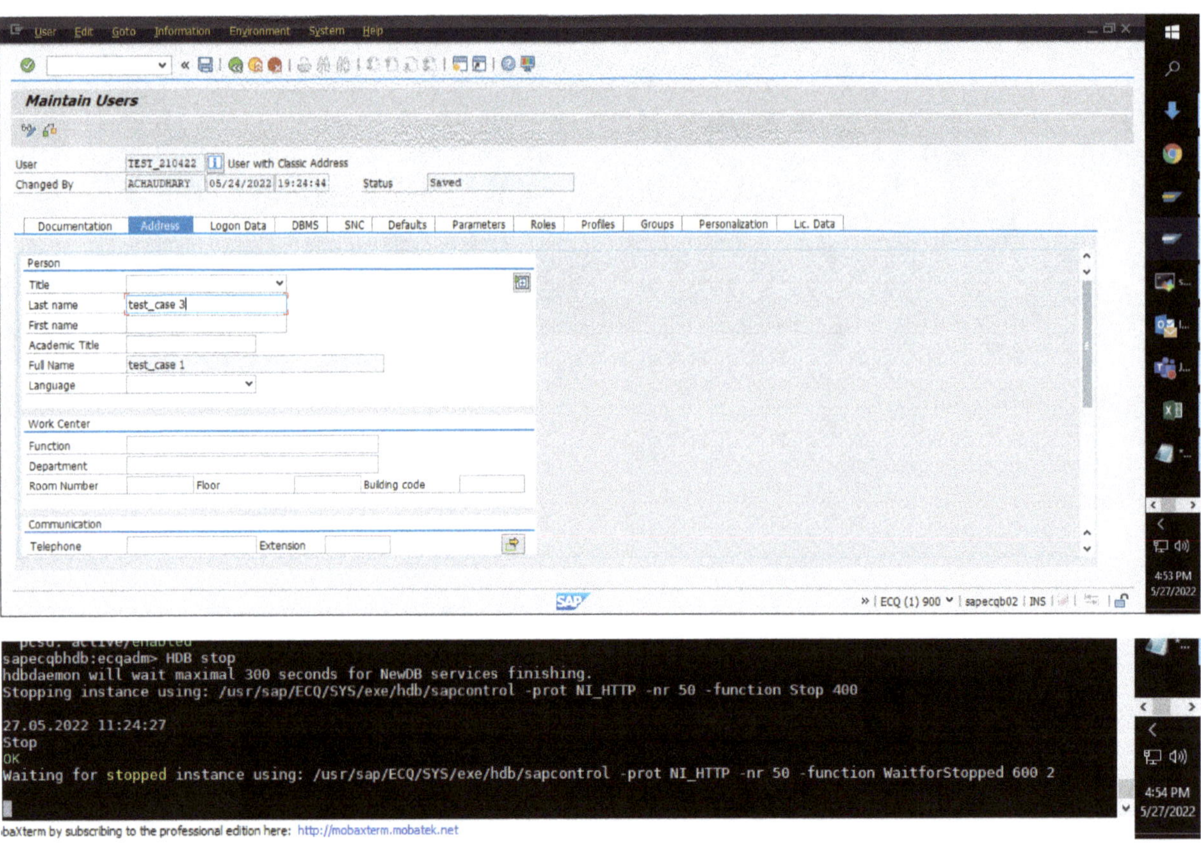

```
  pcsd: active/enabled
sapecqbhdb:ecqadm> HDB stop
hdbdaemon will wait maximal 300 seconds for NewDB services finishing.
Stopping instance using: /usr/sap/ECQ/SYS/exe/hdb/sapcontrol -prot NI_HTTP -nr 50 -function Stop 400

27.05.2022 11:24:27
Stop
OK
Waiting for stopped instance using: /usr/sap/ECQ/SYS/exe/hdb/sapcontrol -prot NI_HTTP -nr 50 -function WaitforStopped 600 2
```

Check cluster:

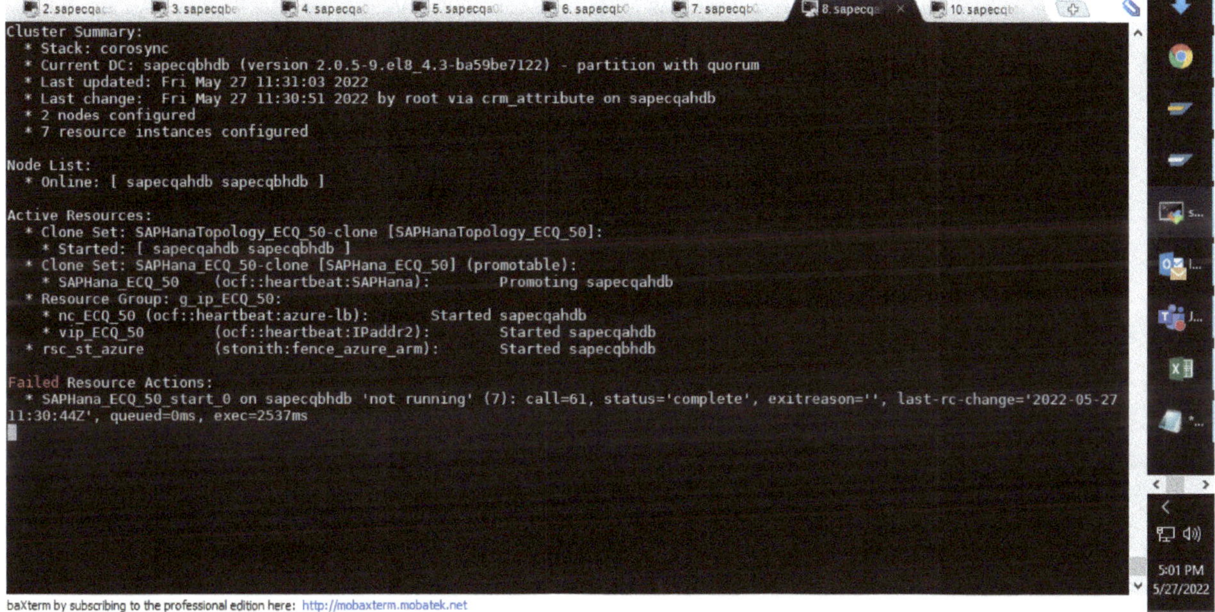

User changes have been saved without any issue.

NodeA:

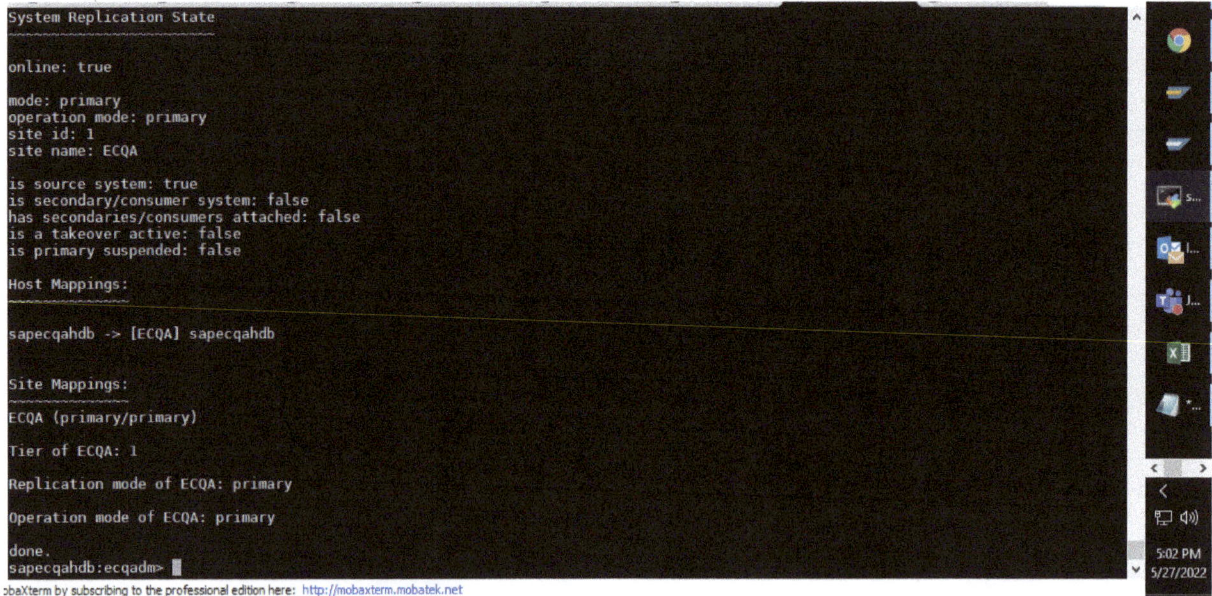

Node B:

Now, re-register Node B as 'secondary' to Node A clear the failed action in cluster

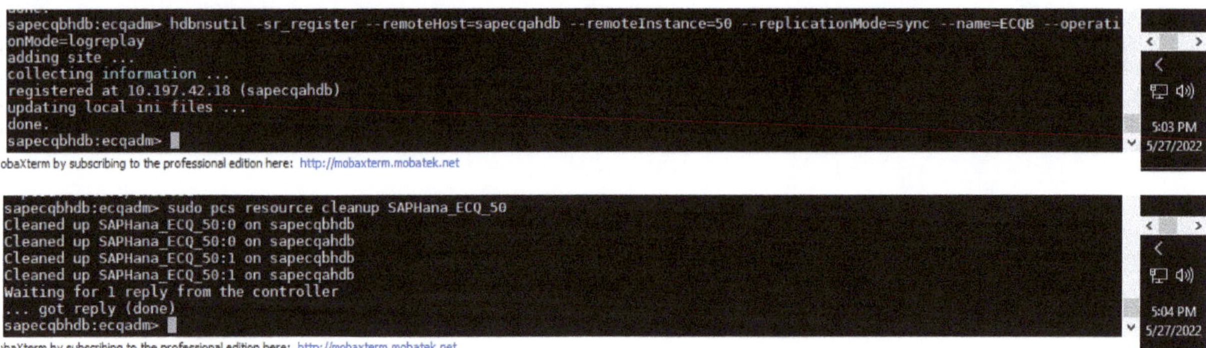

Replication is working fine from node A:

```
sapecqahdb:ecqadm> python systemRe*
|Database |Host       |Port  |Service Name |Volume ID |Site ID |Site Name |Secondary  |Secondary |Secondary |Secondary |Secondary
     |Replication |Replication |Replication            |Secondary    |
|         |           |      |             |          |        |          |Host       |Port      |Site ID   |Site Name |Active Sta
tus |Mode        |Status      |Status Details         |Fully Synced |
|-------- |---------- |----- |------------ |--------- |------- |--------- |---------- |--------- |--------- |--------- |---------
--- |----------- |----------- |---------------------- |------------ |
|SYSTEMDB |sapecqahdb |35001 |nameserver   |        1 |      1 |ECQA      |sapecqbhdb |    35001 |        2 |ECQB      |YES
    |SYNC        |ACTIVE      |                       |        True |
|ECQ      |sapecqahdb |35007 |xsengine     |        2 |      1 |ECQA      |sapecqbhdb |    35007 |        2 |ECQB      |YES
    |SYNC        |ACTIVE      |                       |        True |
|ECQ      |sapecqahdb |35003 |indexserver  |        3 |      1 |ECQA      |sapecqbhdb |    35003 |        2 |ECQB      |YES
    |SYNC        |SYNCING     |Preparing persistence |       False |

status system replication site "2": SYNCING
overall system replication status: SYNCING

Local System Replication State
~~~~~~~~~~~~~~~~~~~~~~~~~~~~~~

mode: PRIMARY
site id: 1
site name: ECQA
sapecqahdb:ecqadm>
```

baXterm by subscribing to the professional edition here: http://mobaxterm.mobatek.net

Check cluster status

```
ecqadm@sapecqbhdb:/usr/sap/ECQ/HDB50/exe/python_support> sudo pcs status
Cluster name: sapecqhdb
Cluster Summary:
  * Stack: corosync
  * Current DC: sapecqbhdb (version 2.0.5-9.el8_4.3-ba59be7122) - partition with quorum
  * Last updated: Mon Mar 28 12:21:45 2022
  * Last change:  Mon Mar 28 12:21:34 2022 by root via crm_attribute on sapecqbhdb
  * 2 nodes configured
  * 7 resource instances configured

Node List:
  * Online: [ sapecqahdb sapecqbhdb ]

Full List of Resources:
  * Clone Set: SAPHanaTopology_ECQ_50-clone [SAPHanaTopology_ECQ_50]:
    * Started: [ sapecqahdb sapecqbhdb ]
  * Clone Set: SAPHana_ECQ_50-clone [SAPHana_ECQ_50] (promotable):
    * Masters: [ sapecqahdb ]
    * Slaves: [ sapecqbhdb ]
  * Resource Group: g_ip_ECQ_50:
    * nc_ECQ_50 (ocf::heartbeat:azure-lb):       Started sapecqahdb
    * vip_ECQ_50        (ocf::heartbeat:IPaddr2):        Started sapecqahdb
  * rsc_st_azure        (stonith:fence_azure_arm):       Started sapecqbhdb

Daemon Status:
  corosync: active/disabled
  pacemaker: active/disabled
  pcsd: active/enabled
ecqadm@sapecqbhdb:/usr/sap/ECQ/HDB50/exe/python_support>
```

baXterm by subscribing to the professional edition here: http://mobaxterm.mobatek.net

8.4. Test case 4: Crash HANA on Primary side

Test Description	Crash HANA on Primary side
Test action	Kill HANA hdb daemon on **sapecqahdb (Primary)**
Result	Pass
Expected results	HANA fails over from sapecqahdb (Primary) to sapecqbhdb (Secondary). Virtual IP (VIP) fails over from sapecqahdb (Primary) to sapecqbhdb (Secondary). Application connectivity to HANA is lost during fail over and re-established.
Desired results	HANA fails over from sapecqahdb (Primary) to sapecqbhdb (Secondary). Virtual IP (VIP) fails over from sapecqahdb (Primary) to sapecqbhdb (Secondary). Application connectivity to HANA is lost during fail over and re-established.
Post-test execution steps	Clean up replication and re-configure system replication with sapecqbhdb as Primary and sapecqahdb as Secondary Restart pacemaker on failed node (sapecqahdb) Check system replication status Check cluster status

Check status of cluster and HANA System replication before starting the test.

```
sapecqahdb:ecqadm> sudo pcs status
Cluster name: sapecqhdb
Cluster Summary:
  * Stack: corosync
  * Current DC: sapecqbhdb (version 2.0.5-9.el8_4.3-ba59be7122) - partition with quorum
  * Last updated: Fri May 27 11:39:49 2022
  * Last change:  Fri May 27 11:39:02 2022 by root via crm_attribute on sapecqbhdb
  * 2 nodes configured
  * 7 resource instances configured

Node List:
  * Online: [ sapecqahdb sapecqbhdb ]

Full List of Resources:
  * Clone Set: SAPHanaTopology_ECQ_50-clone [SAPHanaTopology_ECQ_50]:
    * Started: [ sapecqahdb sapecqbhdb ]
  * Clone Set: SAPHana_ECQ_50-clone [SAPHana_ECQ_50] (promotable):
    * Masters: [ sapecqahdb ]
    * Slaves: [ sapecqbhdb ]
  * Resource Group: g_ip_ECQ_50:
    * nc_ECQ_50 (ocf::heartbeat:azure-lb):        Started sapecqahdb
    * vip_ECQ_50      (ocf::heartbeat:IPaddr2):        Started sapecqahdb
  * rsc_st_azure      (stonith:fence_azure_arm):       Started sapecqbhdb

Daemon Status:
  corosync: active/disabled
  pacemaker: active/disabled
  pcsd: active/enabled
sapecqahdb:ecqadm>
```


Check Replication

```
sapecqahdb:ecqadm> python systemR*
|Database |Host        |Port |Service Name |Volume ID |Site ID |Site Name |Secondary   |Secondary |Secondary |Secondary |Secondary
         |Replication |Replication |Replication  |Secondary |        |          |Host       |Port      |Site ID   |Site Name |Active Sta
tus |Mode        |Status       |Status Details |Fully Synced |
-------- |---------- |----- |-------------- |---------- |------- |--------- |---------- |--------- |--------- |--------- |---------
--- |---------- |---------- |-------------- |------------ |
|SYSTEMDB |sapecqahdb |35001 |nameserver    |      1 |      1 |ECQA    |sapecqbhdb |    35001 |        2 |ECQB      |YES
   |SYNC        |ACTIVE       |             |      True |
|ECQ      |sapecqahdb |35007 |xsengine      |      2 |      1 |ECQA    |sapecqbhdb |    35007 |        2 |ECQB      |YES
   |SYNC        |ACTIVE       |             |      True |
|ECQ      |sapecqahdb |35003 |indexserver   |      3 |      1 |ECQA    |sapecqbhdb |    35003 |        2 |ECQB      |YES
   |SYNC        |ACTIVE       |             |      True |

status system replication site "2": ACTIVE
overall system replication status: ACTIVE

Local System Replication State

mode: PRIMARY
site id: 1
site name: ECQA
sapecqahdb:ecqadm>
```


From node A: hdbnsutil –sr_state

```
sapecqahdb -> [ECQB] sapecqbhdb
sapecqahdb -> [ECQA] sapecqahdb

Site Mappings:

ECQA (primary/primary)
    |---ECQB (sync/logreplay)

Tier of ECQA: 1
Tier of ECQB: 2

Replication mode of ECQA: primary
Replication mode of ECQB: sync

Operation mode of ECQA: primary
Operation mode of ECQB: logreplay

Mapping: ECQA -> ECQB
done.
sapecqahdb:ecqadm>
```


Do changes in user and do node save it, save it after executing below command.

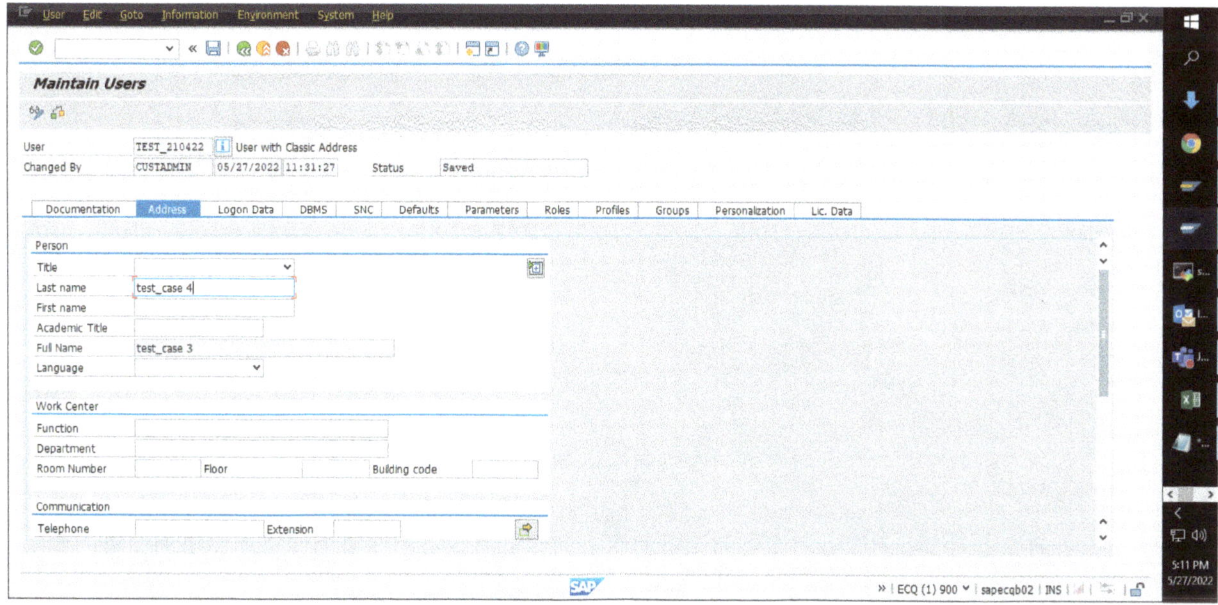

Kill the HANA hdbdaemon process on A side

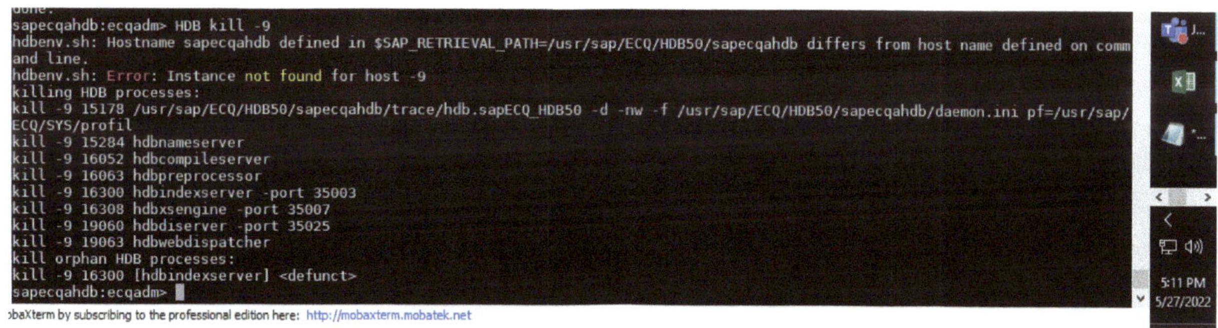

VIP and HANA failed over to B. Now, check the new Primary.

User changes have been saved without any issues.

NodeB:

```
mode: primary
operation mode: primary
site id: 2
site name: ECQB

is source system: true
is secondary/consumer system: false
has secondaries/consumers attached: false
is a takeover active: false
is primary suspended: false

Host Mappings:
~~~~~~~~~~~~~~~

sapecqbhdb -> [ECQB] sapecqbhdb


Site Mappings:
~~~~~~~~~~~~~~~
ECQB (primary/primary)

Tier of ECQB: 1

Replication mode of ECQB: primary

Operation mode of ECQB: primary

done.
sapecqbhdb:ecqadm>
```

Node A:

```
kill -9 10300 [hdbindexserver] <defunct>
sapecqahdb:ecqadm> hdbnsutil -sr_state

System Replication State
~~~~~~~~~~~~~~~~~~~~~~~~~~

online: false

mode: primary
operation mode: unknown
site id: 1
site name: ECQA

is source system: unknown
is secondary/consumer system: false
has secondaries/consumers attached: unknown
is a takeover active: false
is primary suspended: false
done.
sapecqahdb:ecqadm>
```

Re-register A node as secondary and start DB.

```
done.
sapecqahdb:ecqadm> hdbnsutil -sr_register --remoteHost=sapecqbhdb --remoteInstance=50 --replicationMode=sync --name=ECQA --operati
onMode=logreplay
adding site ...
collecting information ...
registered at 10.197.42.19 (sapecqbhdb)
updating local ini files ...
done.
sapecqahdb:ecqadm>
```

Cleanup failed resources:

```
pcsd: active/enabled
sapecqahdb:ecqadm> sudo pcs resource cleanup SAPHana_ECQ_50
Cleaned up SAPHana_ECQ_50:0 on sapecqbhdb
Cleaned up SAPHana_ECQ_50:1 on sapecqahdb
Waiting for 1 reply from the controller
... got reply (done)
sapecqahdb:ecqadm>
```

Check cluster status:

```
sapecqahdb:ecqadm> sudo pcs status
Cluster name: sapecqhdb
Cluster Summary:
  * Stack: corosync
  * Current DC: sapecqbhdb (version 2.0.5-9.el8_4.3-ba59be7122) - partition with quorum
  * Last updated: Fri May 27 11:55:08 2022
  * Last change:  Fri May 27 11:55:00 2022 by root via crm_attribute on sapecqbhdb
  * 2 nodes configured
  * 7 resource instances configured

Node List:
  * Online: [ sapecqahdb sapecqbhdb ]

Full List of Resources:
  * Clone Set: SAPHanaTopology_ECQ_50-clone [SAPHanaTopology_ECQ_50]:
    * Started: [ sapecqahdb sapecqbhdb ]
  * Clone Set: SAPHana_ECQ_50-clone [SAPHana_ECQ_50] (promotable):
    * Masters: [ sapecqbhdb ]
    * Slaves: [ sapecqahdb ]
  * Resource Group: g_ip_ECQ_50:
    * nc_ECQ_50    (ocf::heartbeat:azure-lb):        Started sapecqbhdb
    * vip_ECQ_50        (ocf::heartbeat:IPaddr2):        Started sapecqbhdb
  * rsc_st_azure       (stonith:fence_azure_arm):       Started sapecqahdb

Daemon Status:
  corosync: active/disabled
  pacemaker: active/disabled
  pcsd: active/enabled
sapecqahdb:ecqadm>
```


Replication is looking good now.

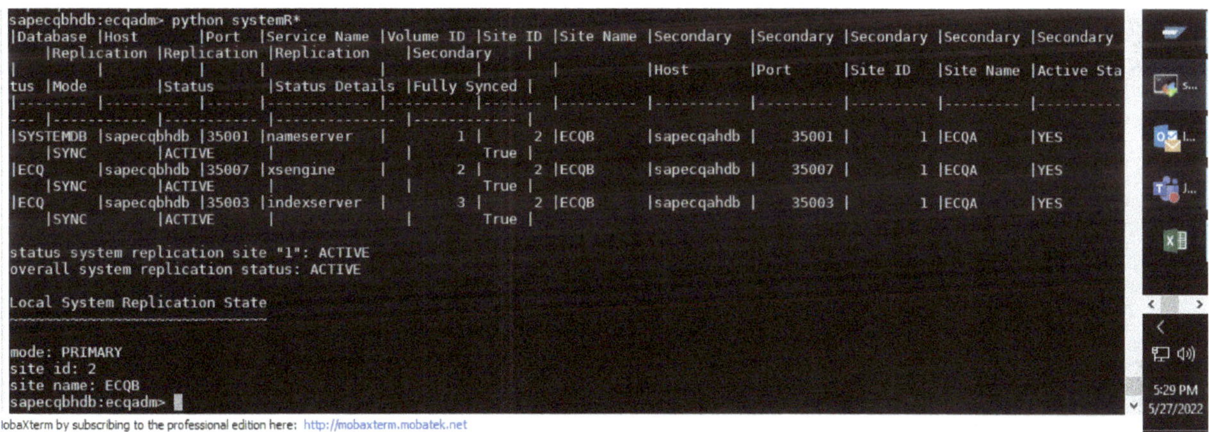
```
sapecqbhdb:ecqadm> python systemR*
|Database |Host       |Port  |Service Name |Volume ID |Site ID |Site Name |Secondary  |Secondary |Secondary |Secondary |Secondary
         |Replication |Replication |Replication      |Secondary   |         |         |Host       |Port      |Site ID   |Site Name |Active Sta
                      |            |                 |            |         |         |
tus |Mode         |Status        |Status Details |Fully Synced |
|--------- |--------- |----- |--------- |--------- |--------- |--------- |--------- |--------- |--------- |--------- |---------
--- |--------- |--------- |--------- |--------- |--------- |
|SYSTEMDB |sapecqbhdb |35001 |nameserver  |      1 |     2 |ECQB    |sapecqahdb |   35001 |       1 |ECQA     |YES
         |SYNC      |ACTIVE    |             |       True |
|ECQ      |sapecqbhdb |35007 |xsengine   |      2 |     2 |ECQB    |sapecqahdb |   35007 |       1 |ECQA     |YES
         |SYNC      |ACTIVE    |             |       True |
|ECQ      |sapecqbhdb |35003 |indexserver |      3 |     2 |ECQB    |sapecqahdb |   35003 |       1 |ECQA     |YES
         |SYNC      |ACTIVE    |             |       True |

status system replication site "1": ACTIVE
overall system replication status: ACTIVE

Local System Replication State


mode: PRIMARY
site id: 2
site name: ECQB
sapecqbhdb:ecqadm>
```


8.5.   Test case 5: Crash HANA on Primary side

Test Description	Crash HANA on Primary side
Test action	Kill HANA hdb daemon on sapecqbhdb (Primary)
Result	Pass
Expected results	HANA fails over from sapecqbhdb (Primary) to sapecqahdb (Secondary). Virtual IP (VIP) fails over from sapecqbhdb (Primary) to sapecqahdb (Secondary). Application connectivity to HANA is lost during fail over and re-established.
Desired results	HANA fails over from sapecqbhdb (Primary) to sapecqahdb (Secondary). Virtual IP (VIP) fails over from sapecqbhdb (Primary) to sapecqahdb (Secondary). Application connectivity to HANA is lost during fail over and re-established.
Post-test execution steps	Clean up replication and re-configure system replication with sapecqahdb as Primary and sapecqbhdb as Secondary Restart pacemaker on failed node (sapecqbhdb) Check system replication status Check cluster status

Test execution steps

Check status of cluster and HANA System replication before starting the test.

Check hdbnsutil –sr_status B node

Replication is running fine on B as Primary node.

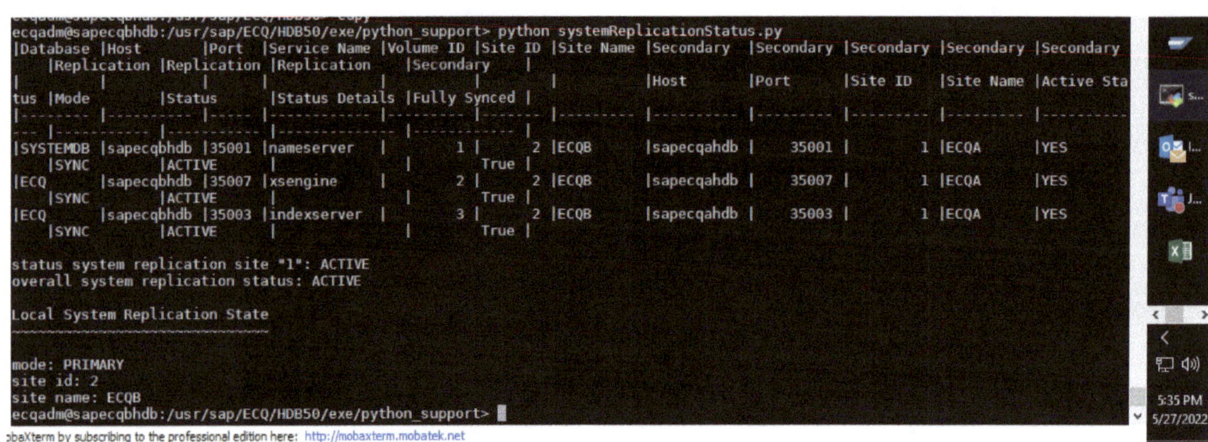

Kill the HANA hdbdaemon process on Primary (B) side. Now, VIP is on the B side (Primary)

```
site name: ECQB
ecqadm@sapecqbhdb:/usr/sap/ECQ/HDB50/exe/python_support> HDB kill -9
hdbenv.sh: Hostname sapecqbhdb defined in $SAP_RETRIEVAL_PATH=/usr/sap/ECQ/HDB50/sapecqbhdb differs from host name defined on comm
and line.
hdbenv.sh: Error: Instance not found for host -9
killing HDB processes:
kill -9 423018 /usr/sap/ECQ/HDB50/sapecqbhdb/trace/hdb.sapECQ_HDB50 -d -nw -f /usr/sap/ECQ/HDB50/sapecqbhdb/daemon.ini pf=/usr/sap
/ECQ/SYS/profile/ECQ_HDB50_sapecqbhdb
kill -9 423040 hdbnameserver
kill -9 423383 hdbcompileserver
kill -9 423386 hdbpreprocessor
kill -9 423426 hdbindexserver -port 35003
kill -9 423429 hdbxsengine -port 35007
kill -9 426739 hdbdiserver -port 35025
kill -9 426742 hdbwebdispatcher
kill orphan HDB processes:
kill -9 423426 [hdbindexserver] <defunct>
kill -9 423429 [hdbxsengine] <defunct>
ecqadm@sapecqbhdb:/usr/sap/ECQ/HDB50/exe/python_support>
```


Save below changes after executing above command.

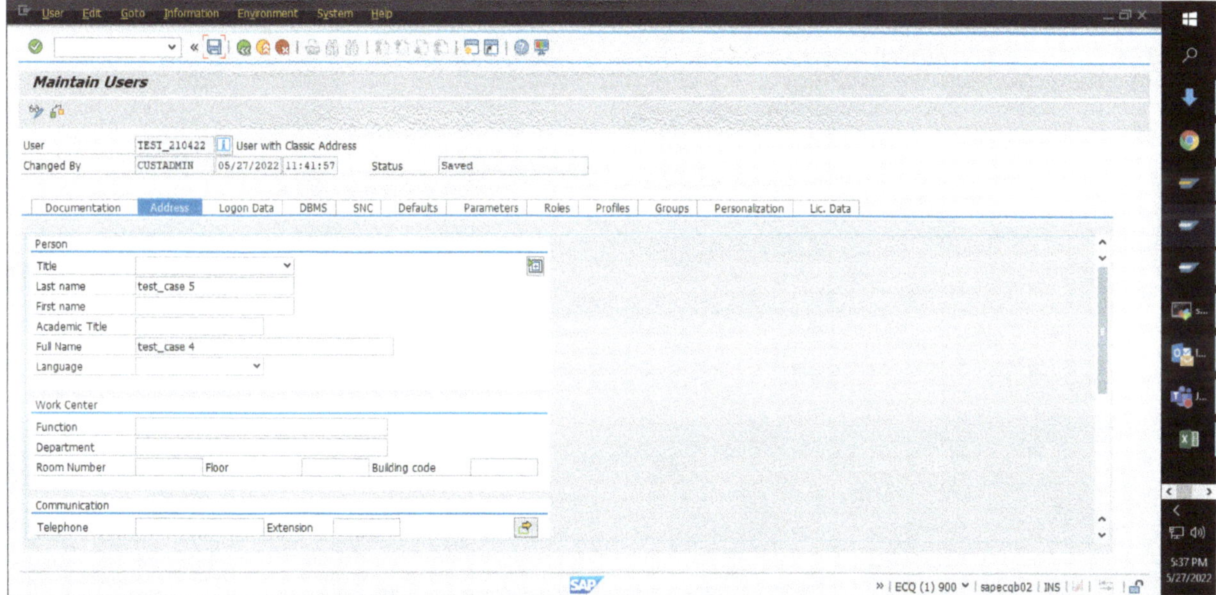

Now, HANA is 'active' on the A side and the VIP has failed over.

```
ecqadm@sapecqbhdb:/usr/sap/ECQ/HDB50/exe/python_support> sudo pcs status
Cluster name: sapecqhdb
Cluster Summary:
  * Stack: corosync
  * Current DC: sapecqbhdb (version 2.0.5-9.el8_4.3-ba59be7122) - partition with quorum
  * Last updated: Fri May 27 12:09:01 2022
  * Last change:  Fri May 27 12:08:33 2022 by root via crm_attribute on sapecqahdb
  * 2 nodes configured
  * 7 resource instances configured

Node List:
  * Online: [ sapecqahdb sapecqbhdb ]

Full List of Resources:
  * Clone Set: SAPHanaTopology_ECQ_50-clone [SAPHanaTopology_ECQ_50]:
    * Started: [ sapecqahdb sapecqbhdb ]
  * Clone Set: SAPHana_ECQ_50-clone [SAPHana_ECQ_50] (promotable):
    * Masters: [ sapecqahdb ]
    * Stopped: [ sapecqbhdb ]
  * Resource Group: g_ip_ECQ_50:
    * nc_ECQ_50 (ocf::heartbeat:azure-lb):          Started sapecqahdb
    * vip_ECQ_50      (ocf::heartbeat:IPaddr2):     Started sapecqahdb
  * rsc_st_azure      (stonith:fence_azure_arm):    Started sapecqbhdb

Failed Resource Actions:
  * SAPHana_ECQ_50_start_0 on sapecqbhdb 'not running' (7): call=107, status='complete', exitreason='', last-rc-change='2022-05-27
12:07:32Z', queued=0ms, exec=2473ms

Daemon Status:
  corosync: active/disabled
  pacemaker: active/disabled
  pcsd: active/enabled
ecqadm@sapecqbhdb:/usr/sap/ECQ/HDB50/exe/python_support>
```

The 'failed action' above is expected as the 'crashed' HANA is not yet configured as 'Secondary'

Changes have been saved without any issues.

Register B node as secondary node and start HDB on node B:

```
pcsd: active/enabled
ecqadm@sapecqbhdb:/usr/sap/ECQ/HDB50/exe/python_support> hdbnsutil -sr_register --remoteHost=sapecqahdb --remoteInstance=50 --repl
icationMode=sync --name=ECQB --operationMode=logreplay
adding site ...
collecting information ...
registered at 10.197.42.18 (sapecqahdb)
updating local ini files ...
done.
```

Cleanup failed actions to start sap HANA

```
ecqadm@sapecqbhdb:/usr/sap/ECQ/HDB50/exe/python_support> sudo pcs resource cleanup SAPHana_ECQ_50
Cleaned up SAPHana_ECQ_50:0 on sapecqbhdb
Cleaned up SAPHana_ECQ_50:0 on sapecqahdb
Cleaned up SAPHana_ECQ_50:1 on sapecqbhdb
Cleaned up SAPHana_ECQ_50:1 on sapecqahdb
Waiting for 1 reply from the controller
... got reply (done)
ecqadm@sapecqbhdb:/usr/sap/ECQ/HDB50/exe/python_support>
```


Check Replication

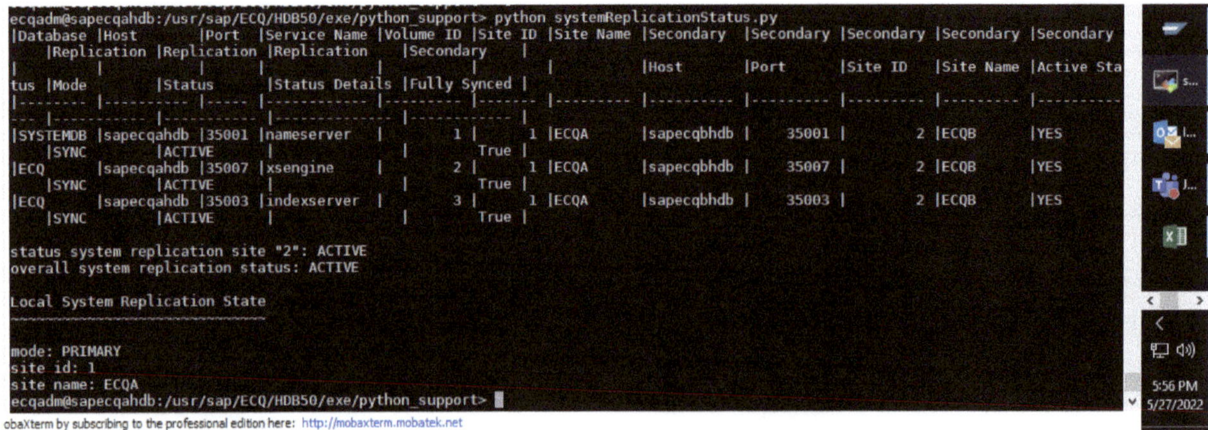

```
ecqadm@sapecqahdb:/usr/sap/ECQ/HDB50/exe/python_support> python systemReplicationStatus.py
|Database |Host       |Port  |Service Name |Volume ID |Site ID |Site Name |Secondary  |Secondary |Secondary |Secondary |Secondary
         |Replication |Replication |Replication    |Secondary  |
                                                                          |Host      |Port     |Site ID   |Site Name |Active Sta
tus |Mode        |Status      |Status Details |Fully Synced |
--- |---------- |----- |------------ |--------- |------- |--------- |--------- |--------- |--------- |--------- |----------
    |---------- |------ |------------ |------------ |
|SYSTEMDB |sapecqahdb |35001 |nameserver   |        1 |      1 |ECQA      |sapecqbhdb |   35001 |        2 |ECQB      |YES
     |SYNC        |ACTIVE      |               |  True |
|ECQ      |sapecqahdb |35007 |xsengine     |        2 |      1 |ECQA      |sapecqbhdb |   35007 |        2 |ECQB      |YES
     |SYNC        |ACTIVE      |               |  True |
|ECQ      |sapecqahdb |35003 |indexserver  |        3 |      1 |ECQA      |sapecqbhdb |   35003 |        2 |ECQB      |YES
     |SYNC        |ACTIVE      |               |  True |

status system replication site "2": ACTIVE
overall system replication status: ACTIVE

Local System Replication State
~~~~~~~~~~~~~~~~~~~~~~~~~~~~~~~~~~~~~~~~~~~~~~~~~~~~~~~~~~~~~~~~~~~~~~~

mode: PRIMARY
site id: 1
site name: ECQA
ecqadm@sapecqahdb:/usr/sap/ECQ/HDB50/exe/python_support>
```


Check cluster status

```
ecqadm@sapecqahdb:/usr/sap/ECQ/HDB50/exe/python_support> sudo pcs status
Cluster name: sapecqhdb
Cluster Summary:
  * Stack: corosync
  * Current DC: sapecqbhdb (version 2.0.5-9.el8_4.3-ba59be7122) - partition with quorum
  * Last updated: Fri May 27 12:27:01 2022
  * Last change:  Fri May 27 12:26:12 2022 by root via crm_attribute on sapecqahdb
  * 2 nodes configured
  * 7 resource instances configured

Node List:
  * Online: [ sapecqahdb sapecqbhdb ]

Full List of Resources:
  * Clone Set: SAPHanaTopology_ECQ_50-clone [SAPHanaTopology_ECQ_50]:
    * Started: [ sapecqahdb sapecqbhdb ]
  * Clone Set: SAPHana_ECQ_50-clone [SAPHana_ECQ_50] (promotable):
    * Masters: [ sapecqahdb ]
    * Slaves: [ sapecqbhdb ]
  * Resource Group: g_ip_ECQ_50:
    * nc_ECQ_50 (ocf::heartbeat:azure-lb):        Started sapecqahdb
    * vip_ECQ_50        (ocf::heartbeat:IPaddr2):        Started sapecqahdb
  * rsc_st_azure        (stonith:fence_azure_arm):        Started sapecqbhdb

Daemon Status:
  corosync: active/disabled
  pacemaker: active/disabled
  pcsd: active/enabled
ecqadm@sapecqahdb:/usr/sap/ECQ/HDB50/exe/python_support>
```


8.6.   Test case 6: Power off HANA server Primary (A) side

Test Description	Power off HANA server on the Primary side (A)
Test action	Perform hard shutdown of sapecpahdb (Primary) server
Result	Pass
Expected results	HANA fails over from sapecpahdb (Primary) to sapecpbhdb (Secondary). Virtual IP (VIP) fails over from sapecpahdb (Primary) to sapecpbhdb (Secondary). Application connectivity to HANA is lost during fail over and re-established.
Desired results	HANA fails over from sapecpahdb (Primary) to sapecpbhdb (Secondary). Virtual IP (VIP) fails over from sapecpahdb (Primary) to sapecpbhdb (Secondary). Application connectivity to HANA is lost during fail over and re-established.
Post-test execution steps	Clean up replication and re-configure system replication with sapecpbhdb as Primary and sapecpahdb as Secondary Restart pacemaker on failed node (sapecpahdb) Check system replication status Check cluster status

Test execution

Check status of cluster and HANA System replication before starting the test.

```
sapecqahdb:ecqadm> sudo pcs status
Cluster name: sapecqhdb
Cluster Summary:
  * Stack: corosync
  * Current DC: sapecqahdb (version 2.0.5-9.el8_4.3-ba59be7122) - partition with quorum
  * Last updated: Fri May 27 10:25:51 2022
  * Last change:  Fri May 27 10:25:26 2022 by root via crm_attribute on sapecqahdb
  * 2 nodes configured
  * 7 resource instances configured

Node List:
  * Online: [ sapecqahdb sapecqbhdb ]

Full List of Resources:
  * Clone Set: SAPHanaTopology_ECQ_50-clone [SAPHanaTopology_ECQ_50]:
    * Started: [ sapecqahdb sapecqbhdb ]
  * Clone Set: SAPHana_ECQ_50-clone [SAPHana_ECQ_50] (promotable):
    * Masters: [ sapecqahdb ]
    * Slaves: [ sapecqbhdb ]
  * Resource Group: g_ip_ECQ_50:
    * nc_ECQ_50 (ocf::heartbeat:azure-lb):         Started sapecqahdb
    * vip_ECQ_50        (ocf::heartbeat:IPaddr2):         Started sapecqahdb
  * rsc_st_azure        (stonith:fence_azure_arm):        Started sapecqbhdb

Daemon Status:
  corosync: active/disabled
  pacemaker: active/disabled
  pcsd: active/enabled
sapecqahdb:ecqadm>
```

Replication is running:

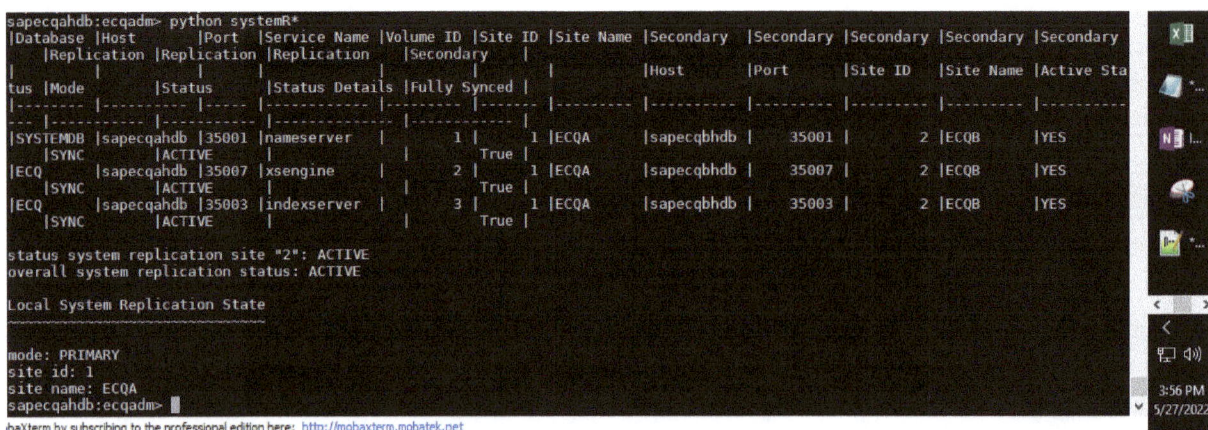

Hdbnsutil –sr_state is fine on A node:

Edit user in su01

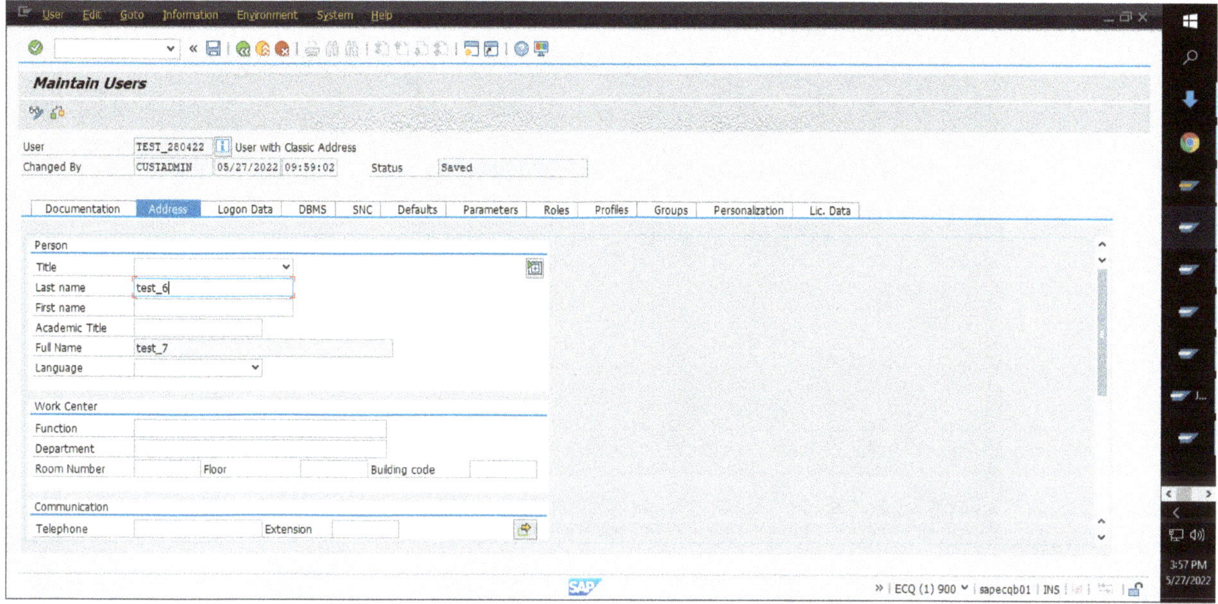

Power off HANA server Primary – A node by using below command:

echo b > /proc/sysrq-trigger

Changes done and clicked save button

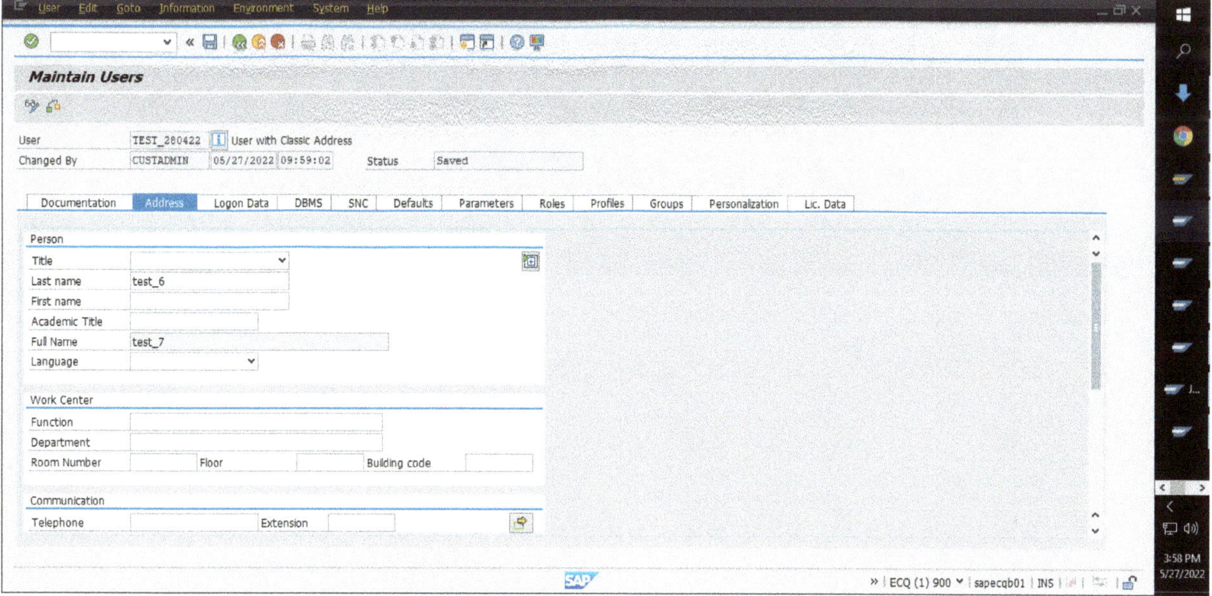

Check cluster status

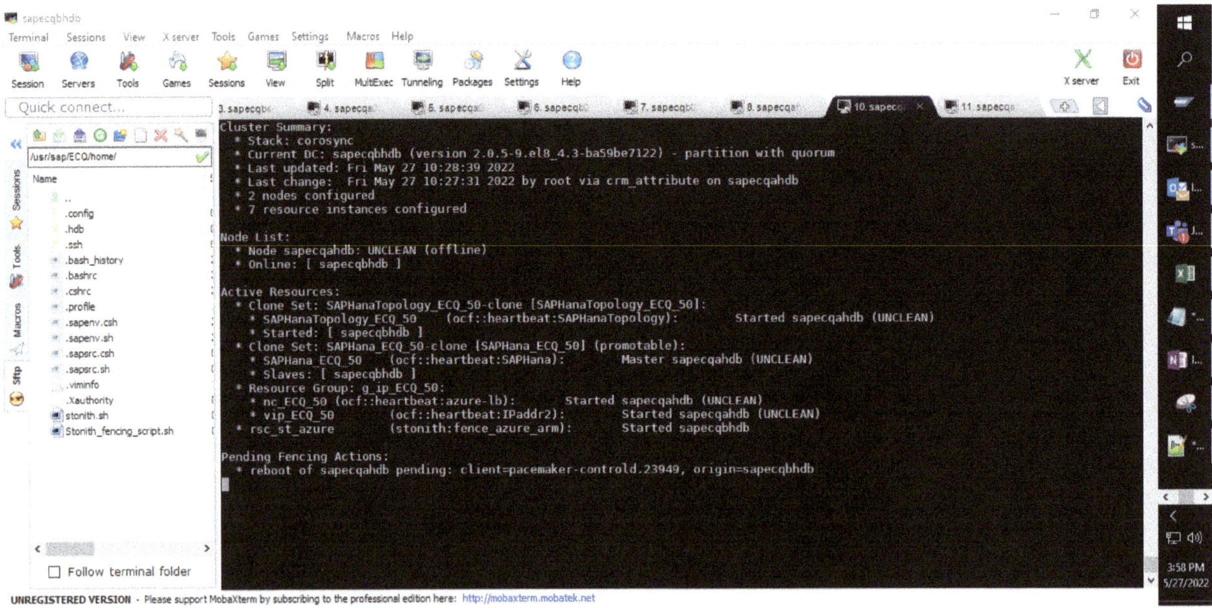

After 4 mins it is started promoting

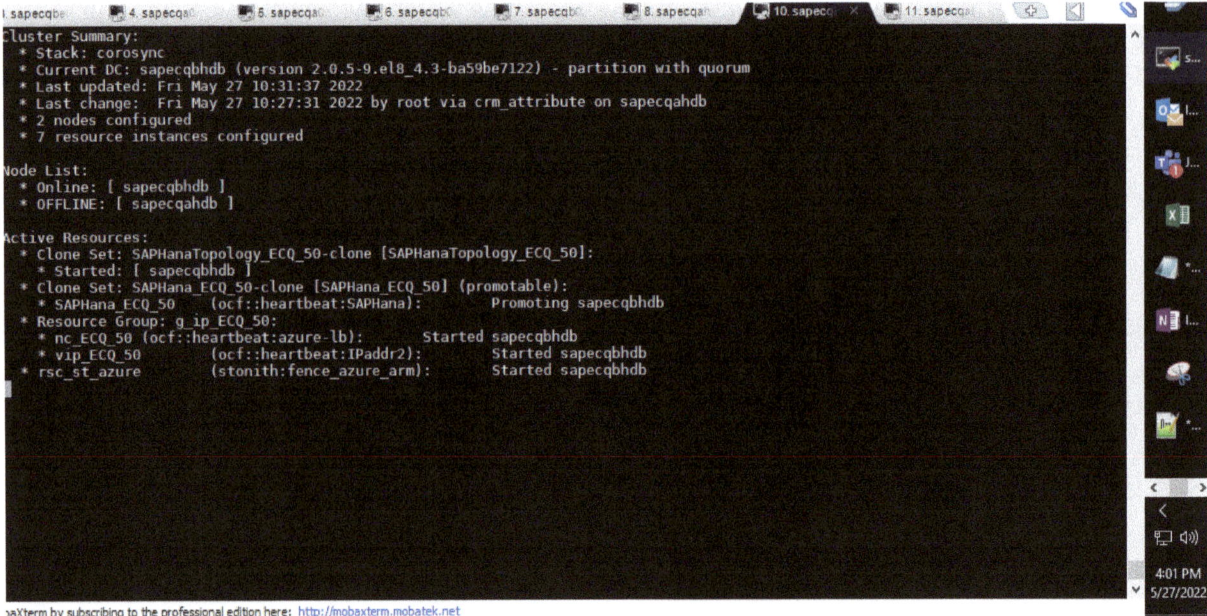

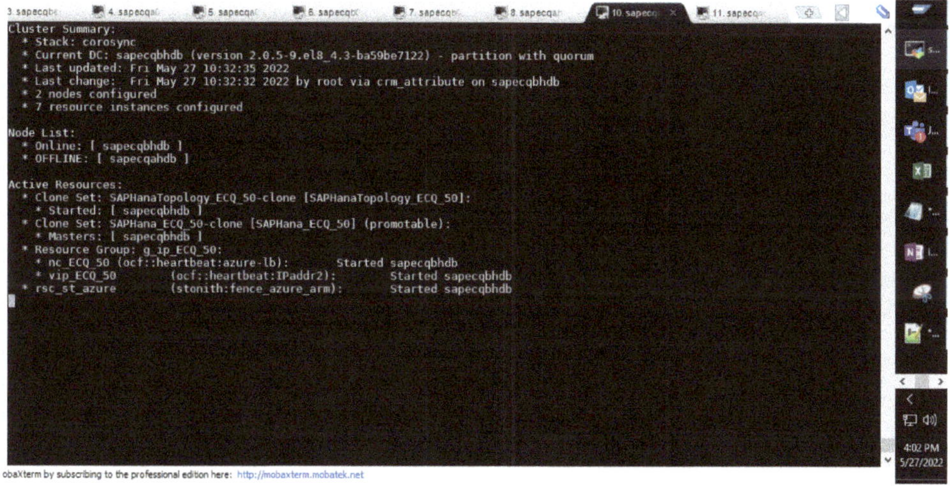

User changes have been saved without any issues..

Register node A as secondary and start cluster

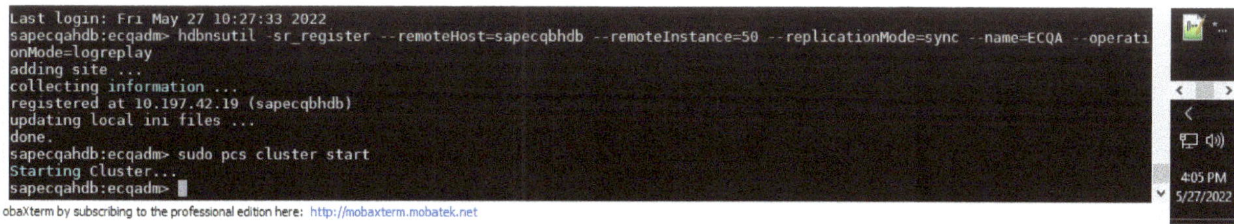

From B node:

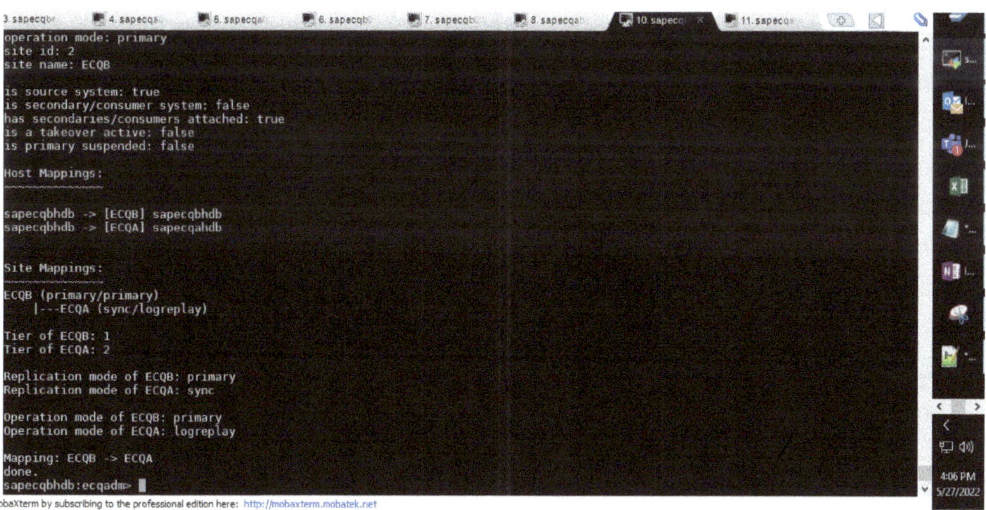

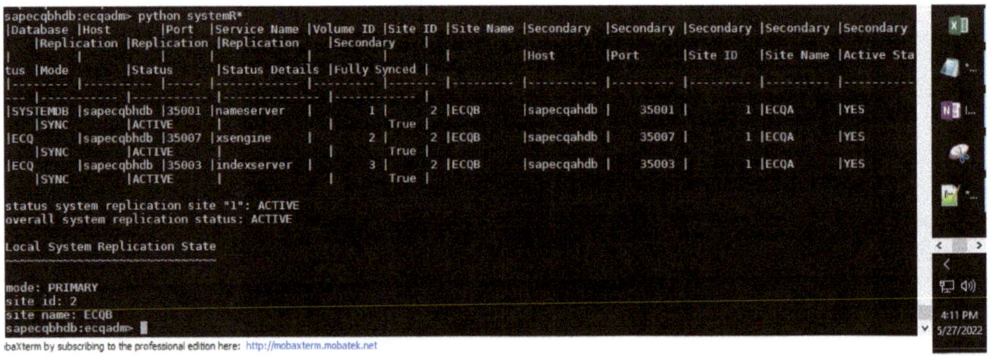

sapecqbhdb:ecqadm> python systemR*
Database	Host	Port	Service Name	Volume ID	Site ID	Site Name	Secondary	Secondary	Secondary	Secondary	Secondary	Replication	Replication	Replication	Secondary
							Host	Port	Site ID	Site Name	Active Status	Mode	Status	Status Details	Fully Synced
SYSTEMDB	sapecqbhdb	35001	nameserver	1	2	ECQB	sapecqahdb	35001	1	ECQA	YES	SYNC	ACTIVE		True
ECQ	sapecqbhdb	35007	xsengine	2	2	ECQB	sapecqahdb	35007	1	ECQA	YES	SYNC	ACTIVE		True
ECQ	sapecqbhdb	35003	indexserver	3	2	ECQB	sapecqahdb	35003	1	ECQA	YES	SYNC	ACTIVE		True
status system replication site "1": ACTIVE
overall system replication status: ACTIVE
Local System Replication State
mode: PRIMARY
site id: 2
site name: ECQB
sapecqbhdb:ecqadm>
baXterm by subscribing to the professional edition here: http://mobaxterm.mobatek.net
4:11 PM
5/27/2022

Cluster status

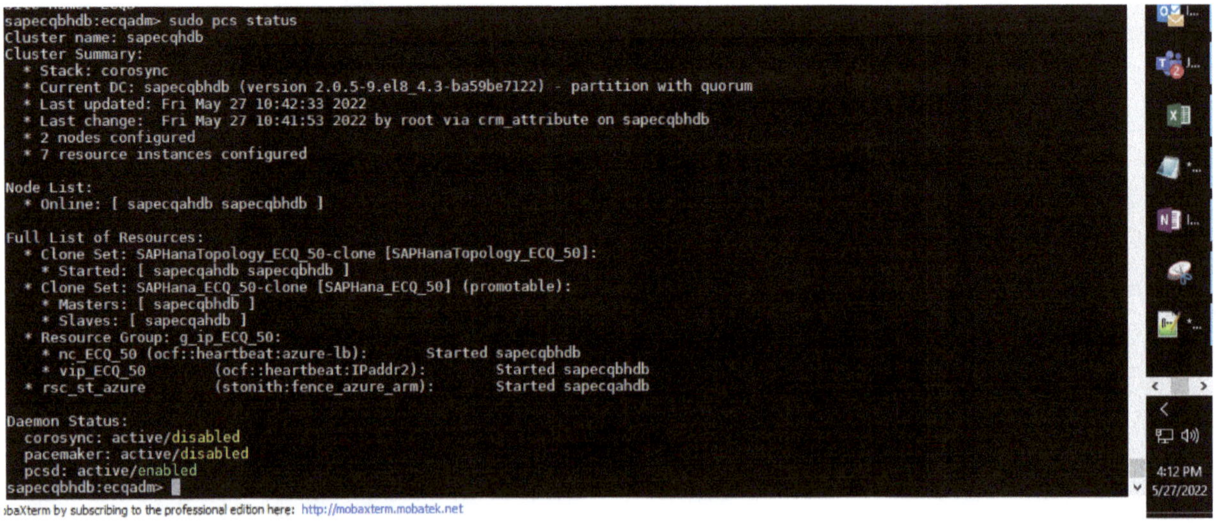

sapecqbhdb:ecqadm> sudo pcs status
Cluster name: sapecqhdb
Cluster Summary:
* Stack: corosync
* Current DC: sapecqbhdb (version 2.0.5-9.el8_4.3-ba59be7122) - partition with quorum
* Last updated: Fri May 27 10:42:33 2022
* Last change: Fri May 27 10:41:53 2022 by root via crm_attribute on sapecqbhdb
* 2 nodes configured
* 7 resource instances configured
Node List:
* Online: [sapecqahdb sapecqbhdb]
Full List of Resources:
* Clone Set: SAPHanaTopology_ECQ_50-clone [SAPHanaTopology_ECQ_50]:
* Started: [sapecqahdb sapecqbhdb]
* Clone Set: SAPHana_ECQ_50-clone [SAPHana_ECQ_50] (promotable):
* Masters: [sapecqbhdb]
* Slaves: [sapecqahdb]
* Resource Group: g_ip_ECQ_50:
* nc_ECQ_50 (ocf::heartbeat:azure-lb): Started sapecqbhdb
* vip_ECQ_50 (ocf::heartbeat:IPaddr2): Started sapecqbhdb
* rsc_st_azure (stonith:fence_azure_arm): Started sapecqahdb
Daemon Status:
corosync: active/disabled
pacemaker: active/disabled
pcsd: active/enabled
sapecqbhdb:ecqadm>
baXterm by subscribing to the professional edition here: http://mobaxterm.mobatek.net
4:12 PM
5/27/2022

8.7. Test case 7: Power off HANA server Primary (B) side

Test Description	Power off HANA server on the Primary side (B)
Test action	Perform hard shutdown of sapecpbhdb (Primary) server
Result	Pass
Expected results	HANA fails over from sapecpbhdb (Primary) to sapecpahdb (Secondary). Virtual IP (VIP) fails over from sapecpbhdb (Primary) to sapecpahdb (Secondary). Application connectivity to HANA is lost during fail over and re-established.
Desired results	HANA fails over from sapecpbhdb (Primary) to sapecpahdb (Secondary). Virtual IP (VIP) fails over from sapecpbhdb (Primary) to sapecpahdb (Secondary). Application connectivity to HANA is lost during fail over and re-established.
Post-test execution steps	Clean up replication and re-configure system replication with sapecpahdb as Primary and sapecpbhdb as Secondary Restart pacemaker on failed node (sapecpbhdb) Check system replication status Check cluster status

Test execution

Check status of cluster and HANA System replication before starting the test.

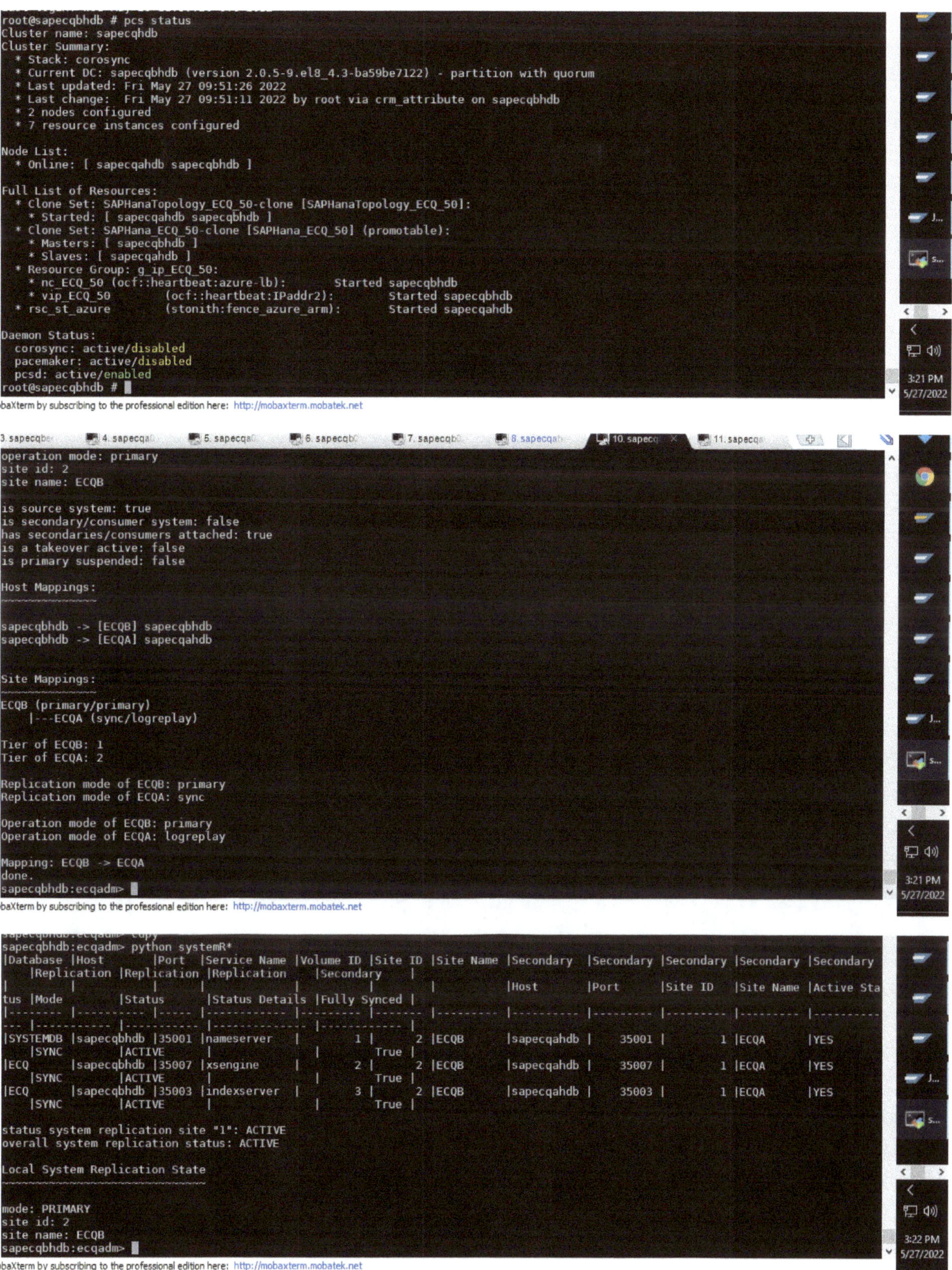

Will try to save below changes in su01

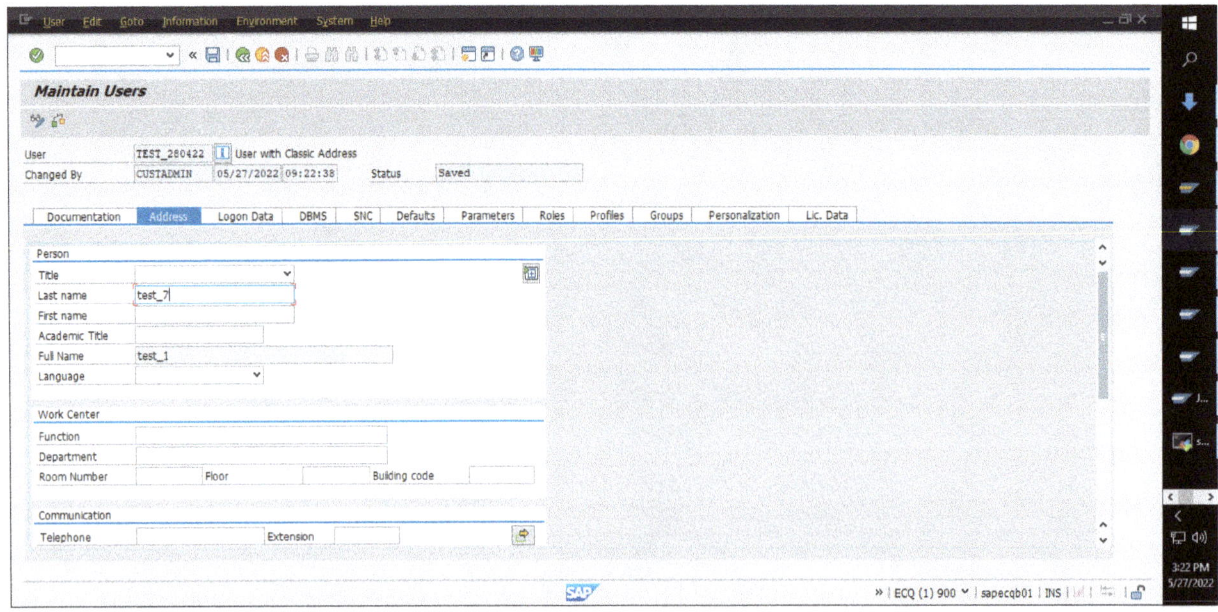

Shut down B node

Cluster status immediately after shutting down B node

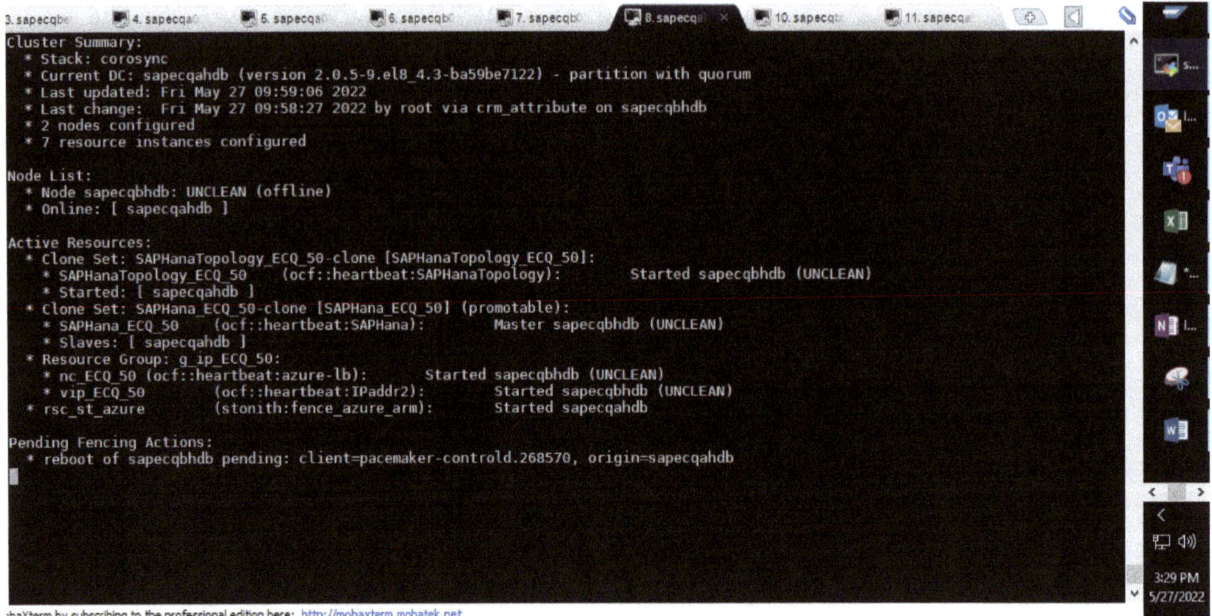

It took 3 mins to start promoting node A as master

```
Cluster Summary:
  * Stack: corosync
  * Current DC: sapecqahdb (version 2.0.5-9.el8_4.3-ba59be7122) - partition with quorum
  * Last updated: Fri May 27 10:02:41 2022
  * Last change:  Fri May 27 10:02:35 2022 by root via crm_attribute on sapecqahdb
  * 2 nodes configured
  * 7 resource instances configured

Node List:
  * Online: [ sapecqahdb ]
  * OFFLINE: [ sapecqbhdb ]

Active Resources:
  * Clone Set: SAPHanaTopology_ECQ_50-clone [SAPHanaTopology_ECQ_50]:
    * Started: [ sapecqahdb ]
  * Clone Set: SAPHana_ECQ_50-clone [SAPHana_ECQ_50] (promotable):
    * SAPHana_ECQ_50    (ocf::heartbeat:SAPHana):        Promoting sapecqahdb
  * Resource Group: g_ip_ECQ_50:
    * nc_ECQ_50 (ocf::heartbeat:azure-lb):      Started sapecqahdb
    * vip_ECQ_50        (ocf::heartbeat:IPaddr2):        Started sapecqahdb
  * rsc_st_azure        (stonith:fence_azure_arm):       Started sapecqahdb
```


Now Node A is master

```
Cluster Summary:
  * Stack: corosync
  * Current DC: sapecqahdb (version 2.0.5-9.el8_4.3-ba59be7122) - partition with quorum
  * Last updated: Fri May 27 10:03:35 2022
  * Last change:  Fri May 27 10:03:32 2022 by root via crm_attribute on sapecqahdb
  * 2 nodes configured
  * 7 resource instances configured

Node List:
  * Online: [ sapecqahdb ]
  * OFFLINE: [ sapecqbhdb ]

Active Resources:
  * Clone Set: SAPHanaTopology_ECQ_50-clone [SAPHanaTopology_ECQ_50]:
    * Started: [ sapecqahdb ]
  * Clone Set: SAPHana_ECQ_50-clone [SAPHana_ECQ_50] (promotable):
    * Masters: [ sapecqahdb ]
  * Resource Group: g_ip_ECQ_50:
    * nc_ECQ_50 (ocf::heartbeat:azure-lb):      Started sapecqahdb
    * vip_ECQ_50        (ocf::heartbeat:IPaddr2):        Started sapecqahdb
  * rsc_st_azure        (stonith:fence_azure_arm):       Started sapecqahdb
```


User TEST_280422 has changed   SAP   » | ECQ (1) 900 ∨ | sapecqb01 | INS | ...

Register node B as secondary and start the cluster

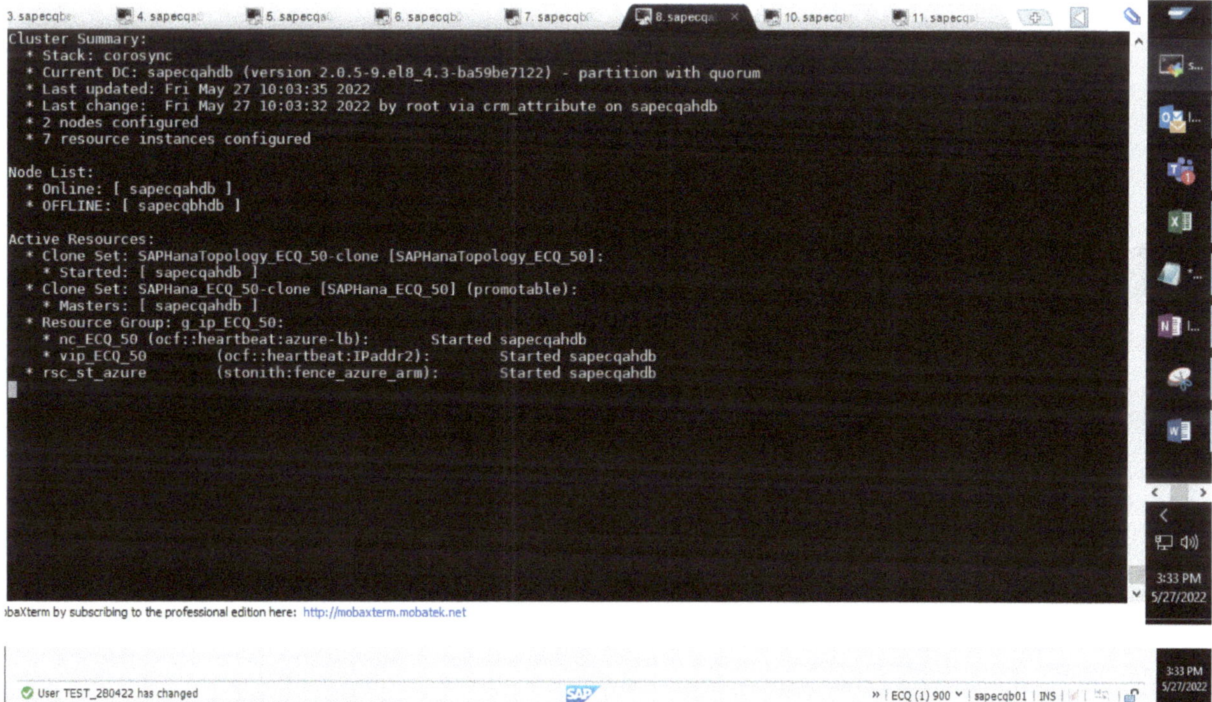

```
sapecqbhdb:ecqadm> hdbnsutil -sr_register --remoteHost=sapecqahdb --remoteInstance=50 --replicationMode=sync --name=ECQB --operati
onMode=logreplay
adding site ...
collecting information ...
registered at 10.197.42.18 (sapecqahdb)
updating local ini files ...
done.
sapecqbhdb:ecqadm> sudo pcs cluster start
Starting Cluster...
sapecqbhdb:ecqadm>
```

```
sapecqahdb:ecqadm> python systemR*
|Database |Host         |Port  |Service Name |Volume ID |Site ID |Site Name |Secondary  |Secondary |Secondary |Secondary |Secondary
    |Replication |Replication |Replication  |Secondary    |
|            |            |      |             |          |        |          |Host       |Port      |Site ID   |Site Name |Active Sta
tus |Mode       |Status       |Status Details |Fully Synced |
|-------- |---------- |----- |------------ |--------- |-------- |--------- |---------- |--------- |--------- |--------- |----------
--- |---------- |---------- |------------- |------------ |
|SYSTEMDB |sapecqahdb |35001 |nameserver   |       1 |       1 |ECQA      |sapecqbhdb |    35001 |        2 |ECQB      |YES
    |SYNC       |ACTIVE       |             |     True |
|ECQ      |sapecqahdb |35007 |xsengine     |       2 |       1 |ECQA      |sapecqbhdb |    35007 |        2 |ECQB      |YES
    |SYNC       |ACTIVE       |             |     True |
|ECQ      |sapecqahdb |35003 |indexserver  |       3 |       1 |ECQA      |sapecqbhdb |    35003 |        2 |ECQB      |YES
    |SYNC       |ACTIVE       |             |     True |

status system replication site "2": ACTIVE
overall system replication status: ACTIVE

Local System Replication State
~~~~~~~~~~~~~~~~~~~~~~~~~~~~~~~~

mode: PRIMARY
site id: 1
site name: ECQA
sapecqahdb:ecqadm>
```


Cluster status

```
sapecqahdb:ecqadm> sudo pcs status
Cluster name: sapecqhdb
Cluster Summary:
  * Stack: corosync
  * Current DC: sapecqahdb (version 2.0.5-9.el8_4.3-ba59be7122) - partition with quorum
  * Last updated: Fri May 27 10:23:42 2022
  * Last change:  Fri May 27 10:23:21 2022 by root via crm_attribute on sapecqahdb
  * 2 nodes configured
  * 7 resource instances configured

Node List:
  * Online: [ sapecqahdb sapecqbhdb ]

Full List of Resources:
  * Clone Set: SAPHanaTopology_ECQ_50-clone [SAPHanaTopology_ECQ_50]:
    * Started: [ sapecqahdb sapecqbhdb ]
  * Clone Set: SAPHana_ECQ_50-clone [SAPHana_ECQ_50] (promotable):
    * Masters: [ sapecqahdb ]
    * Slaves: [ sapecqbhdb ]
  * Resource Group: g_ip_ECQ_50:
    * nc_ECQ_50 (ocf::heartbeat:azure-lb):          Started sapecqahdb
    * vip_ECQ_50       (ocf::heartbeat:IPaddr2):         Started sapecqahdb
  * rsc_st_azure       (stonith:fence_azure_arm):        Started sapecqbhdb

Daemon Status:
  corosync: active/disabled
  pacemaker: active/disabled
  pcsd: active/enabled
sapecqahdb:ecqadm>
```


8.8.   Test case 8: Stop HANA on the 'Secondary' side (B)

Test Description	Stop HANA on the Secondary node (B)
Test action	Shutdown HANA on sapecqbhdb (secondary)
Result	Pass
Expected results	HANA does not fail over from sapecqahdb (Primary) to sapecqbhdb (Secondary). Virtual IP (VIP) does not fail over from sapecqahdb (Primary) to sapecqbhdb (Secondary). Application connectivity to HANA is not lost
Desired results	HANA does not fail over from sapecqahdb (Primary) to sapecqbhdb (Secondary). Virtual IP (VIP) does not fail over from sapecqahdb (Primary) to sapecqbhdb (Secondary). Application connectivity to HANA is not lost
Post-test execution steps	Restart pacemaker on secondary node (sapecqbhdb) Check system replication status Check cluster status

Test execution

Check status of cluster and HANA System replication before starting the test.

```
ecqadm@sapecqahdb:/usr/sap/ECQ/home> sudo pcs status
Cluster name: sapecqhdb
Cluster Summary:
  * Stack: corosync
  * Current DC: sapecqbhdb (version 2.0.5-9.el8_4.3-ba59be7122) - partition with quorum
  * Last updated: Fri May 27 12:37:44 2022
  * Last change:  Fri May 27 12:37:36 2022 by root via crm_attribute on sapecqahdb
  * 2 nodes configured
  * 7 resource instances configured

Node List:
  * Online: [ sapecqahdb sapecqbhdb ]

Full List of Resources:
  * Clone Set: SAPHanaTopology_ECQ_50-clone [SAPHanaTopology_ECQ_50]:
    * Started: [ sapecqahdb sapecqbhdb ]
  * Clone Set: SAPHana_ECQ_50-clone [SAPHana_ECQ_50] (promotable):
    * Masters: [ sapecqahdb ]
    * Slaves: [ sapecqbhdb ]
  * Resource Group: g_ip_ECQ_50:
    * nc_ECQ_50 (ocf::heartbeat:azure-lb):        Started sapecqahdb
    * vip_ECQ_50      (ocf::heartbeat:IPaddr2):        Started sapecqahdb
  * rsc_st_azure      (stonith:fence_azure_arm):        Started sapecqbhdb

Daemon Status:
  corosync: active/disabled
  pacemaker: active/disabled
  pcsd: active/enabled
ecqadm@sapecqahdb:/usr/sap/ECQ/home>
```


Node A: Hdbnsutil –sr_state

```
site id: 1
site name: ECQA

is source system: true
is secondary/consumer system: false
has secondaries/consumers attached: true
is a takeover active: false
is primary suspended: false

Host Mappings:
~~~~~~~~~~~~~~~

sapecqahdb -> [ECQB] sapecqbhdb
sapecqahdb -> [ECQA] sapecqahdb


Site Mappings:
~~~~~~~~~~~~~~~
ECQA (primary/primary)
    |---ECQB (sync/logreplay)

Tier of ECQA: 1
Tier of ECQB: 2

Replication mode of ECQA: primary
Replication mode of ECQB: sync

Operation mode of ECQA: primary
Operation mode of ECQB: logreplay

Mapping: ECQA -> ECQB
done.
ecqadm@sapecqahdb:/usr/sap/ECQ/home>
```


Check replication

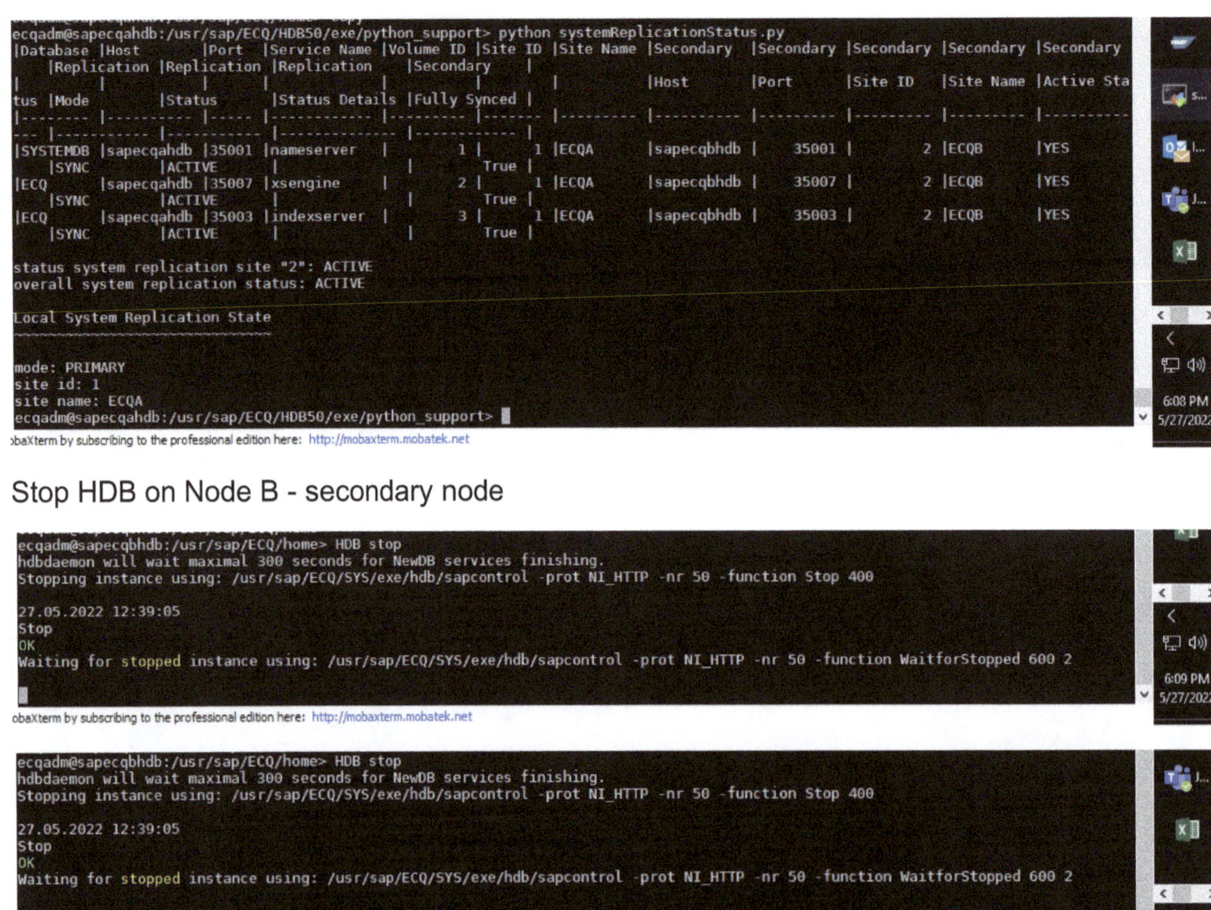

Stop HDB on Node B - secondary node

Once secondary DB is down

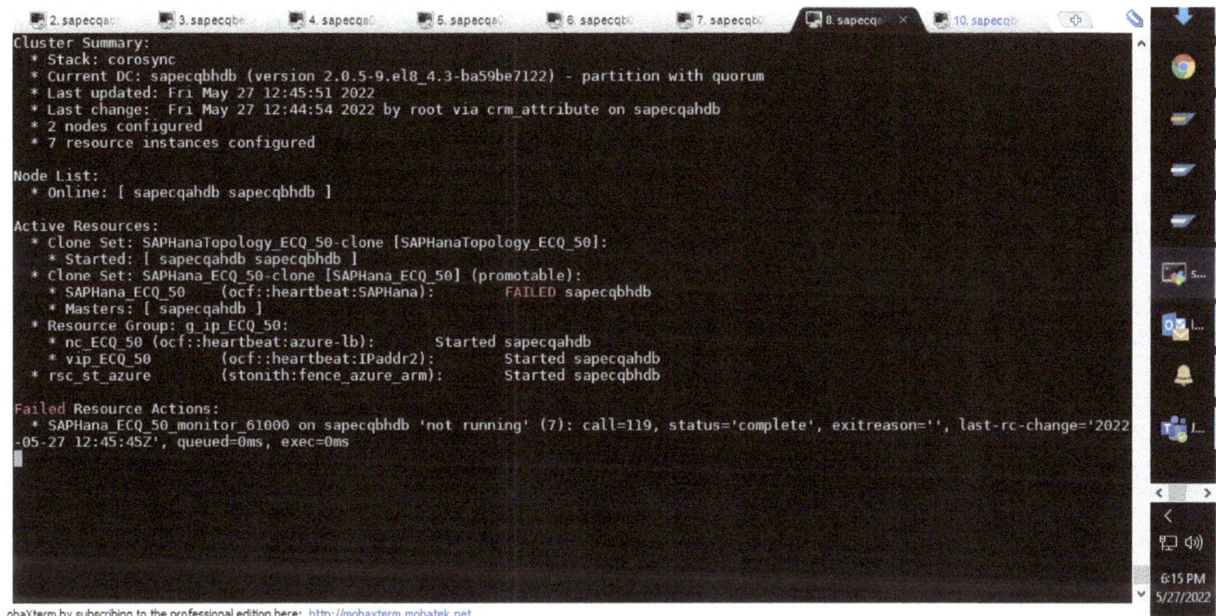

HDB is up and running automatically on node B –secondary.

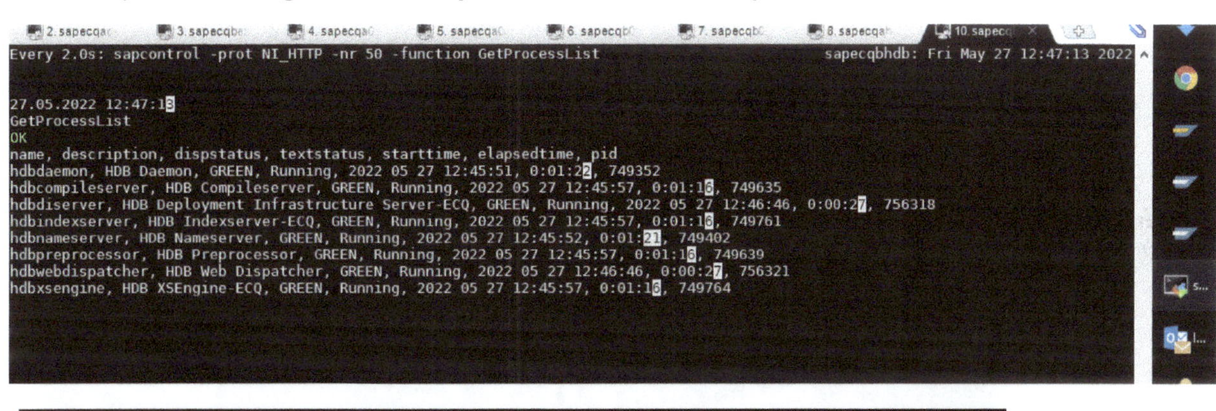

Check overall replication status

Checking from A (primary) node:

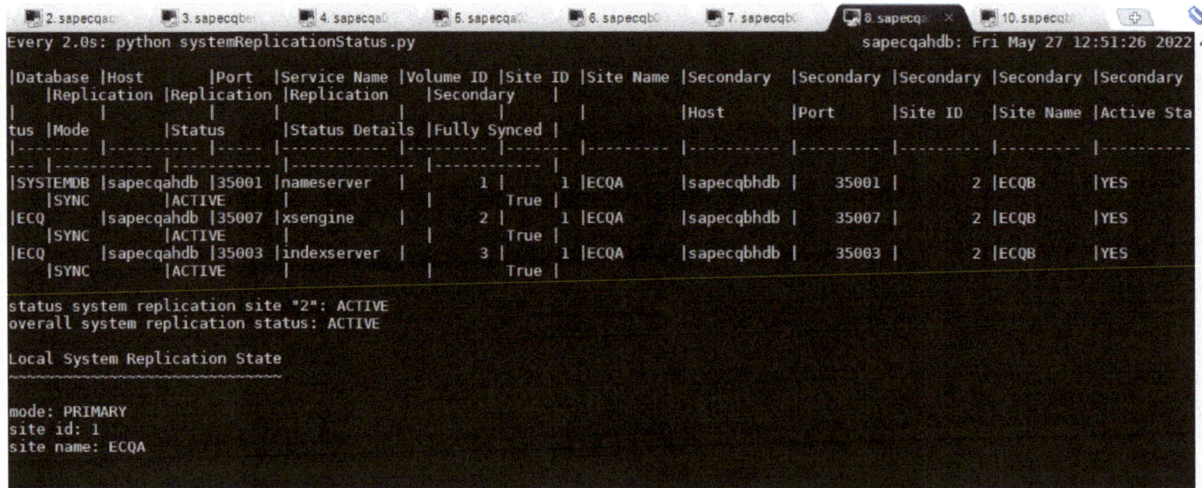

Cleanup failed action

Check cluster status

8.9. Test case 9: Kill HANA on the 'Secondary' side (B)

Test Description	Kill HANA on the Secondary node (B)
Test action	Kill hdb daemon on sapecqbhdb (secondary)
Result	Pass
Expected results	HANA does not fail over from sapecqahdb (Primary) to sapecqbhdb (Secondary). Virtual IP (VIP) does not fail over from sapecqahdb (Primary) to sapecqbhdb (Secondary). Application connectivity to HANA is not lost
Desired results	HANA does not fail over from sapecqahdb (Primary) to sapecqbhdb (Secondary). Virtual IP (VIP) does not fail over from sapecqahdb (Primary) to sapecqbhdb (Secondary). Application connectivity to HANA is not lost

<table>
<tr><td>Post-test execution
steps</td><td>Restart pacemaker on secondary node (sapecqbhdb)
Check system replication status
Check cluster status</td></tr>
</table>

Test execution

Check status of cluster and HANA System replication before starting the test.

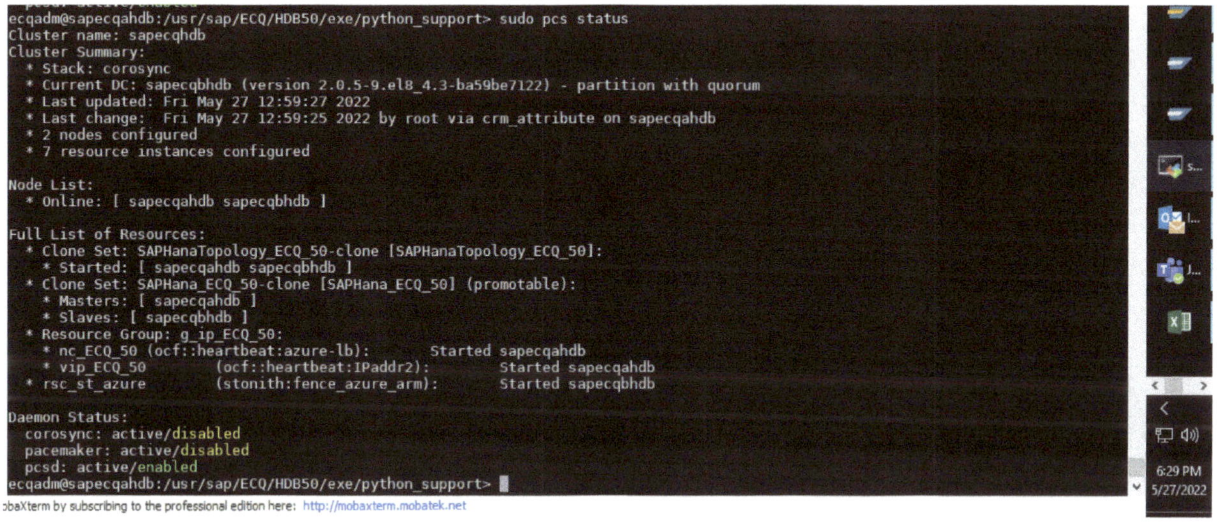

```
ecqadm@sapecqahdb:/usr/sap/ECQ/HDB50/exe/python_support> sudo pcs status
Cluster name: sapecqhdb
Cluster Summary:
  * Stack: corosync
  * Current DC: sapecqbhdb (version 2.0.5-9.el8_4.3-ba59be7122) - partition with quorum
  * Last updated: Fri May 27 12:59:27 2022
  * Last change:  Fri May 27 12:59:25 2022 by root via crm_attribute on sapecqahdb
  * 2 nodes configured
  * 7 resource instances configured

Node List:
  * Online: [ sapecqahdb sapecqbhdb ]

Full List of Resources:
  * Clone Set: SAPHanaTopology_ECQ_50-clone [SAPHanaTopology_ECQ_50]:
    * Started: [ sapecqahdb sapecqbhdb ]
  * Clone Set: SAPHana_ECQ_50-clone [SAPHana_ECQ_50] (promotable):
    * Masters: [ sapecqahdb ]
    * Slaves: [ sapecqbhdb ]
  * Resource Group: g_ip_ECQ_50:
    * nc_ECQ_50 (ocf::heartbeat:azure-lb):        Started sapecqahdb
    * vip_ECQ_50         (ocf::heartbeat:IPaddr2):        Started sapecqahdb
  * rsc_st_azure         (stonith:fence_azure_arm):       Started sapecqahdb

Daemon Status:
  corosync: active/disabled
  pacemaker: active/disabled
  pcsd: active/enabled
ecqadm@sapecqahdb:/usr/sap/ECQ/HDB50/exe/python_support>
```

Hdbnsutil –sr_state

```
is primary suspended: false

Host Mappings:
~~~~~~~~~~~~~~

sapecqahdb -> [ECQB] sapecqbhdb
sapecqahdb -> [ECQA] sapecqahdb


Site Mappings:
~~~~~~~~~~~~~~

ECQA (primary/primary)
    |---ECQB (sync/logreplay)

Tier of ECQA: 1
Tier of ECQB: 2

Replication mode of ECQA: primary
Replication mode of ECQB: sync

Operation mode of ECQA: primary
Operation mode of ECQB: logreplay

Mapping: ECQA -> ECQB
done.
ecqadm@sapecqahdb:/usr/sap/ECQ/HDB50/exe/python_support>
```

Replication is running

```
ecqadm@sapecqahdb:/usr/sap/ECQ/HDB50/exe/python_support> python systemReplicationStatus.py
|Database |Host         |Port  |Service Name |Volume ID |Site ID |Site Name |Secondary  |Secondary |Secondary |Secondary  |Secondary
         |Replication |Replication |Replication    |Secondary    |         |           |Host     |Port     |Site ID  |Site Name |Active Sta
tus |Mode        |Status      |Status Details |Fully Synced |
--- |----------- |----------- |-------------- |------------ |------- |--------- |--------- |-------- |-------- |-------- |----------
|SYSTEMDB |sapecqahdb |35001 |nameserver   |        1 |      1 |ECQA     |sapecqbhdb |  35001 |       2 |ECQB     |YES
         |SYNC       |ACTIVE      |               |       True |
|ECQ      |sapecqahdb |35007 |xsengine     |        2 |      1 |ECQA     |sapecqbhdb |  35007 |       2 |ECQB     |YES
         |SYNC       |ACTIVE      |               |       True |
|ECQ      |sapecqahdb |35003 |indexserver  |        3 |      1 |ECQA     |sapecqbhdb |  35003 |       2 |ECQB     |YES
         |SYNC       |ACTIVE      |               |       True |

status system replication site "2": ACTIVE
overall system replication status: ACTIVE

Local System Replication State
~~~~~~~~~~~~~~~~~~~~~~~~~~~~~~~~

mode: PRIMARY
site id: 1
site name: ECQA
ecqadm@sapecqahdb:/usr/sap/ECQ/HDB50/exe/python_support>
```

Kill hdbdaemon on **Secondary**. It automatically restarts HANA on B side, without affecting Primary A.

```
ecqadm@sapecqbhdb:/usr/sap/ECQ/home> HDB kill -9
hdbenv.sh: Hostname sapecqbhdb defined in $SAP_RETRIEVAL_PATH=/usr/sap/ECQ/HDB50/sapecqbhdb differs from host name defined on comm
and line.
hdbenv.sh: Error: Instance not found for host -9
killing HDB processes:
kill -9 749352 /usr/sap/ECQ/HDB50/sapecqbhdb/trace/hdb.sapECQ_HDB50 -d -nw -f /usr/sap/ECQ/HDB50/sapecqbhdb/daemon.ini pf=/usr/sap
/ECQ/SYS/profile/ECQ_HDB50_sapecqbhdb
kill -9 749402 hdbnameserver
kill -9 749635 hdbcompileserver
kill -9 749639 hdbpreprocessor
kill -9 749761 hdbindexserver -port 35003
kill -9 749764 hdbxsengine -port 35007
kill -9 756318 hdbdiserver -port 35025
kill -9 756321 hdbwebdispatcher
kill orphan HDB processes:
kill -9 749402 [hdbnameserver] <defunct>
kill -9 749761 [hdbindexserver] <defunct>
kill -9 749764 [hdbxsengine] <defunct>
ecqadm@sapecqbhdb:/usr/sap/ECQ/home>
```

Cluster status, just after killing hdbdeamon in node B

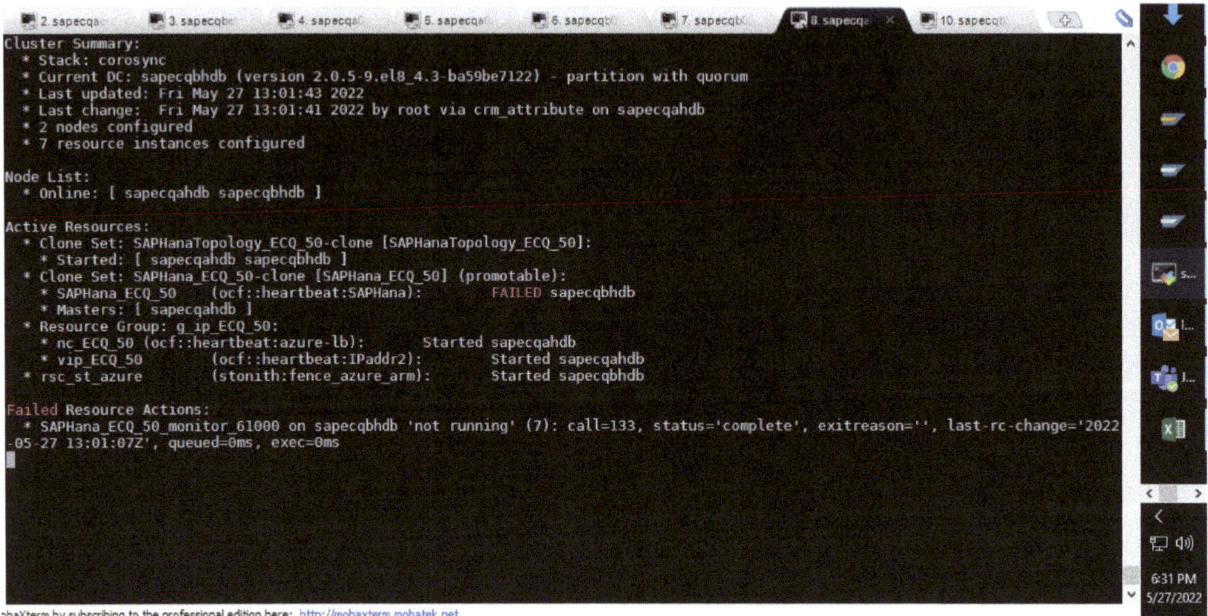

Once secondary DB is started by cluster

```
ecqadm@sapecqahdb:/usr/sap/ECQ/HDB50/exe/python_support> sudo pcs status
Cluster name: sapecqhdb
Cluster Summary:
  * Stack: corosync
  * Current DC: sapecqbhdb (version 2.0.5-9.el8_4.3-ba59be7122) - partition with quorum
  * Last updated: Fri May 27 13:03:30 2022
  * Last change:  Fri May 27 13:03:17 2022 by root via crm_attribute on sapecqbhdb
  * 2 nodes configured
  * 7 resource instances configured

Node List:
  * Online: [ sapecqahdb sapecqbhdb ]

Full List of Resources:
  * Clone Set: SAPHanaTopology_ECQ_50-clone [SAPHanaTopology_ECQ_50]:
    * Started: [ sapecqahdb sapecqbhdb ]
  * Clone Set: SAPHana_ECQ_50-clone [SAPHana_ECQ_50] (promotable):
    * Masters: [ sapecqahdb ]
    * Slaves: [ sapecqbhdb ]
  * Resource Group: g_ip_ECQ_50:
    * nc_ECQ_50 (ocf::heartbeat:azure-lb):        Started sapecqahdb
    * vip_ECQ_50        (ocf::heartbeat:IPaddr2):        Started sapecqahdb
  * rsc_st_azure        (stonith:fence_azure_arm):        Started sapecqbhdb

Failed Resource Actions:
  * SAPHana_ECQ_50_monitor_61000 on sapecqbhdb 'not running' (7): call=133, status='complete', exitreason='', last-rc-change='2022
-05-27 13:01:07Z', queued=0ms, exec=0ms

Daemon Status:
  corosync: active/disabled
  pacemaker: active/disabled
  pcsd: active/enabled
ecqadm@sapecqahdb:/usr/sap/ECQ/HDB50/exe/python_support>
```

Replication is running.

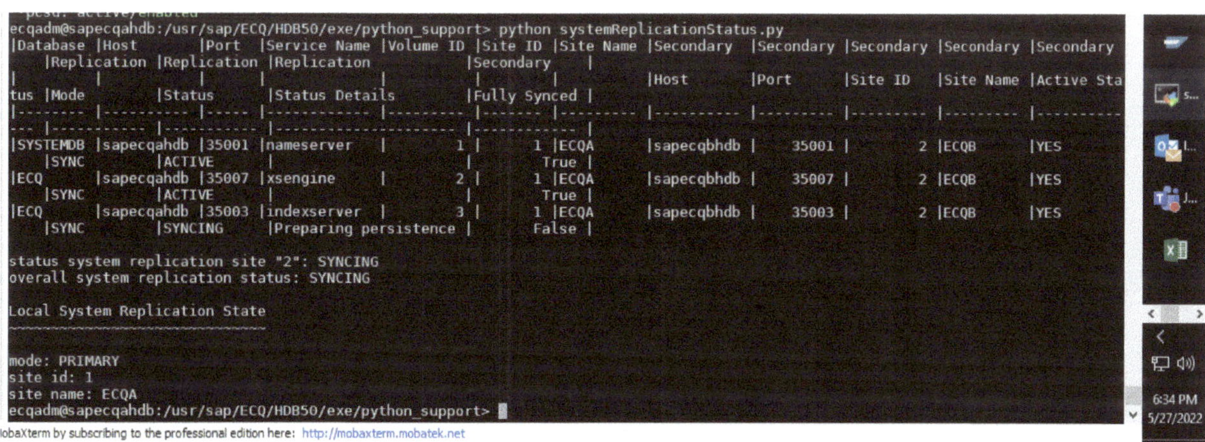

```
ecqadm@sapecqahdb:/usr/sap/ECQ/HDB50/exe/python_support> python systemReplicationStatus.py
|Database |Host       |Port  |Service Name |Volume ID |Site ID |Site Name |Secondary  |Secondary |Secondary |Secondary |Secondary
|         |Replication |Replication |Replication |          |Secondary |          |           |          |          |          |
|         |            |      |             |          |          |          |Host       |Port      |Site ID   |Site Name |Active Sta
tus      |Mode        |Status       |Status Details |          |Fully Synced |          |           |          |          |
|-------- |----------- |----- |------------ |--------- |------- |--------- |---------- |--------- |--------- |--------- |---------
---      |----------- |----------- |------------ |--------- |------------ |
|SYSTEMDB |sapecqahdb |35001 |nameserver   |        1 |        1 |ECQA      |sapecqbhdb |   35001  |        2 |ECQB      |YES
         |SYNC        |ACTIVE       |             |          |        True |
|ECQ      |sapecqahdb |35007 |xsengine     |        2 |        1 |ECQA      |sapecqbhdb |   35007  |        2 |ECQB      |YES
         |SYNC        |ACTIVE       |             |          |        True |
|ECQ      |sapecqahdb |35003 |indexserver  |        3 |        1 |ECQA      |sapecqbhdb |   35003  |        2 |ECQB      |YES
         |SYNC        |SYNCING      |Preparing persistence |   False |

status system replication site "2": SYNCING
overall system replication status: SYNCING

Local System Replication State
~~~~~~~~~~~~~~~~~~~~~~~~~~~~~~~~

mode: PRIMARY
site id: 1
site name: ECQA
ecqadm@sapecqahdb:/usr/sap/ECQ/HDB50/exe/python_support>
```

Clear failed actions

```
ecqadm@sapecqahdb:/usr/sap/ECQ/HDB50/exe/python_support> sudo pcs resource cleanup SAPHana_ECQ_50
Cleaned up SAPHana_ECQ_50:0 on sapecqbhdb
Cleaned up SAPHana_ECQ_50:1 on sapecqahdb
Waiting for 1 reply from the controller
... got reply (done)
ecqadm@sapecqahdb:/usr/sap/ECQ/HDB50/exe/python_support>
```

Check cluster status.

```
ecqadm@sapecqahdb:/usr/sap/ECQ/HDB50/exe/python_support> sudo pcs status
Cluster name: sapecqhdb
Cluster Summary:
  * Stack: corosync
  * Current DC: sapecqbhdb (version 2.0.5-9.el8_4.3-ba59be7122) - partition with quorum
  * Last updated: Fri May 27 13:07:08 2022
  * Last change:  Fri May 27 13:06:54 2022 by root via crm_attribute on sapecqbhdb
  * 2 nodes configured
  * 7 resource instances configured

Node List:
  * Online: [ sapecqahdb sapecqbhdb ]

Full List of Resources:
  * Clone Set: SAPHanaTopology_ECQ_50-clone [SAPHanaTopology_ECQ_50]:
    * Started: [ sapecqahdb sapecqbhdb ]
  * Clone Set: SAPHana_ECQ_50-clone [SAPHana_ECQ_50] (promotable):
    * Masters: [ sapecqahdb ]
    * Slaves: [ sapecqbhdb ]
  * Resource Group: g_ip_ECQ_50:
    * nc_ECQ_50 (ocf::heartbeat:azure-lb):        Started sapecqahdb
    * vip_ECQ_50        (ocf::heartbeat:IPaddr2):        Started sapecqahdb
  * rsc_st_azure        (stonith:fence_azure_arm):        Started sapecqbhdb

Daemon Status:
  corosync: active/disabled
  pacemaker: active/disabled
  pcsd: active/enabled
ecqadm@sapecqahdb:/usr/sap/ECQ/HDB50/exe/python_support>
```

obaXterm by subscribing to the professional edition here: http://mobaxterm.mobatek.net

8.10. Test case 10: Power off 'Secondary' HANA server (B)

Test Description	Power off HANA server on the Secondary node (B)
Test action	Perform hard shutdown of HANA server sapecpbhdb (secondary)
Result	Pass
Expected results	HANA does not fail over from sapecpahdb (Primary) to sapecpbhdb (Secondary). Virtual IP (VIP) does not fail over from sapecpahdb (Primary) to sapecpbhdb (Secondary). Application connectivity to HANA is not lost
Desired results	HANA does not fail over from sapecpahdb (Primary) to sapecpbhdb (Secondary). Virtual IP (VIP) does not fail over from sapecpahdb (Primary) to sapecpbhdb (Secondary). Application connectivity to HANA is not lost
Post-test execution steps	Restart pacemaker on secondary node (sapecpbhdb) Check system replication status Check cluster status

Test execution

Check status of cluster and HANA System replication before starting the test.

```
ecqadm@sapecqbhdb:/usr/sap/ECQ/HDB50> sudo pcs status
Cluster name: sapecqhdb
Cluster Summary:
  * Stack: corosync
  * Current DC: sapecqahdb (version 2.0.5-9.el8_4.3-ba59be7122) - partition with quorum
  * Last updated: Mon May 30 16:39:09 2022
  * Last change:  Mon May 30 16:38:59 2022 by root via crm_attribute on sapecqahdb
  * 2 nodes configured
  * 7 resource instances configured

Node List:
  * Online: [ sapecqahdb sapecqbhdb ]

Full List of Resources:
  * Clone Set: SAPHanaTopology_ECQ_50-clone [SAPHanaTopology_ECQ_50]:
    * Started: [ sapecqahdb sapecqbhdb ]
  * Clone Set: SAPHana_ECQ_50-clone [SAPHana_ECQ_50] (promotable):
    * Masters: [ sapecqahdb ]
    * Slaves: [ sapecqbhdb ]
  * Resource Group: g_ip_ECQ_50:
    * nc_ECQ_50 (ocf::heartbeat:azure-lb):        Started sapecqahdb
    * vip_ECQ_50        (ocf::heartbeat:IPaddr2):        Started sapecqahdb
  * rsc_st_azure        (stonith:fence_azure_arm):        Started sapecqbhdb

Daemon Status:
  corosync: active/disabled
  pacemaker: active/disabled
  pcsd: active/enabled
ecqadm@sapecqbhdb:/usr/sap/ECQ/HDB50>
```


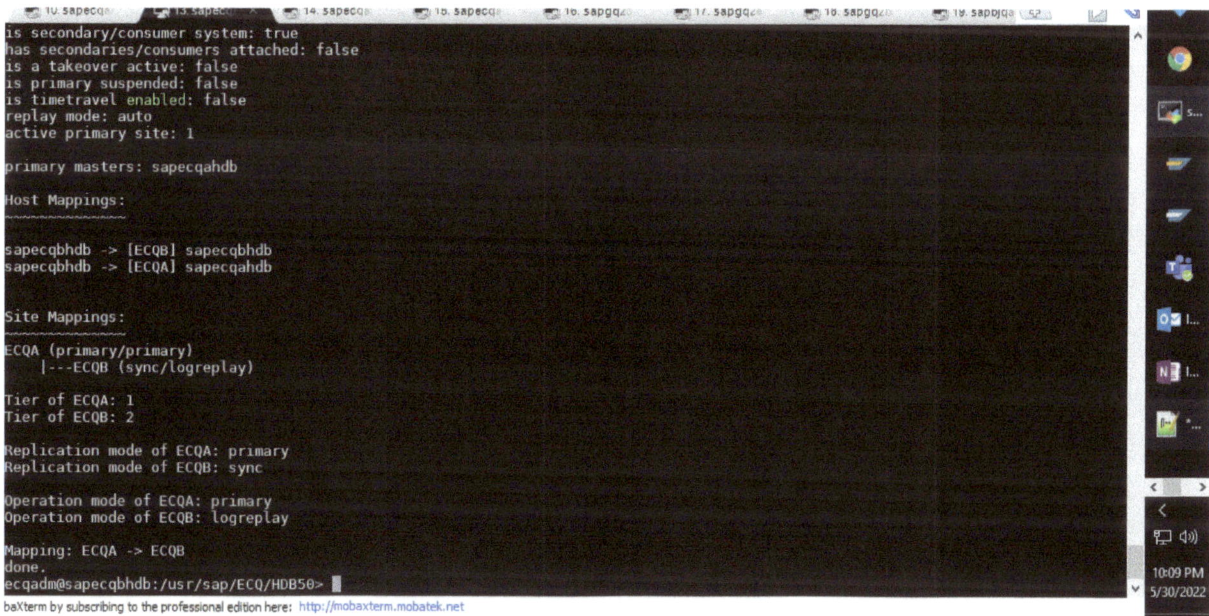
```
is secondary/consumer system: true
has secondaries/consumers attached: false
is a takeover active: false
is primary suspended: false
is timetravel enabled: false
replay mode: auto
active primary site: 1

primary masters: sapecqahdb

Host Mappings:


sapecqbhdb -> [ECQB] sapecqbhdb
sapecqbhdb -> [ECQA] sapecqahdb


Site Mappings:

ECQA (primary/primary)
    |---ECQB (sync/logreplay)

Tier of ECQA: 1
Tier of ECQB: 2

Replication mode of ECQA: primary
Replication mode of ECQB: sync

Operation mode of ECQA: primary
Operation mode of ECQB: logreplay

Mapping: ECQA -> ECQB
done.
ecqadm@sapecqbhdb:/usr/sap/ECQ/HDB50>
```


Replication is active and running.

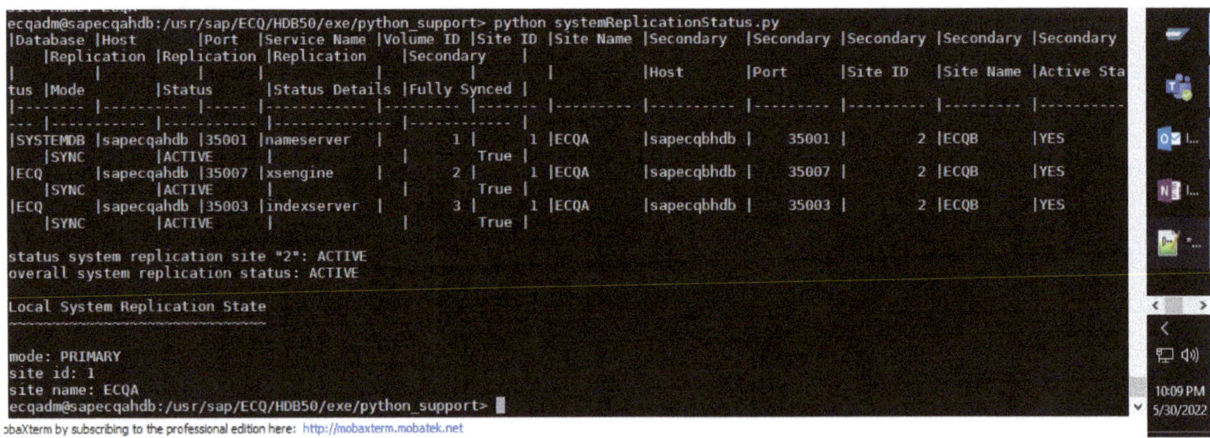

Power of 'Secondary' HANA server using below command:

echo b > /proc/sysrq-trigger

Just after shutting down B node

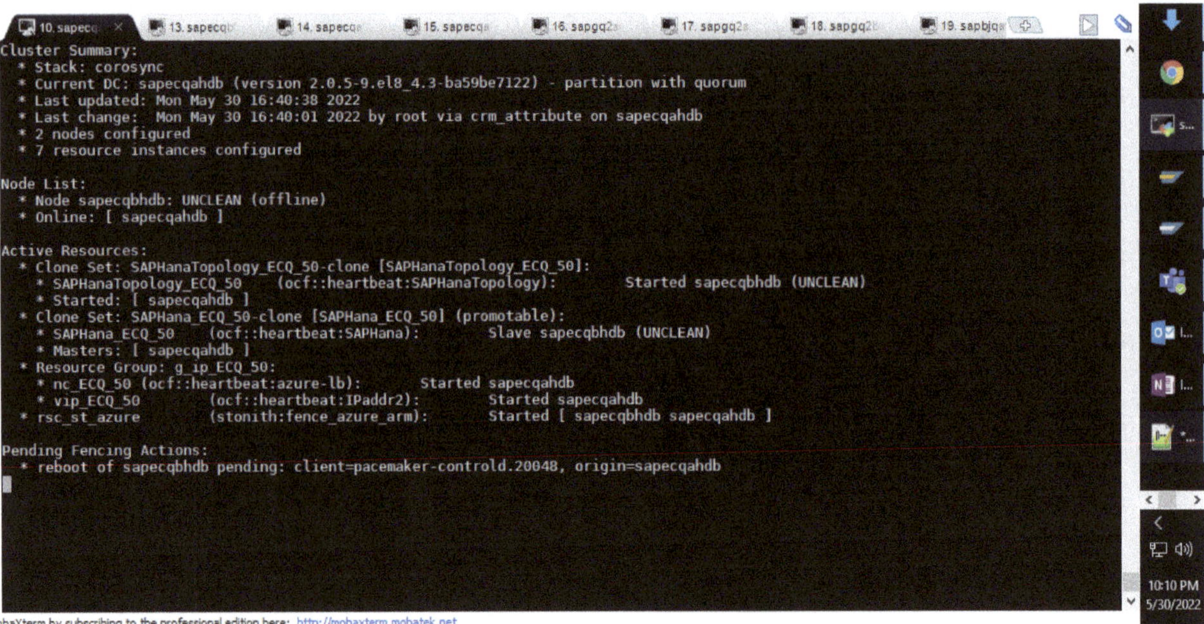

```
ecqadm@sapecqahdb:/usr/sap/ECQ/HDB50/exe/python_support> sudo pcs status
Cluster name: sapecqhdb
Cluster Summary:
  * Stack: corosync
  * Current DC: sapecqahdb (version 2.0.5-9.el8_4.3-ba59be7122) - partition with quorum
  * Last updated: Mon May 30 16:44:46 2022
  * Last change:  Mon May 30 16:44:24 2022 by root via crm_attribute on sapecqahdb
  * 2 nodes configured
  * 7 resource instances configured

Node List:
  * Online: [ sapecqahdb ]
  * OFFLINE: [ sapecqbhdb ]

Full List of Resources:
  * Clone Set: SAPHanaTopology_ECQ_50-clone [SAPHanaTopology_ECQ_50]:
    * Started: [ sapecqahdb ]
    * Stopped: [ sapecqbhdb ]
  * Clone Set: SAPHana_ECQ_50-clone [SAPHana_ECQ_50] (promotable):
    * Masters: [ sapecqahdb ]
    * Stopped: [ sapecqbhdb ]
  * Resource Group: g_ip_ECQ_50:
    * nc_ECQ_50 (ocf::heartbeat:azure-lb):       Started sapecqahdb
    * vip_ECQ_50        (ocf::heartbeat:IPaddr2):      Started sapecqahdb
    * rsc_st_azure      (stonith:fence_azure_arm):     Started sapecqahdb

Daemon Status:
  corosync: active/disabled
  pacemaker: active/disabled
  pcsd: active/enabled
ecqadm@sapecqahdb:/usr/sap/ECQ/HDB50/exe/python_support>
```

Replication is reporting error because Node B is down

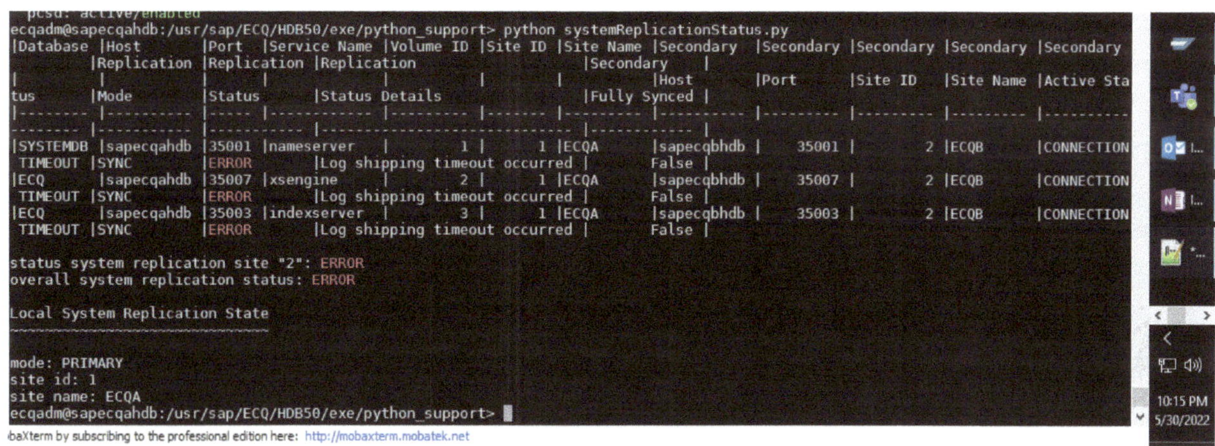

```
  pcsd: active/enabled
ecqadm@sapecqahdb:/usr/sap/ECQ/HDB50/exe/python_support> python systemReplicationStatus.py
|Database |Host       |Port  |Service Name |Volume ID |Site ID |Site Name |Secondary  |Secondary |Secondary |Secondary |Secondary
|         |Replication|Replication |Replication |          |        |          |Secondary  |          |          |          |
|         |           |      |             |          |        |          |Host       |Port      |Site ID   |Site Name |Active Sta
tus      |Mode       |Status |     |Status Details |          |        |          |Fully Synced |          |          |          |
|-------- |---------- |----- |------------ |--------- |------- |--------- |---------- |--------- |--------- |--------- |----------
|-------- |---------- |----- |------------ |--------- |------- |--------- |---------- |--------- |--------- |--------- |----------
|SYSTEMDB |sapecqahdb |35001 |nameserver   |        1 |      1 |ECQA      |sapecqbhdb |   35001  |        2 |ECQB      |CONNECTION
 TIMEOUT  |SYNC       |ERROR  |     |Log shipping timeout occurred |     False |          |          |          |
|ECQ      |sapecqahdb |35007 |xsengine     |        2 |      1 |ECQA      |sapecqbhdb |   35007  |        2 |ECQB      |CONNECTION
 TIMEOUT  |SYNC       |ERROR  |     |Log shipping timeout occurred |     False |          |          |          |
|ECQ      |sapecqahdb |35003 |indexserver  |        3 |      1 |ECQA      |sapecqbhdb |   35003  |        2 |ECQB      |CONNECTION
 TIMEOUT  |SYNC       |ERROR  |     |Log shipping timeout occurred |     False |          |          |          |

status system replication site "2": ERROR
overall system replication status: ERROR

Local System Replication State
~~~~~~~~~~~~~~~~~~~~~~~~~~~~~~~~

mode: PRIMARY
site id: 1
site name: ECQA
ecqadm@sapecqahdb:/usr/sap/ECQ/HDB50/exe/python_support>
```

Start cluster in node B manually, this will start DB in node B also.

```
ecqadm@sapecqbhdb:/usr/sap/ECQ/HDB50> hdbnsutil -sr_state

System Replication State
~~~~~~~~~~~~~~~~~~~~~~~~~

online: false

mode: sync
operation mode: unknown
site id: 2
site name: ECQB

is source system: unknown
is secondary/consumer system: true
has secondaries/consumers attached: unknown
is a takeover active: false
is primary suspended: false
is timetravel enabled: false
replay mode: auto
active primary site: 1

primary masters: sapecqahdb
done.
ecqadm@sapecqbhdb:/usr/sap/ECQ/HDB50> sudo pcs cluster start
Starting Cluster...
ecqadm@sapecqbhdb:/usr/sap/ECQ/HDB50>
```

```
ecqadm@sapecqahdb:/usr/sap/ECQ/HDB50/exe/python_support> python systemReplicationStatus.py
|Database |Host          |Port  |Service Name |Volume ID |Site ID |Site Name |Secondary   |Secondary |Secondary |Secondary  |Secondary
         |Replication |Replication |Replication  |Secondary  |
|        |            |            |             |          |        |          |Host        |Port      |Site ID   |Site Name |Active Sta
tus |Mode         |Status       |Status Details |Fully Synced |
|---------- |---------- |----- |------------- |--------- |------- |--------- |---------- |--------- |--------- |--------- |----------
--- |---------- |---------- |------------- |----------- |
|SYSTEMDB |sapecqahdb |35001 |nameserver   |        1 |      1 |ECQA      |sapecqbhdb |    35001 |        2 |ECQB      |YES
         |SYNC         |ACTIVE       |             |      True |
|ECQ      |sapecqahdb |35007 |xsengine     |        2 |      1 |ECQA      |sapecqbhdb |    35007 |        2 |ECQB      |YES
         |SYNC         |ACTIVE       |             |      True |
|ECQ      |sapecqahdb |35003 |indexserver  |        3 |      1 |ECQA      |sapecqbhdb |    35003 |        2 |ECQB      |YES
         |SYNC         |ACTIVE       |             |      True |

status system replication site "2": ACTIVE
overall system replication status: ACTIVE

Local System Replication State
~~~~~~~~~~~~~~~~~~~~~~~~~~~~~~~~~~~~~~~~~~

mode: PRIMARY
site id: 1
site name: ECQA
ecqadm@sapecqahdb:/usr/sap/ECQ/HDB50/exe/python_support>
```

Check cluster status

```
ecqadm@sapecqahdb:/usr/sap/ECQ/HDB50/exe/python_support> sudo pcs status
Cluster name: sapecqhdb
Cluster Summary:
  * Stack: corosync
  * Current DC: sapecqahdb (version 2.0.5-9.el8_4.3-ba59be7122) - partition with quorum
  * Last updated: Mon May 30 16:52:31 2022
  * Last change:  Mon May 30 16:52:11 2022 by root via crm_attribute on sapecqbhdb
  * 2 nodes configured
  * 7 resource instances configured

Node List:
  * Online: [ sapecqahdb sapecqbhdb ]

Full List of Resources:
  * Clone Set: SAPHanaTopology_ECQ_50-clone [SAPHanaTopology_ECQ_50]:
    * Started: [ sapecqahdb sapecqbhdb ]
  * Clone Set: SAPHana_ECQ_50-clone [SAPHana_ECQ_50] (promotable):
    * Masters: [ sapecqahdb ]
    * Slaves: [ sapecqbhdb ]
  * Resource Group: g_ip_ECQ_50:
    * nc_ECQ_50 (ocf::heartbeat:azure-lb):          Started sapecqahdb
    * vip_ECQ_50        (ocf::heartbeat:IPaddr2):          Started sapecqahdb
  * rsc_st_azure        (stonith:fence_azure_arm):         Started sapecqbhdb

Daemon Status:
  corosync: active/disabled
  pacemaker: active/disabled
  pcsd: active/enabled
ecqadm@sapecqahdb:/usr/sap/ECQ/HDB50/exe/python_support>
```

8.11. Test case 11: Stop the network interfaces on Secondary HANA node B

Test Description	Stop network interfaces on Secondary HANA node sapecqbhdb
Test action	Shutdown eth interfaces on server
Result	Pass
Expected results	sapecqbhdb (secondary) gets fenced and rebooted HANA does not fail over from sapecqahdb (Primary) to sapecqbhdb (Secondary). Virtual IP (VIP) does not fail over from sapecqahdb (Primary) to sapecqbhdb (Secondary). Application connectivity to HANA is not lost
Desired results	sapecqbhdb (secondary) gets fenced and rebooted HANA does not fail over from sapecqahdb (Primary) to sapecqbhdb (Secondary). Virtual IP (VIP) does not fail over from sapecqahdb (Primary) to sapecqbhdb (Secondary). Application connectivity to HANA is not lost
Post-test execution steps	Start pacemaker on secondary node (sapecqbhdb) Check system replication status Check cluster status

Test execution

Check status of cluster and HANA System replication before starting the test.

```
ecqadm@sapecqahdb:/usr/sap/ECQ/HDB50/exe/python_support> sudo pcs status
Cluster name: sapecqhdb
Cluster Summary:
  * Stack: corosync
  * Current DC: sapecqahdb (version 2.0.5-9.el8_4.3-ba59be7122) - partition with quorum
  * Last updated: Mon May 30 16:53:09 2022
  * Last change:  Mon May 30 16:52:43 2022 by root via crm_attribute on sapecqahdb
  * 2 nodes configured
  * 7 resource instances configured

Node List:
  * Online: [ sapecqahdb sapecqbhdb ]

Full List of Resources:
  * Clone Set: SAPHanaTopology_ECQ_50-clone [SAPHanaTopology_ECQ_50]:
    * Started: [ sapecqahdb sapecqbhdb ]
  * Clone Set: SAPHana_ECQ_50-clone [SAPHana_ECQ_50] (promotable):
    * Masters: [ sapecqahdb ]
    * Slaves: [ sapecqbhdb ]
  * Resource Group: g_ip_ECQ_50:
    * nc_ECQ_50  (ocf::heartbeat:azure-lb):      Started sapecqahdb
    * vip_ECQ_50      (ocf::heartbeat:IPaddr2):      Started sapecqahdb
  * rsc_st_azure      (stonith:fence_azure_arm):      Started sapecqbhdb

Daemon Status:
  corosync: active/disabled
  pacemaker: active/disabled
  pcsd: active/enabled
ecqadm@sapecqahdb:/usr/sap/ECQ/HDB50/exe/python_support>
```

Node A (primary) hdbnsutil –sr_state

```
is source system: true
is secondary/consumer system: false
has secondaries/consumers attached: true
is a takeover active: false
is primary suspended: false

Host Mappings:
~~~~~~~~~~~~~~~~

sapecqahdb -> [ECQB] sapecqbhdb
sapecqahdb -> [ECQA] sapecqahdb


Site Mappings:
~~~~~~~~~~~~~~~
ECQA (primary/primary)
    |---ECQB (sync/logreplay)

Tier of ECQA: 1
Tier of ECQB: 2

Replication mode of ECQA: primary
Replication mode of ECQB: sync

Operation mode of ECQA: primary
Operation mode of ECQB: logreplay

Mapping: ECQA -> ECQB
done.
ecqadm@sapecqahdb:/usr/sap/ECQ/HDB50/exe/python_support>
```

Replication is running fine

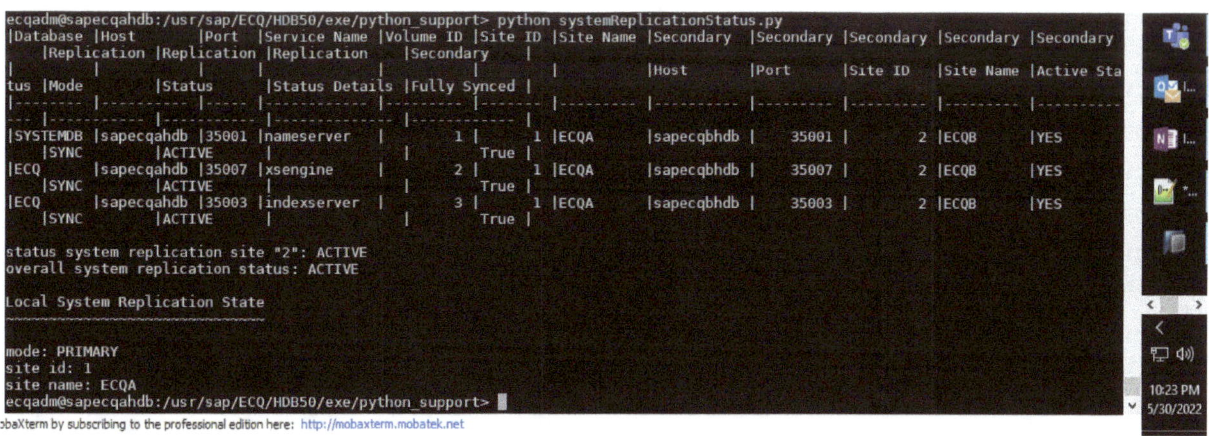

```
ecqadm@sapecqahdb:/usr/sap/ECQ/HDB50/exe/python_support> python systemReplicationStatus.py
```

Database	Host	Port	Service Name	Volume ID	Site ID	Site Name	Secondary Host	Secondary Port	Secondary Site ID	Secondary Site Name	Secondary Active Status	Replication Mode	Replication Status	Replication Status Details	Secondary Fully Synced
SYSTEMDB	sapecqahdb	35001	nameserver	1	1	ECQA	sapecqbhdb	35001	2	ECQB	YES	SYNC	ACTIVE		True
ECQ	sapecqahdb	35007	xsengine	2	1	ECQA	sapecqbhdb	35007	2	ECQB	YES	SYNC	ACTIVE		True
ECQ	sapecqahdb	35003	indexserver	3	1	ECQA	sapecqbhdb	35003	2	ECQB	YES	SYNC	ACTIVE		True

```
status system replication site "2": ACTIVE
overall system replication status: ACTIVE

Local System Replication State
~~~~~~~~~~~~~~~~~~~~~~~~~~~~~~~~

mode: PRIMARY
site id: 1
site name: ECQA
ecqadm@sapecqahdb:/usr/sap/ECQ/HDB50/exe/python_support>
```

Upload below script in node A (make sure put B node's physical hostname in plug section)

```
ecqadm@sapecqahdb:/usr/sap/ECQ/home> cat Stonith_fencing_script.sh
#!/bin/bash
action=reboot
login="b1e5bbbf-3c38-4125-8c3f-c00b5fa4a457"
passwd="wAu7Q~i4p.EhseZkR6A5t.opV~1VvHv5gz2jm"
pcmk_reboot_timeout=900
power_timeout=240
resourceGroup=RSG-SAP-PreProd

subscriptionId=91cbd599-d354-48e3-b7b9-380006e84af6
tenantId=4e9dbbfb-394a-4583-8810-53f81f819e3b
verbose=1
plug=azusapecqbhdb


fence_azure_arm --action=$action --username=$login --password="$passwd" \
--resourceGroup=$resourceGroup --tenantId=$tenantId --subscriptionId=$subscriptionId \
--power-timeout=$power_timeout --verbose --plug=$plug
echo "Return Value $?"
ecqadm@sapecqahdb:/usr/sap/ECQ/home>
```


Run this script with root user, Secondary HANA server gets STONITHed by the Primary HANA server. Secondary HANA server gets rebooted. Application connectivity is not lost.

```
[root@sapecqahdb home]# ls -ltr
total 68440
-rw------- 1 ecqadm sapsys 12377596 Mar  6 03:44 messages-20220306
-rw------- 1 ecqadm sapsys 12547466 Mar 13 03:40 messages-20220313
-rw------- 1 root   root   40256234 Mar 20 03:10 messages-20220320
-rw-r----- 1 ecqadm sapsys  4887997 Mar 21 10:56 indexserver_sapecqthdb.35003.000.trc
-rwxrwxr-x 1 root   root        558 Mar 29 12:37 Stonith_fencing_script.sh
[root@sapecqahdb home]# ./Stonith_fencing_script.sh
```


Node B got rebooted

```
2022-05-30 16:59:15,893 DEBUG: Starting new HTTPS connection (1): management.azure.com:443
2022-05-30 16:59:16,282 DEBUG: https://management.azure.com:443 "GET /subscriptions/91cbd599-d354-48e3-b7b9-380006e84af6/resourceG
roups/RSG-SAP-PreProd/providers/Microsoft.Compute/virtualMachines/azusapecqbhdb?$expand=instanceView&api-version=2019-03-01 HTTP/1
.1" 200 None
2022-05-30 16:59:16,290 INFO: Found power state of VM: unknown (starting)
2022-05-30 16:59:17,291 INFO: getting power status for VM azusapecqbhdb
2022-05-30 16:59:17,292 DEBUG: bdf5e858-9b20-44ef-8b99-84a23e2a40be - Authority:Instance discovery/validation has either already b
een completed or is turned off: ...
2022-05-30 16:59:17,293 INFO: bdf5e858-9b20-44ef-8b99-84a23e2a40be - TokenRequest:Getting token with client credentials.
2022-05-30 16:59:17,293 DEBUG: bdf5e858-9b20-44ef-8b99-84a23e2a40be - TokenRequest:No user_id passed for cache query
2022-05-30 16:59:17,293 DEBUG: bdf5e858-9b20-44ef-8b99-84a23e2a40be - CacheDriver:finding with query keys: {'_clientId': '...'}
2022-05-30 16:59:17,293 DEBUG: bdf5e858-9b20-44ef-8b99-84a23e2a40be - CacheDriver:Looking for potential cache entries: {'_clientId
': '...'}
2022-05-30 16:59:17,293 DEBUG: bdf5e858-9b20-44ef-8b99-84a23e2a40be - CacheDriver:Found 1 potential entries.
2022-05-30 16:59:17,293 DEBUG: bdf5e858-9b20-44ef-8b99-84a23e2a40be - CacheDriver:Resource specific token found.
2022-05-30 16:59:17,293 DEBUG: bdf5e858-9b20-44ef-8b99-84a23e2a40be - CacheDriver:Returning token from cache lookup, AccessTokenId
: b'Vtpt4haU/Ig94m7ORW3mRAWqeKP6CyBpGWO1/rcOhNw='
2022-05-30 16:59:17,293 DEBUG: Configuring redirects: allow=True, max=30
2022-05-30 16:59:17,294 DEBUG: Configuring request: timeout=100, verify=True, cert=None
2022-05-30 16:59:17,294 DEBUG: Configuring proxies: ''
2022-05-30 16:59:17,294 DEBUG: Evaluate proxies against ENV settings: True
2022-05-30 16:59:17,295 DEBUG: Starting new HTTPS connection (1): management.azure.com:443
2022-05-30 16:59:17,685 DEBUG: https://management.azure.com:443 "GET /subscriptions/91cbd599-d354-48e3-b7b9-380006e84af6/resourceG
roups/RSG-SAP-PreProd/providers/Microsoft.Compute/virtualMachines/azusapecqbhdb?$expand=instanceView&api-version=2019-03-01 HTTP/1
.1" 200 None
2022-05-30 16:59:17,693 INFO: Found power state of VM: on (running)
Success: Rebooted
Return Value 0
[root@sapecqahdb home]#
```


Uptime in node B

```
Last login: Mon May 30 16:59:49 2022
ecqadm@sapecqbhdb:/usr/sap/ECQ/HDB50> uptime
 17:00:23 up 0 min,  1 user,  load average: 1.21, 0.39, 0.13
ecqadm@sapecqbhdb:/usr/sap/ECQ/HDB50>
```


Cluster will be in stopped state in B node

```
ecqadm@sapecqbhdb:/usr/sap/ECQ/HDB50> sudo pcs status
Error: error running crm_mon, is pacemaker running?
  crm_mon: Error: cluster is not available on this node
ecqadm@sapecqbhdb:/usr/sap/ECQ/HDB50>
```



```
```

Cluster status

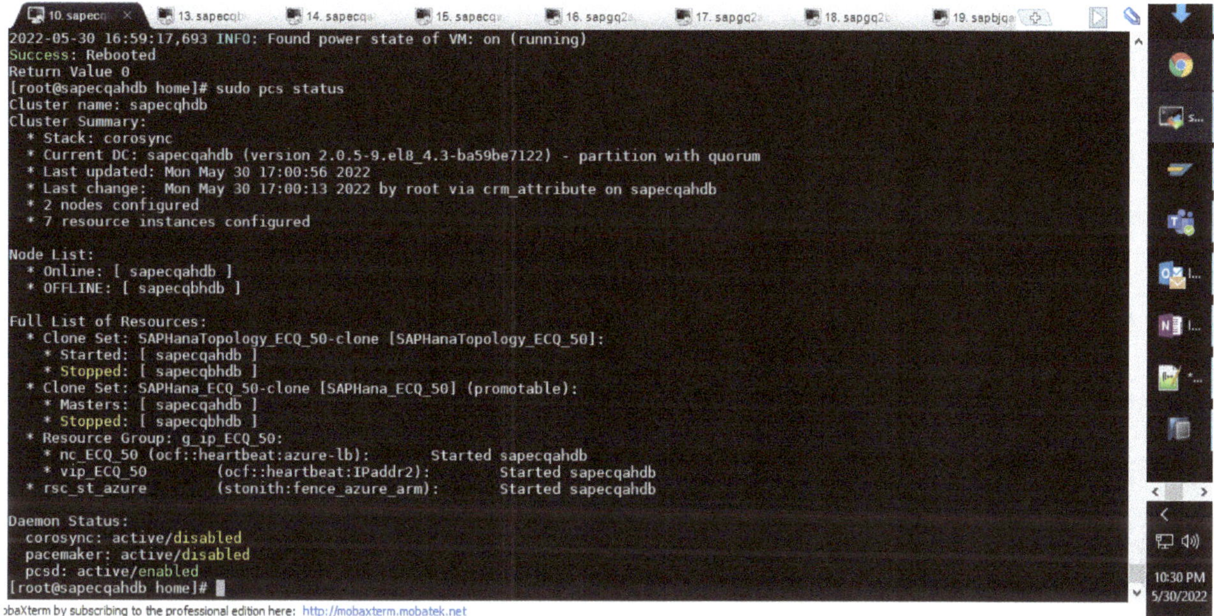

Replication status

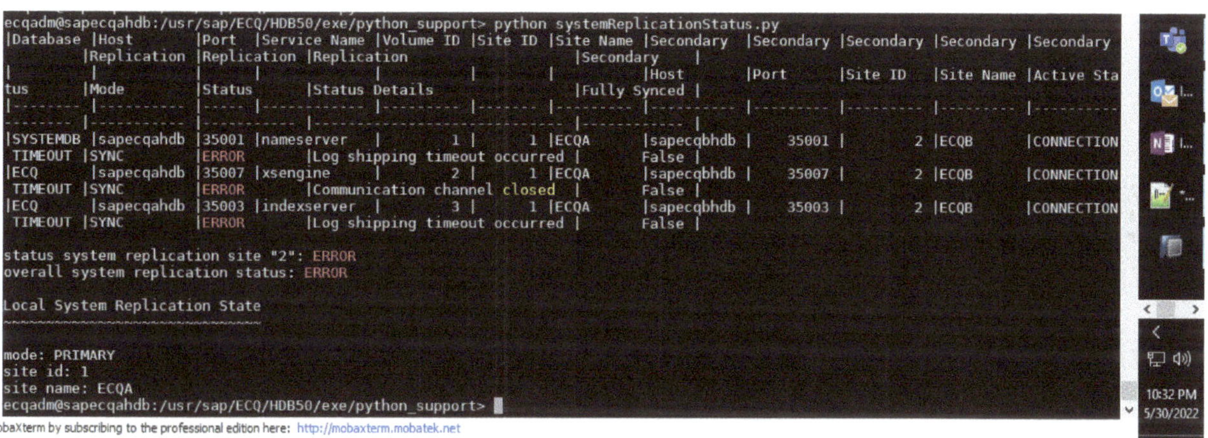

Start cluster in node B, it will start DB

Replication status after starting HANA node B

```
ecqadm@sapecqahdb:/usr/sap/ECQ/HDB50/exe/python_support> python systemReplicationStatus.py
|Database |Host        |Port   |Service Name |Volume ID |Site ID |Site Name |Secondary  |Secondary |Secondary |Secondary |Secondary
|         |Replication |Replication |Replication |          |Secondary |          |          |          |          |          |
|         |            |            |            |          |          |          |Host      |Port      |Site ID   |Site Name |Active Sta
|tus      |Mode        |Status      |Status Details |          |Fully Synced |          |          |          |          |          |
|-------- |----------- |----------- |-------------- |-------- |------- |--------- |--------- |--------- |--------- |--------- |-----------
--- |----------- |----------- |-------------- |-------- |----------- |
|SYSTEMDB |sapecqahdb |35001 |nameserver   |        1 |      1 |ECQA      |sapecqbhdb |   35001 |        2 |ECQB      |YES
|         |SYNC        |ACTIVE      |            |          |     True |          |          |          |          |          |
|ECQ      |sapecqahdb |35007 |xsengine     |        2 |      1 |ECQA      |sapecqbhdb |   35007 |        2 |ECQB      |YES
|         |SYNC        |ACTIVE      |            |          |     True |          |          |          |          |          |
|ECQ      |sapecqahdb |35003 |indexserver  |        3 |      1 |ECQA      |sapecqbhdb |   35003 |        2 |ECQB      |YES
|         |SYNC        |SYNCING     |Preparing persistence | |    False |          |          |          |          |          |

status system replication site "2": SYNCING
overall system replication status: SYNCING


Local System Replication State
~~~~~~~~~~~~~~~~~~~~~~~~~~~~~~~~~~~~~~~~~~~~~~~

mode: PRIMARY
site id: 1
site name: ECQA
ecqadm@sapecqahdb:/usr/sap/ECQ/HDB50/exe/python_support>
```

Cluster status

```
ecqadm@sapecqahdb:/usr/sap/ECQ/HDB50/exe/python_support> sudo pcs status
Cluster name: sapecqhdb
Cluster Summary:
  * Stack: corosync
  * Current DC: sapecqahdb (version 2.0.5-9.el8_4.3-ba59be7122) - partition with quorum
  * Last updated: Mon May 30 17:07:50 2022
  * Last change:  Mon May 30 17:07:31 2022 by root via crm_attribute on sapecqahdb
  * 2 nodes configured
  * 7 resource instances configured

Node List:
  * Online: [ sapecqahdb sapecqbhdb ]

Full List of Resources:
  * Clone Set: SAPHanaTopology_ECQ_50-clone [SAPHanaTopology_ECQ_50]:
    * Started: [ sapecqahdb sapecqbhdb ]
  * Clone Set: SAPHana_ECQ_50-clone [SAPHana_ECQ_50] (promotable):
    * Masters: [ sapecqahdb ]
    * Slaves: [ sapecqbhdb ]
  * Resource Group: g_ip_ECQ_50:
    * nc_ECQ_50   (ocf::heartbeat:azure-lb):       Started sapecqahdb
    * vip_ECQ_50       (ocf::heartbeat:IPaddr2):       Started sapecqahdb
  * rsc_st_azure       (stonith:fence_azure_arm):      Started sapecqbhdb

Daemon Status:
  corosync: active/disabled
  pacemaker: active/disabled
  pcsd: active/enabled
ecqadm@sapecqahdb:/usr/sap/ECQ/HDB50/exe/python_support>
```

8.12. Test case 12: Stop the network interfaces on Primary HANA node A

Test Description	Stop network interfaces on Primary HANA node
Test action	Shutdown eth interfaces on server sapecqahdb
Result	Pass
Expected results	sapecqahdb (Primary) gets fenced and rebooted HANA fails over from sapecqahdb (Primary) to sapecqbhdb (Secondary). Virtual IP (VIP) fails over from sapecqahdb (Primary) to sapecqbhdb (Secondary). Application connectivity to HANA is lost and re-established
Desired results	sapecqahdb (Primary) gets fenced and rebooted HANA fails over from sapecqahdb (Primary) to sapecqbhdb (Secondary). Virtual IP (VIP) fails over from sapecqahdb (Primary) to sapecqbhdb (Secondary). Application connectivity to HANA is lost and re-established
Post-test execution steps	Re-configure system replication with sapecqbhdb as Primary and sapecqahdb as Secondary Start pacemaker on failed node (sapecqahdb) Check system replication status Check cluster status

Test execution

Check status of cluster and HANA System replication before starting the test.

```
ecqadm@sapecqahdb:/usr/sap/ECQ/HDB50/exe/python_support> sudo pcs status
Cluster name: sapecqhdb
Cluster Summary:
  * Stack: corosync
  * Current DC: sapecqahdb (version 2.0.5-9.el8_4.3-ba59be7122) - partition with quorum
  * Last updated: Tue May 31 12:14:26 2022
  * Last change:  Tue May 31 12:14:05 2022 by root via crm_attribute on sapecqahdb
  * 2 nodes configured
  * 7 resource instances configured

Node List:
  * Online: [ sapecqahdb sapecqbhdb ]

Full List of Resources:
  * Clone Set: SAPHanaTopology_ECQ_50-clone [SAPHanaTopology_ECQ_50]:
    * Started: [ sapecqahdb sapecqbhdb ]
  * Clone Set: SAPHana_ECQ_50-clone [SAPHana_ECQ_50] (promotable):
    * Masters: [ sapecqahdb ]
    * Slaves: [ sapecqbhdb ]
  * Resource Group: g_ip_ECQ_50:
    * nc_ECQ_50   (ocf::heartbeat:azure-lb):      Started sapecqahdb
    * vip_ECQ_50      (ocf::heartbeat:IPaddr2):       Started sapecqahdb
  * rsc_st_azure       (stonith:fence_azure_arm):      Started sapecqbhdb

Daemon Status:
  corosync: active/disabled
  pacemaker: active/disabled
  pcsd: active/enabled
ecqadm@sapecqahdb:/usr/sap/ECQ/HDB50/exe/python_support>
```

Node A (primary) hdbnsutil –sr_state

```
operation mode: primary
site id: 1
site name: ECQA

is source system: true
is secondary/consumer system: false
has secondaries/consumers attached: true
is a takeover active: false
is primary suspended: false

Host Mappings:
~~~~~~~~~~~~~~

sapecqahdb -> [ECQB] sapecqbhdb
sapecqahdb -> [ECQA] sapecqahdb


Site Mappings:
~~~~~~~~~~~~~~

ECQA (primary/primary)
    |---ECQB (sync/logreplay)

Tier of ECQA: 1
Tier of ECQB: 2

Replication mode of ECQA: primary
Replication mode of ECQB: sync

Operation mode of ECQA: primary
Operation mode of ECQB: logreplay

Mapping: ECQA -> ECQB
done.
ecqadm@sapecqahdb:/usr/sap/ECQ/HDB50/exe/python_support>
```

```
ecqadm@sapecqahdb:/usr/sap/ECQ/HDB50/exe/python_support> python systemReplicationStatus.py
|Database |Host       |Port  |Service Name |Volume ID |Site ID |Site Name |Secondary  |Secondary |Secondary |Secondary |Secondary
|    |Replication |Replication |Replication |Secondary |        |          |Host       |Port      |Site ID   |Site Name |Active Sta
|    |        |           |        |             |          |        |          |           |          |          |          |
tus |Mode    |Status     |Status Details |Fully Synced |
|------- |------- |-------- |------- |------------ |----------- |------- |--------- |---------- |--------- |--------- |--------- |
--- |------- |--------- |------- |------------ |----------- |
|SYSTEMDB |sapecqahdb |35001 |nameserver  |          1 |      1 |ECQA     |sapecqbhdb |   35001 |        2 |ECQB     |YES
|    |SYNC    |ACTIVE     |        |        True |
|ECQ      |sapecqahdb |35007 |xsengine    |          2 |      1 |ECQA     |sapecqbhdb |   35007 |        2 |ECQB     |YES
|    |SYNC    |ACTIVE     |        |        True |
|ECQ      |sapecqahdb |35003 |indexserver |          3 |      1 |ECQA     |sapecqbhdb |   35003 |        2 |ECQB     |YES
|    |SYNC    |ACTIVE     |        |        True |

status system replication site "2": ACTIVE
overall system replication status: ACTIVE

Local System Replication State
~~~~~~~~~~~~~~~~~~~~~~~~~~~~~~~~

mode: PRIMARY
site id: 1
site name: ECQA
ecqadm@sapecqahdb:/usr/sap/ECQ/HDB50/exe/python_support>
```


Changed user in su01

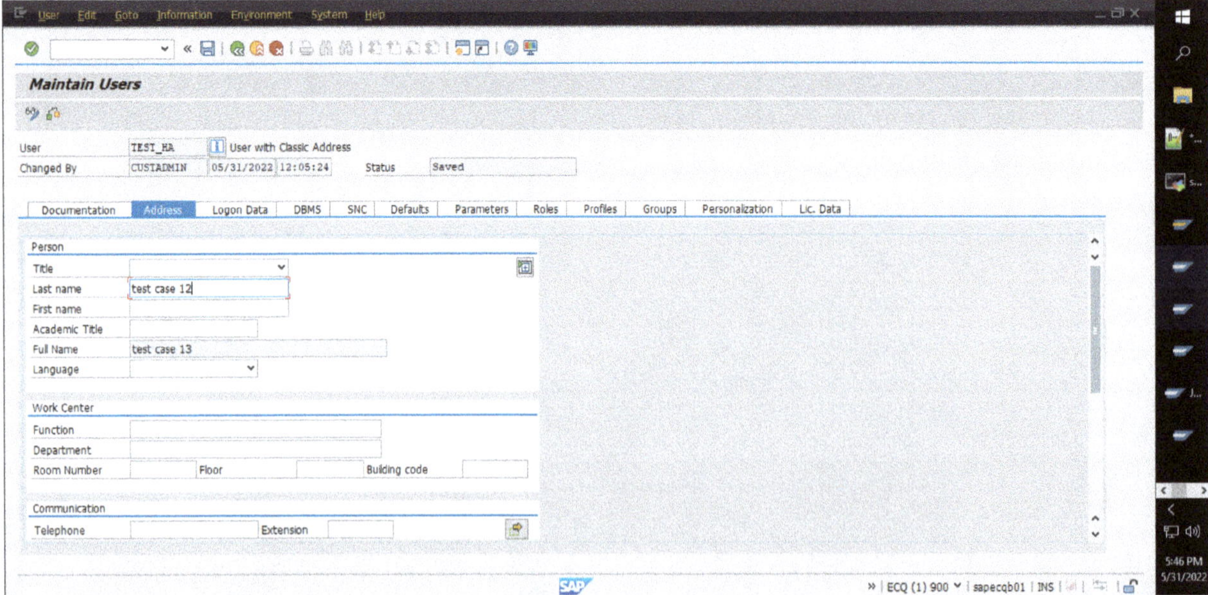

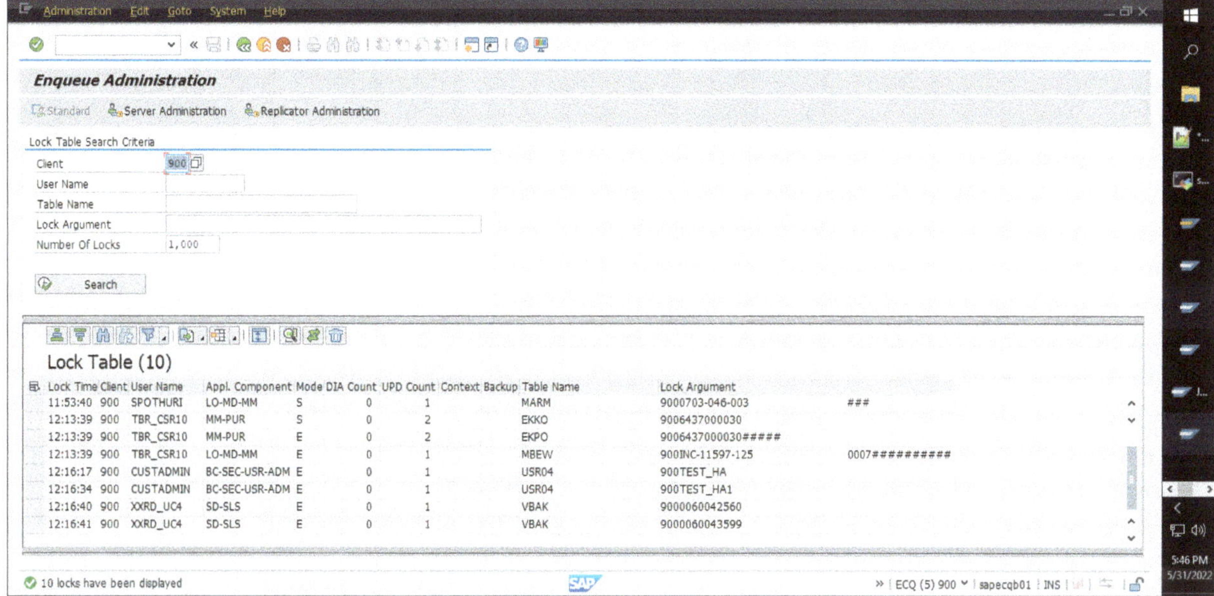

Replication is running fine

Upload below script in node B (make sure put A node's physical hostname in plug section)

Copy the stonith script from /auto/media to /usr/sap/ECQ/home

```
ecqadm@sapecqbhdb:/usr/sap/ECQ/HDB50/exe/python_support> cd
ecqadm@sapecqbhdb:/usr/sap/ECQ/home> ls -ltr
total 8
-rwxr-xr-x 1 ecqadm sapsys 565 Mar 29 07:16 stonith.sh
-rwxrwxr-x 1 ecqadm sapsys 558 Apr  1 14:29 Stonith_fencing_script.sh
ecqadm@sapecqbhdb:/usr/sap/ECQ/home> cat Stonith_fencing_script.sh
#!/bin/bash
action=reboot
login="b1e5bbbf-3c38-4125-8c3f-c00b5fa4a457"
passwd="wAu7Q~i4p.EhseZkR6A5t.opV~1VvHv5gz2jm"
pcmk_reboot_timeout=900
power_timeout=240
resourceGroup=RSG-SAP-PreProd

subscriptionId=91cbd599-d354-48e3-b7b9-380006e84af6
tenantId=4e9dbbfb-394a-4583-8810-53f81f819e3b
verbose=1
plug=azusapecqahdb


fence_azure_arm --action=$action --username=$login --password="$passwd" \
--resourceGroup=$resourceGroup --tenantId=$tenantId --subscriptionId=$subscriptionId \
--power-timeout=$power_timeout --verbose --plug=$plug
echo "Return Value $?"
ecqadm@sapecqbhdb:/usr/sap/ECQ/home> 
```

Run this script with root user, Primary HANA server gets STONITHed by the B HANA server.
Primary HANA server gets rebooted. Application connectivity is not lost.

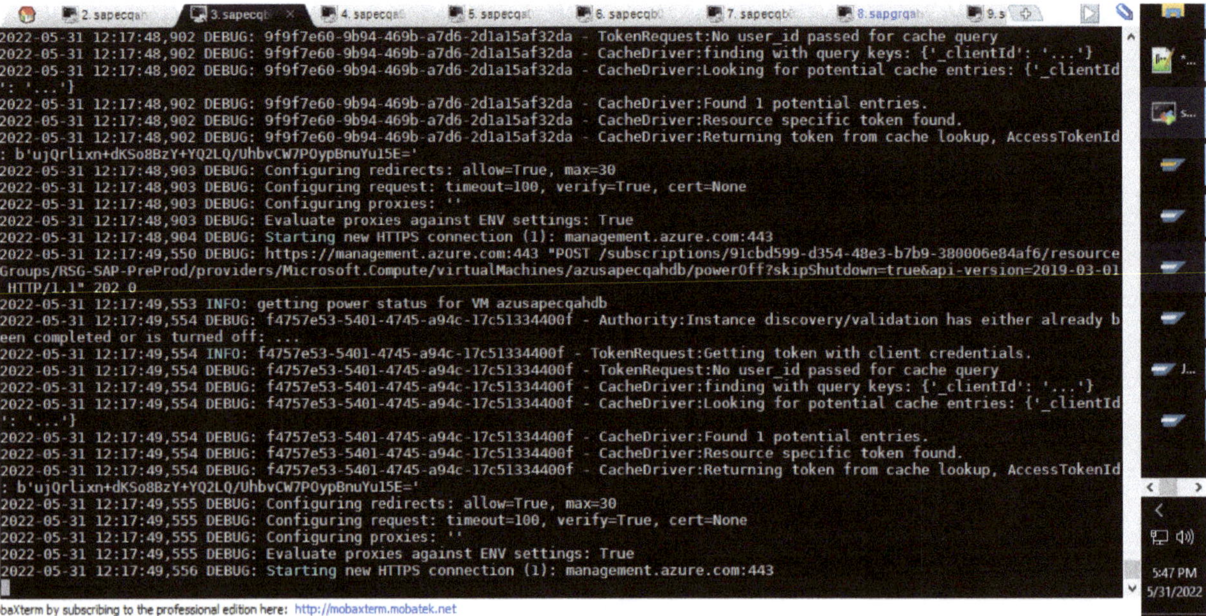

Save the user

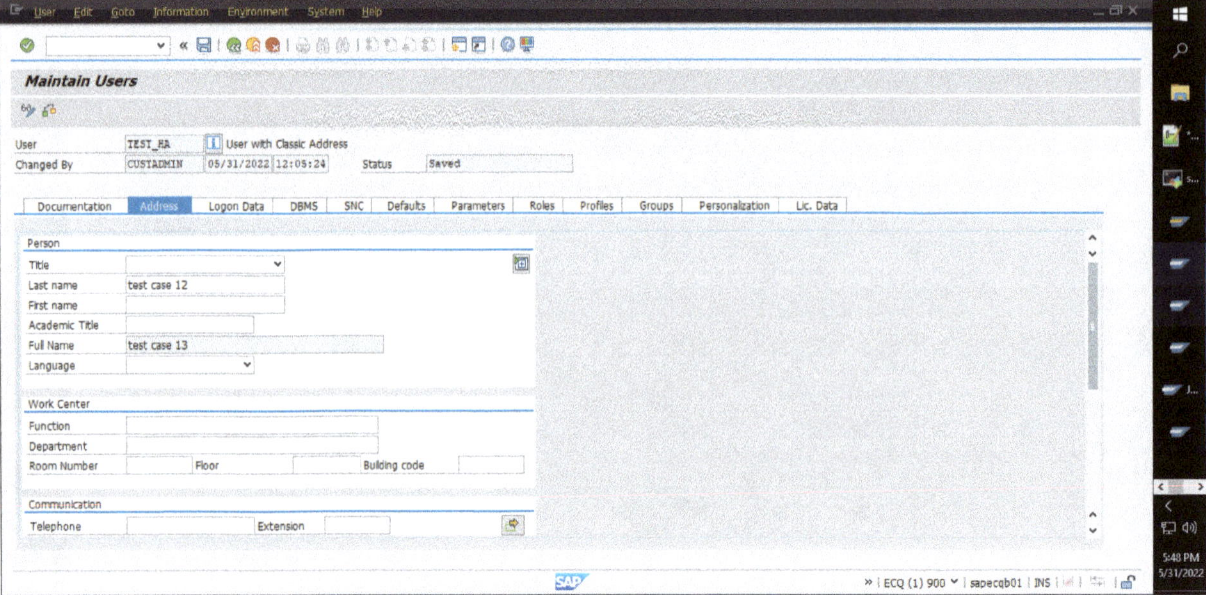

Only one lock entry should exist → since one of the user was saved

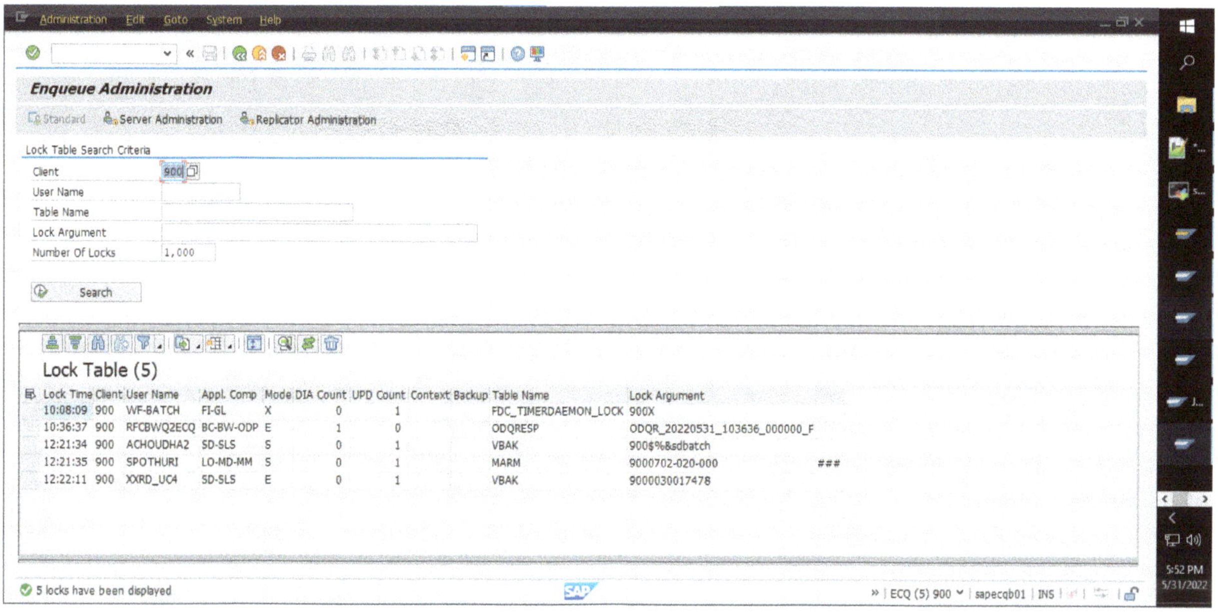
Administration Edit Goto System Help
Enqueue Administration
Standard Server Administration Replicator Administration
Lock Table Search Criteria
Client 900
User Name
Table Name
Lock Argument
Number Of Locks 1,000
Search
Lock Table (5)
Lock Time Client User Name Appl. Comp Mode DIA Count UPD Count Context Backup Table Name Lock Argument
10:08:09 900 WF-BATCH FI-GL X 0 1 FDC_TIMERDAEMON_LOCK 900X
10:36:37 900 RFCBWQ2ECQ BC-BW-ODP E 1 0 ODQRESP ODQR_20220531_103636_000000_F
12:21:34 900 ACHOUDHA2 SD-SLS S 0 1 VBAK 900$%&sdbatch
12:21:35 900 SPOTHURI LO-MD-MM S 0 1 MARM 9000702-020-000 ###
12:22:11 900 XXRD_UC4 SD-SLS E 0 1 VBAK 9000030017478
5 locks have been displayed
ECQ (5) 900 sapecqb01 INS
5:52 PM
5/31/2022

Took 4 mins to save the user

Node A got rebooted

Uptime in node A

Last login: Tue May 31 12:17:12 2022
ecqadm@sapecqahdb:/usr/sap/ECQ/HDB50> uptime
12:23:22 up 2 min, 1 user, load average: 1.05, 1.01, 0.42
ecqadm@sapecqahdb:/usr/sap/ECQ/HDB50>
obaXterm by subscribing to the professional edition here: http://mobaxterm.mobatek.net
5:53 PM
5/31/2022

Cluster status

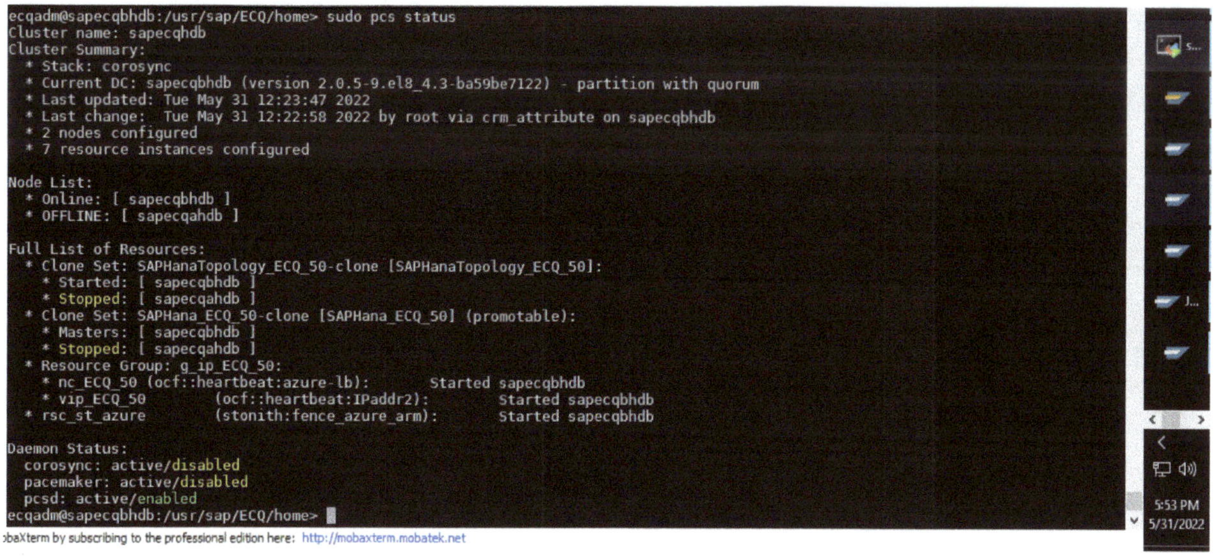
ecqadm@sapecqbhdb:/usr/sap/ECQ/home> sudo pcs status
Cluster name: sapecqhdb
Cluster Summary:
* Stack: corosync
* Current DC: sapecqbhdb (version 2.0.5-9.el8_4.3-ba59be7122) - partition with quorum
* Last updated: Tue May 31 12:23:47 2022
* Last change: Tue May 31 12:22:58 2022 by root via crm_attribute on sapecqbhdb
* 2 nodes configured
* 7 resource instances configured
Node List:
* Online: [sapecqbhdb]
* OFFLINE: [sapecqahdb]
Full List of Resources:
* Clone Set: SAPHanaTopology_ECQ_50-clone [SAPHanaTopology_ECQ_50]:
* Started: [sapecqbhdb]
* Stopped: [sapecqahdb]
* Clone Set: SAPHana_ECQ_50-clone [SAPHana_ECQ_50] (promotable):
* Masters: [sapecqbhdb]
* Stopped: [sapecqahdb]
* Resource Group: g_ip_ECQ_50:
* nc_ECQ_50 (ocf::heartbeat:azure-lb): Started sapecqbhdb
* vip_ECQ_50 (ocf::heartbeat:IPaddr2): Started sapecqbhdb
* rsc_st_azure (stonith:fence_azure_arm): Started sapecqbhdb
Daemon Status:
corosync: active/disabled
pacemaker: active/disabled
pcsd: active/enabled
ecqadm@sapecqbhdb:/usr/sap/ECQ/home>
obaXterm by subscribing to the professional edition here: http://mobaxterm.mobatek.net
5:53 PM
5/31/2022

Register A node as secondary and start cluster

```
ecqadm@sapecqahdb:/usr/sap/ECQ/HDB50> hdbnsutil -sr_register --remoteHost=sapecqbhdb --remoteInstance=50 --replicationMode=sync --name=ECQA --operationMode=logreplay
adding site ...
collecting information ...
registered at 10.197.42.19 (sapecqbhdb)
updating local ini files ...
done.
ecqadm@sapecqahdb:/usr/sap/ECQ/HDB50> sudo pcs status
Error: error running crm_mon, is pacemaker running?
  crm_mon: Error: cluster is not available on this node
ecqadm@sapecqahdb:/usr/sap/ECQ/HDB50> sudo pcs cluster start
Starting Cluster...
ecqadm@sapecqahdb:/usr/sap/ECQ/HDB50>
```


Replication status after starting cluster in node A

```
ecqadm@sapecqbhdb:/usr/sap/ECQ/HDB50/exe/python_support> python systemReplicationStatus.py
```

Database	Host	Port	Service Name	Volume ID	Site ID	Site Name	Secondary Host	Secondary Port	Secondary Site ID	Secondary Site Name	Secondary Active Status	Replication Mode	Replication Status	Replication Status Details	Secondary Fully Synced
SYSTEMDB	sapecqbhdb	35001	nameserver	1	2	ECQB	sapecqahdb	35001	1	ECQA	YES	SYNC	ACTIVE		True
ECQ	sapecqbhdb	35007	xsengine	2	2	ECQB	sapecqahdb	35007	1	ECQA	YES	SYNC	ACTIVE		True
ECQ	sapecqbhdb	35003	indexserver	3	2	ECQB	sapecqahdb	35003	1	ECQA	YES	SYNC	SYNCING	Preparing persistence	False

```
status system replication site "1": SYNCING
overall system replication status: SYNCING

Local System Replication State
~~~~~~~~~~~~~~~~~~~~~~~~~~~~~~~~

mode: PRIMARY
site id: 2
site name: ECQB
ecqadm@sapecqbhdb:/usr/sap/ECQ/HDB50/exe/python_support>
```


Cluster status

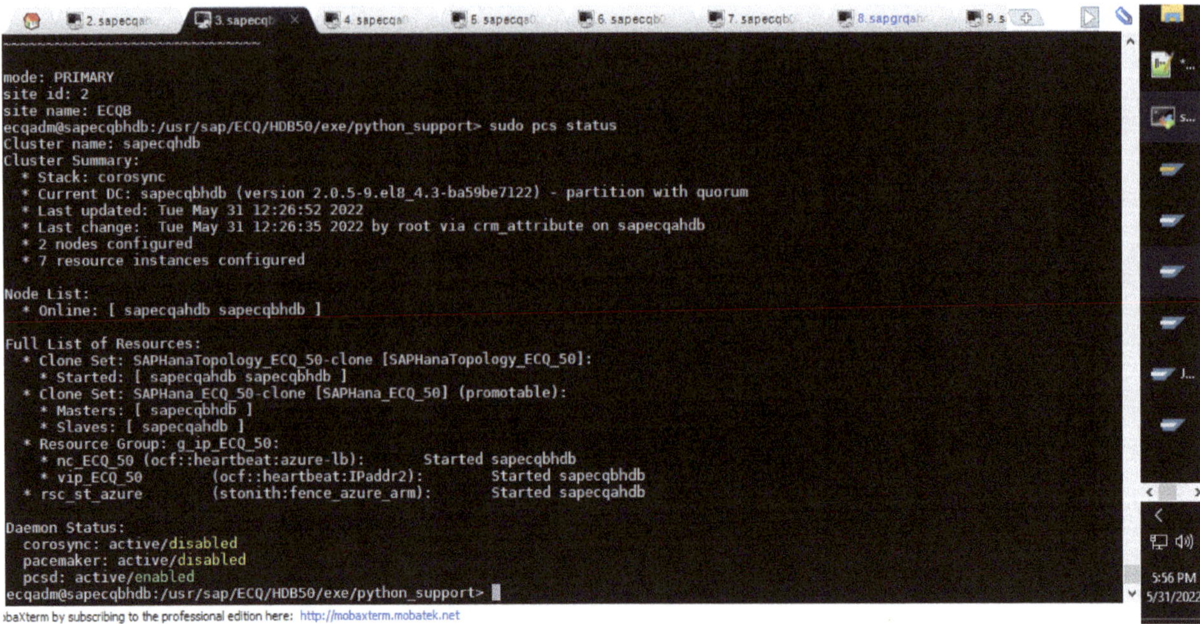

```
mode: PRIMARY
site id: 2
site name: ECQB
ecqadm@sapecqbhdb:/usr/sap/ECQ/HDB50/exe/python_support> sudo pcs status
Cluster name: sapecqhdb
Cluster Summary:
  * Stack: corosync
  * Current DC: sapecqbhdb (version 2.0.5-9.el8_4.3-ba59be7122) - partition with quorum
  * Last updated: Tue May 31 12:26:52 2022
  * Last change:  Tue May 31 12:26:35 2022 by root via crm_attribute on sapecqahdb
  * 2 nodes configured
  * 7 resource instances configured

Node List:
  * Online: [ sapecqahdb sapecqbhdb ]

Full List of Resources:
  * Clone Set: SAPHanaTopology_ECQ_50-clone [SAPHanaTopology_ECQ_50]:
    * Started: [ sapecqahdb sapecqbhdb ]
  * Clone Set: SAPHana_ECQ_50-clone [SAPHana_ECQ_50] (promotable):
    * Masters: [ sapecqbhdb ]
    * Slaves: [ sapecqahdb ]
  * Resource Group: g_ip_ECQ_50:
    * nc_ECQ_50       (ocf::heartbeat:azure-lb):       Started sapecqbhdb
    * vip_ECQ_50      (ocf::heartbeat:IPaddr2):        Started sapecqbhdb
  * rsc_st_azure      (stonith:fence_azure_arm):       Started sapecqahdb

Daemon Status:
  corosync: active/disabled
  pacemaker: active/disabled
  pcsd: active/enabled
ecqadm@sapecqbhdb:/usr/sap/ECQ/HDB50/exe/python_support>
```

Test Description	Intentionally fail over from Node B to Node A
Test action	Restart Pacemaker on Primary HANA node (Node B)
Result	Pass
Expected results	HANA fails over from sapecpbhdb (Primary) to sapecpahdb (Secondary). Virtual IP (VIP) fails over from sapecpbhdb (Primary) to sapecpahdb (Secondary). After failover, System replication continues to work between the new Primary sapecpahdb and DR sapecpdhdb Application connectivity to HANA is lost and re-established
Desired results	HANA fails over from sapecpbhdb (Primary) to sapecpahdb (Secondary). Virtual IP (VIP) fails over from sapecpbhdb (Primary) to sapecpahdb (Secondary). After failover, System replication continues to work between the new Primary sapecpahdb and DR sapecpdhdb Application connectivity to HANA is lost and re-established
Post-test execution steps	Re-configure system replication with sapecpahdb as Primary and sapecpbhdb as Secondary Re-start pacemaker on old primary node (sapecpbhdb) Check system replication status Check cluster status

Check cluster Status

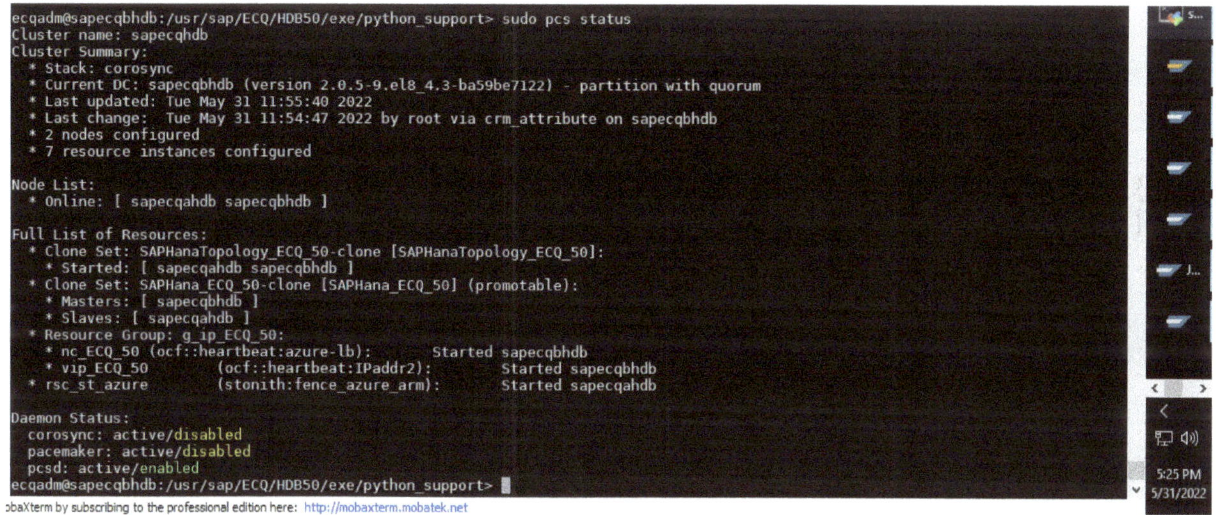

Check Replication in Node B

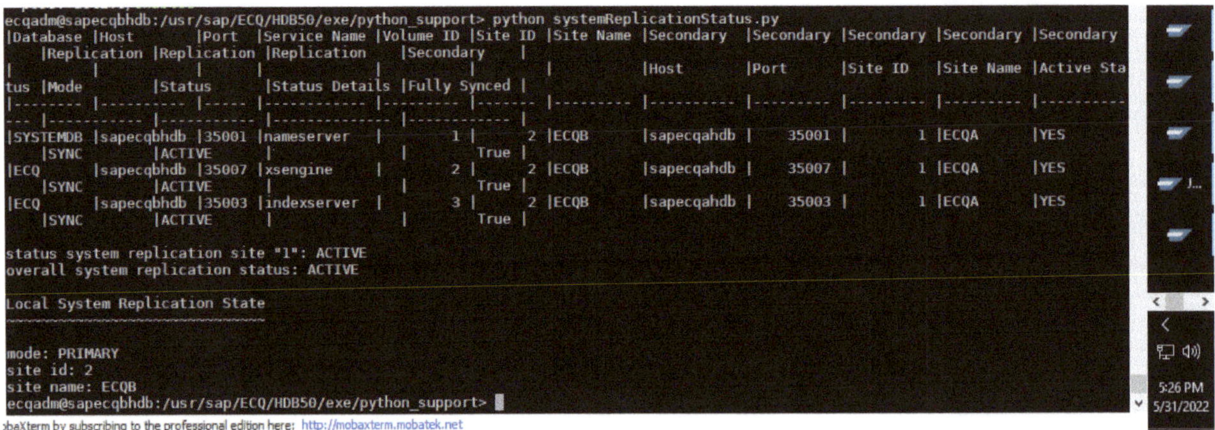

Check hdbnsutil –sr_state

Edit the user and do not save

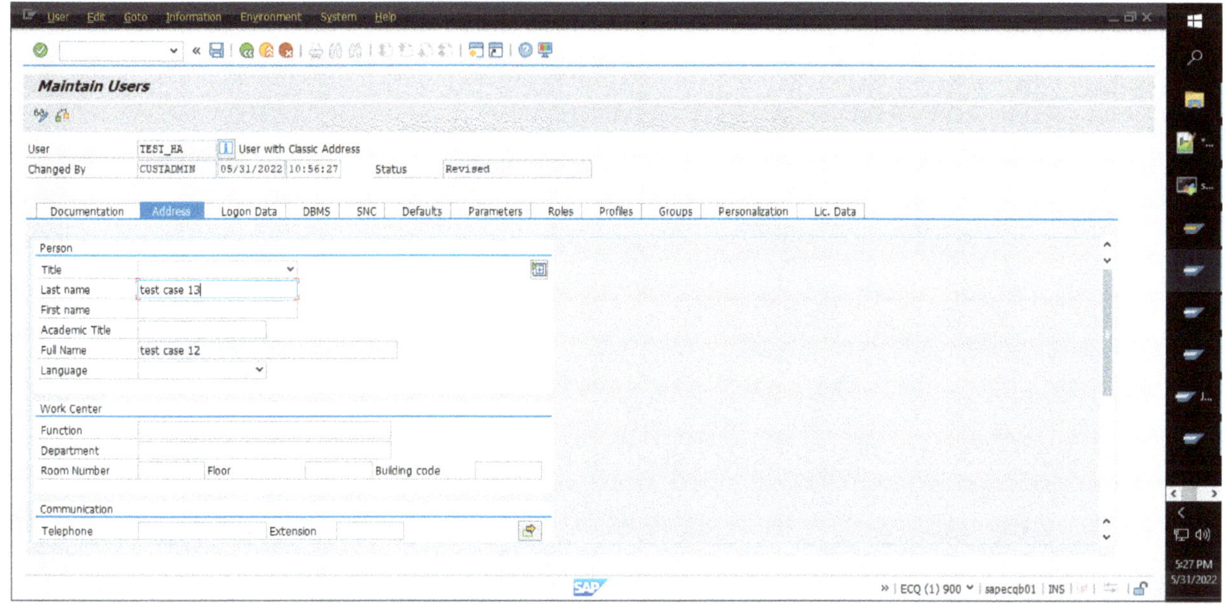

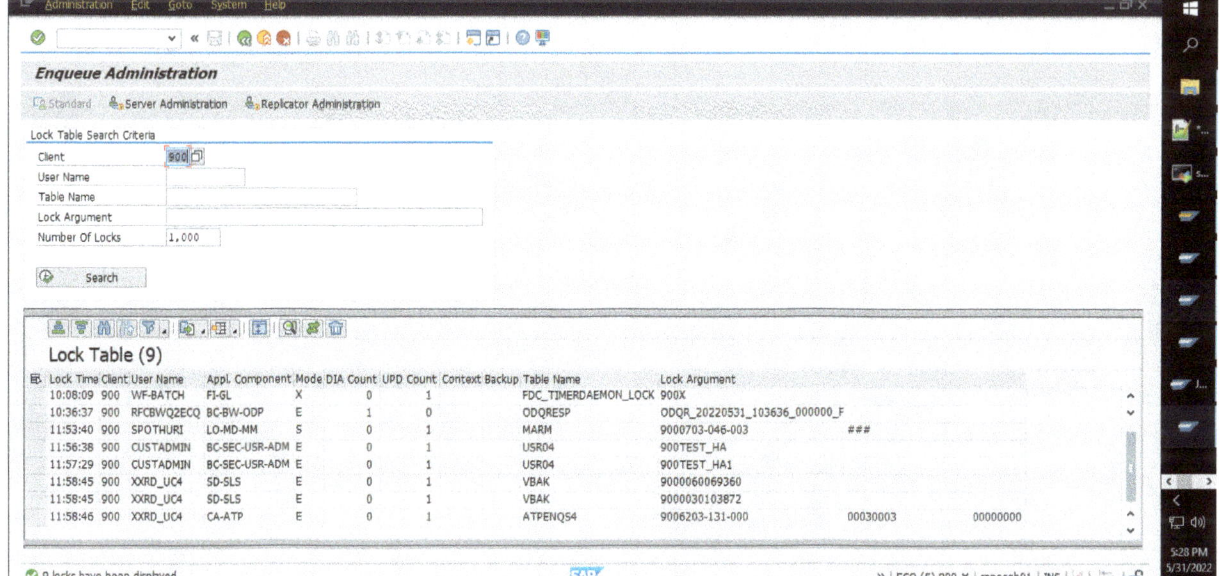

Restart Pacemaker on Node B

Pcs cluster stop

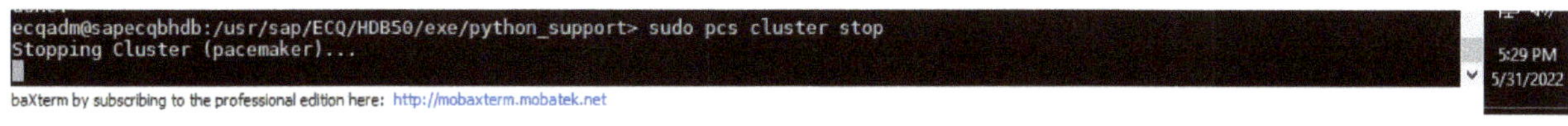

baXterm by subscribing to the professional edition here: http://mobaxterm.mobatek.net

Save user in su01

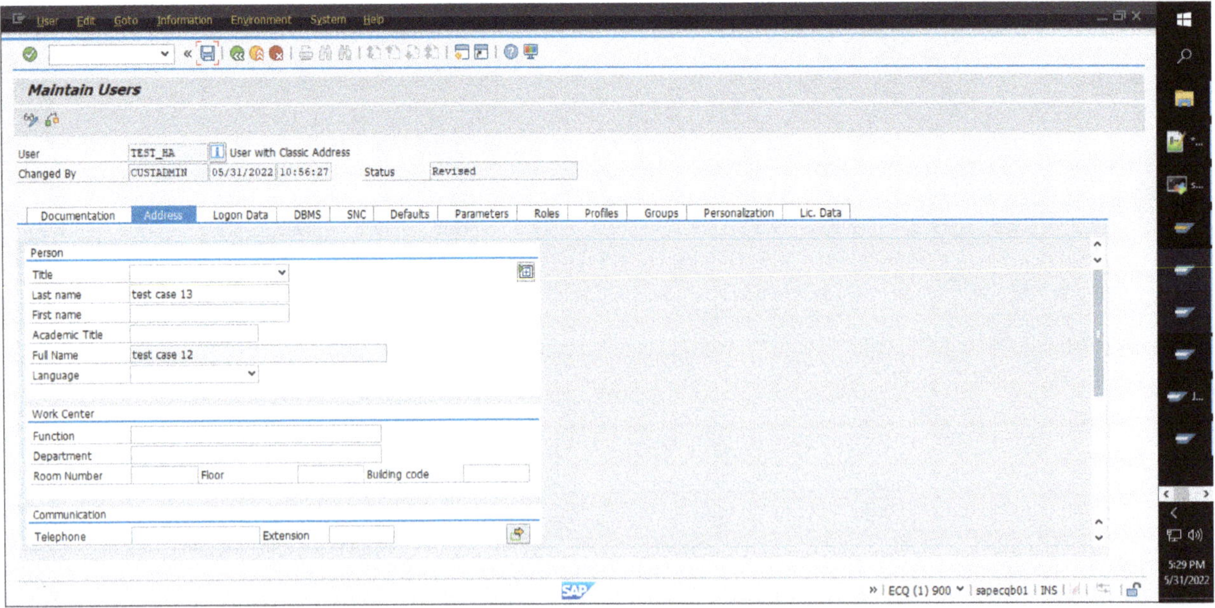

Cluster status from node A

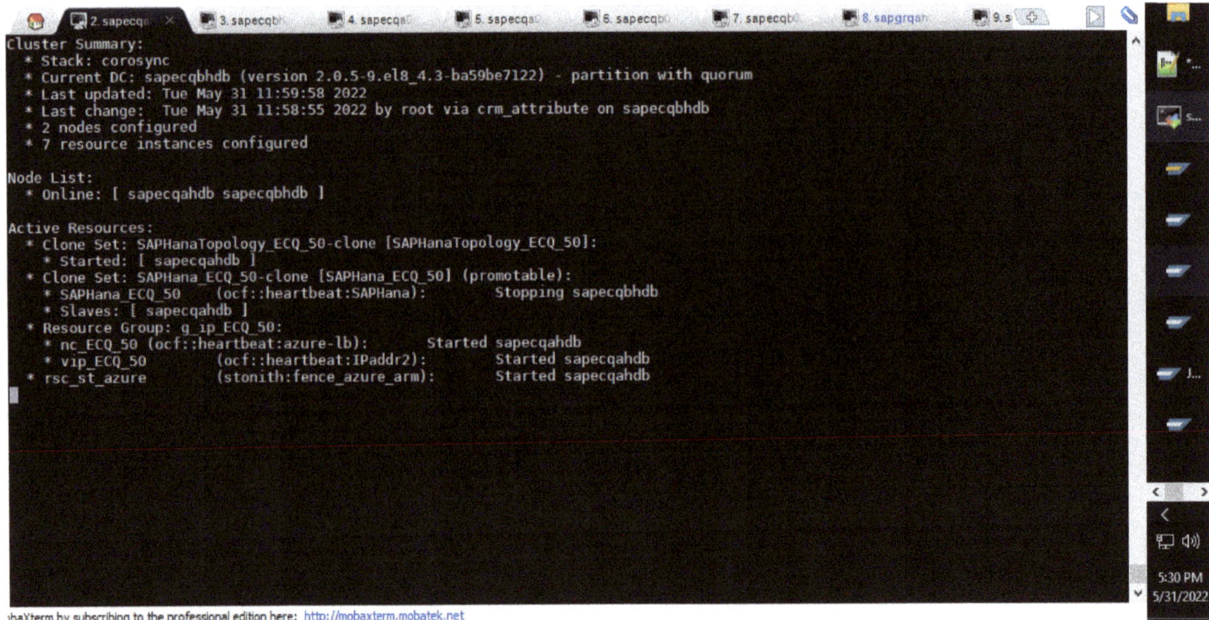

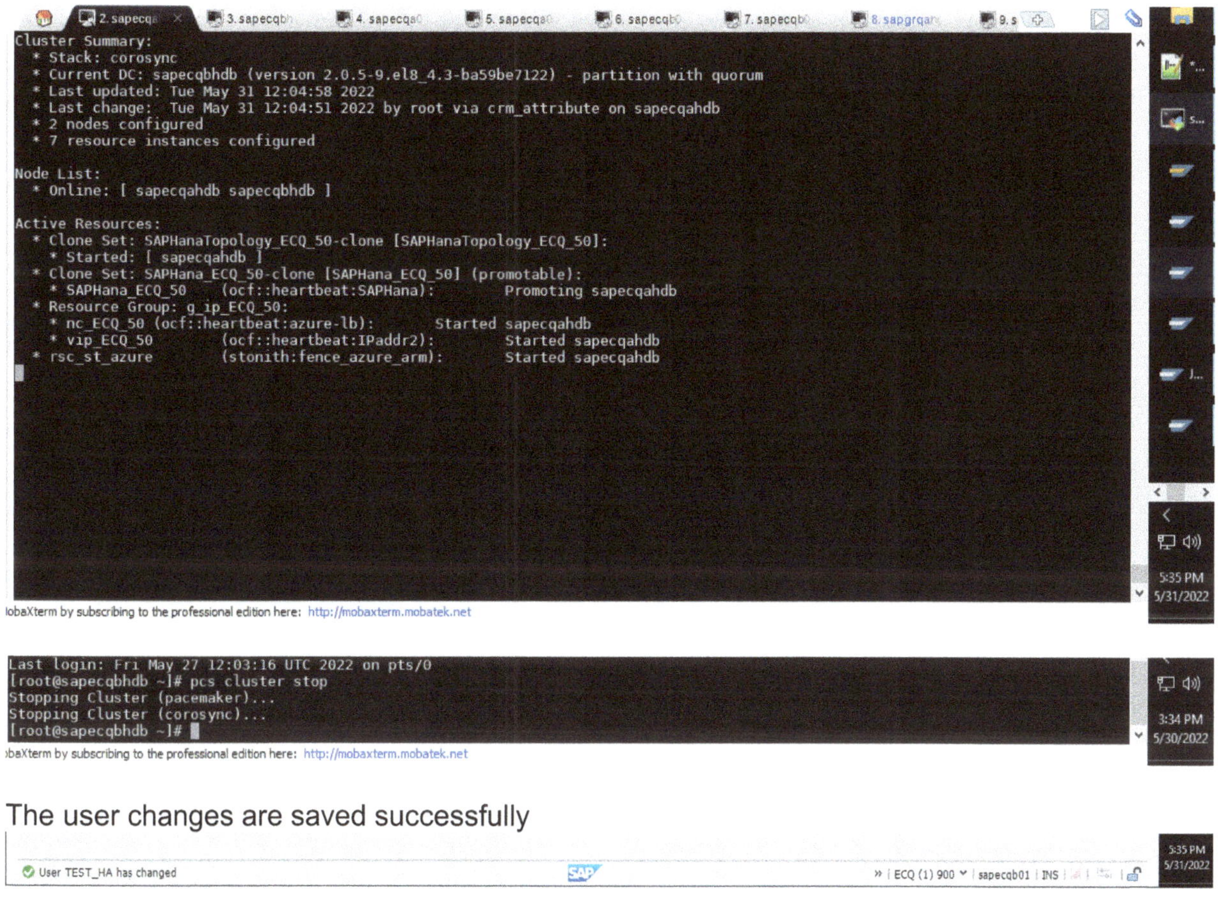

The user changes are saved successfully

Hdbnsutil –sr_state
Node A

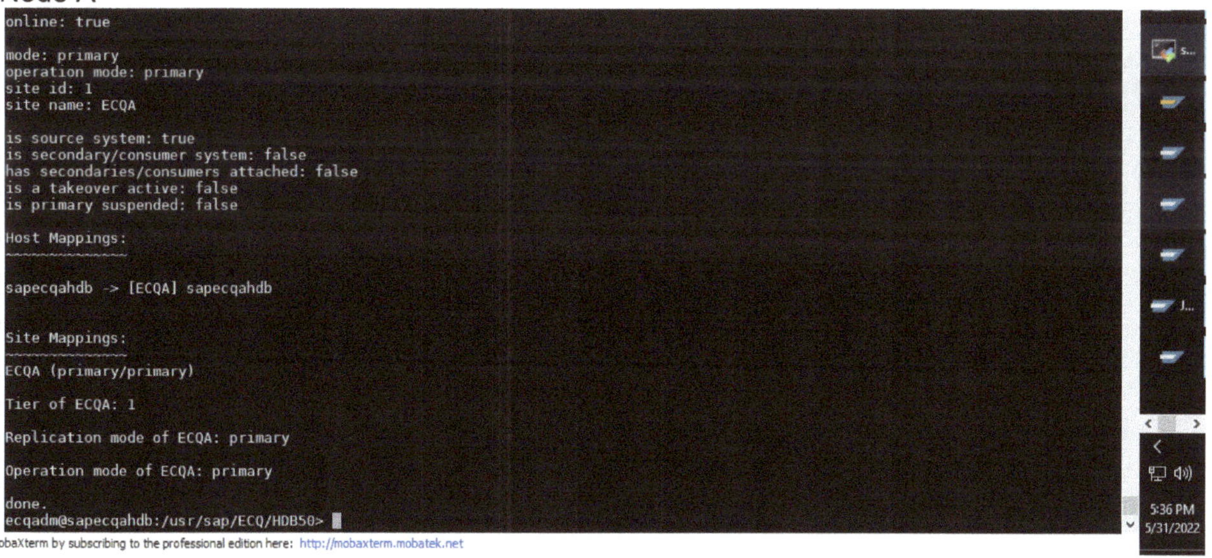

Node B

```
ecqadm@sapecqbhdb:/usr/sap/ECQ/HDB50/exe/python_support> hdbnsutil -sr_state

System Replication State
~~~~~~~~~~~~~~~~~~~~~~~~~

online: false

mode: primary
operation mode: unknown
site id: 2
site name: ECQB

is source system: unknown
is secondary/consumer system: false
has secondaries/consumers attached: unknown
is a takeover active: false
is primary suspended: false
done.
ecqadm@sapecqbhdb:/usr/sap/ECQ/HDB50/exe/python_support>
```

Register Node B as secondary and start cluster

```
ecqadm@sapecqbhdb:/usr/sap/ECQ/HDB50/exe/python_support> hdbnsutil -sr_register --remoteHost=sapecqahdb --remoteInstance=50 --repl
icationMode=sync --name=ECQB --operationMode=logreplay
adding site ...
collecting information ...
registered at 10.197.42.18 (sapecqahdb)
updating local ini files ...
done.
ecqadm@sapecqbhdb:/usr/sap/ECQ/HDB50/exe/python_support> sudo pcs status
Error: error running crm_mon, is pacemaker running?
  crm_mon: Error: cluster is not available on this node
ecqadm@sapecqbhdb:/usr/sap/ECQ/HDB50/exe/python_support> sudo pcs cluster start
Starting Cluster...
ecqadm@sapecqbhdb:/usr/sap/ECQ/HDB50/exe/python_support>
```

In A Node

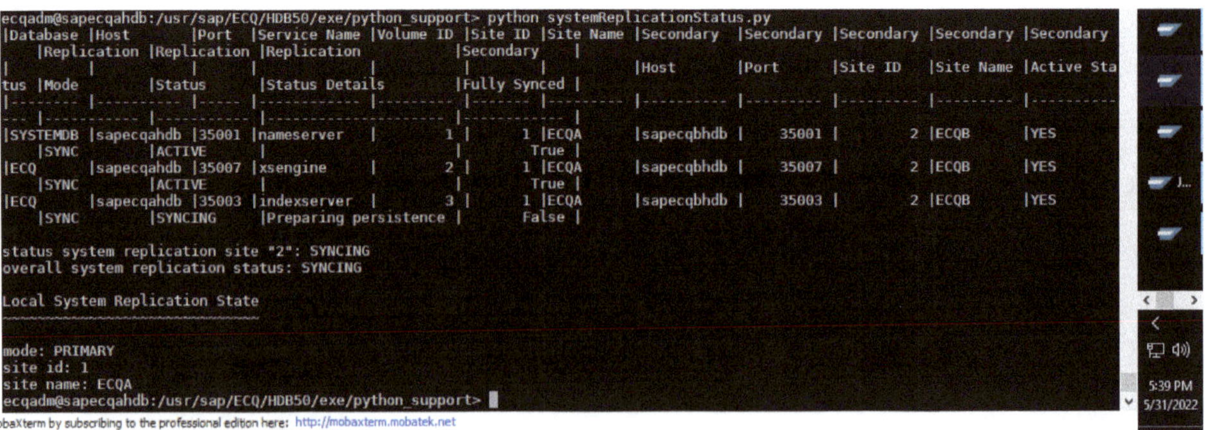

```
ecqadm@sapecqahdb:/usr/sap/ECQ/HDB50/exe/python_support> python systemReplicationStatus.py
```

Database	Host	Port	Service Name	Volume ID	Site ID	Site Name	Secondary Host	Secondary Port	Secondary Site ID	Secondary Site Name	Secondary Active Status	Replication Mode	Replication Status	Replication Status Details	Secondary Fully Synced
SYSTEMDB	sapecqahdb	35001	nameserver	1	1	ECQA	sapecqbhdb	35001	2	ECQB	YES	SYNC	ACTIVE		True
ECQ	sapecqahdb	35007	xsengine	2	1	ECQA	sapecqbhdb	35007	2	ECQB	YES	SYNC	ACTIVE		True
ECQ	sapecqahdb	35003	indexserver	3	1	ECQA	sapecqbhdb	35003	2	ECQB	YES	SYNC	SYNCING	Preparing persistence	False

```
status system replication site "2": SYNCING
overall system replication status: SYNCING

Local System Replication State
~~~~~~~~~~~~~~~~~~~~~~~~~~~~~~~~

mode: PRIMARY
site id: 1
site name: ECQA
ecqadm@sapecqahdb:/usr/sap/ECQ/HDB50/exe/python_support>
```

9. CONCLUSION

This comprehensive guide explores the real time execution scenarios, natural occurring disaster situations for both Application, HANA Databases, Operating Systems & other infrastructure critical components of achieving high availability (HA) in SAP HANA environments through effective system replication strategies. It explores into the architecture of SAP HANA HSR methodologies, detailing how system replication can be configured/performed to ensure business continuity, minimize downtime, and protect against data loss.

This book covers various replication techniques, including synchronous and asynchronous modes, and explains their advantages and limitations. It includes best practices for implementing and managing high-availability configurations, monitoring performance, and conducting disaster recovery tests.

Real-world case studies illustrate successful deployments and the lessons learned from organizations that have navigated the complexities of SAP HANA high availability. Additionally, the book offers troubleshooting tips, maintenance strategies, and insights into emerging trends in database replication and HA solutions.

10.   SUGGESTION & REFERENCES

- https://docs.microsoft.com/en-us/azure/virtual-machines/workloads/sap/high-availability-guide-rhel
- SAP Support Portal accessiable with S-User or SAP Universal IDs
- SAP Community Network – SCN blogs
- SAP Best Practice and Guides about SAP HANA HIGH Availability
- SAP HANA Administration Guide
- SAP HANA System Replication – Technical Implementation
- Other Online learnings